GUARDING THE FRONTIER

Guarding the Frontier

A STUDY OF FRONTIER DEFENSE
FROM 1815 TO 1825

BY

EDGAR BRUCE WESLEY

HEAD OF THE HISTORY DEPARTMENT
UNIVERSITY HIGH SCHOOL
AND ASSOCIATE PROFESSOR OF EDUCATION
UNIVERSITY OF MINNESOTA

GREENWOOD PRESS, PUBLISHERS
WESTPORT, CONNECTICUT

Originally published in 1935
by The University of Minnesota Press

First Greenwood Reprinting 1970

Library of Congress Catalogue Card Number 70-110883

SBN 8371-4567-8

Printed in the United States of America

To a Great Teacher
Thomas Maitland Marshall

PREFACE

MANY phases of the westward movement of the American people have received adequate treatment at the hands of historians. The significance of the frontier has been stated, recognized, and to some extent appreciated. Yet some important aspects of the westward advance have been all but ignored. The heroic frontiersman battling against hostile Indians has become a stereotyped figure, and that picture has tended to obscure the fact that the United States government made a systematic attempt to protect the settler, not only against the Indians but against the greater danger of a frontier restricted by foreign powers. By its Indian and frontier defense policies the United States made the westward movement possible.

This study is concerned with the official aspects of frontier defense in the decade following the War of 1812. From the standpoint of time I have treated only a small part of a large subject, but within the period selected the scope is comprehensive. Such comprehensiveness naturally increases the liability of error, but the value of an inclusive study justifies the risk. Detailed studies of local aspects may bring forth new facts and perhaps disclose errors in this volume, but the significance of such studies will be enhanced by the present attempt to show the subject in its broader aspects.

In the preparation of this study, I had access to valuable manuscripts and other source materials, which are described in the bibliography. The letter books of Jacob Brown, preserved in the Library of Congress, yielded invaluable information concerning military policy, army administration, and conditions in the Northern Division. The voluminous files of letters to the secretary of war, which are preserved in the Old Records Division of the War Department, furnished indisputable information on frontier conditions. The orderly books, general orders, department orders, letters sent, division and department returns, Gaines's Letter Book, and Jackson's Letter Book and orders were used, though by no means exhausted. In the inspection reports, preserved in the office of the inspector general, were recorded the confidential opinions as well as the general observations of trained men who made the rounds of the military posts. The reports of the Corps of Engineers were concerned largely with coast defenses, but they furnished some incidental information. Copies of letters to Indian agents and factors preserved in the Indian Office also yielded indispensable information. The factory accounts are preserved in the same office.

The manuscripts of the Missouri Historical Society are a mine of information which no one person could exhaust in a lifetime. Only the collections that proved most valuable are here mentioned. The papers of two Indian agents, Richard Graham and Thomas Forsyth, furnished the greater part of the material utilized in the discussion of Indian agents. Of special value were the letter books of George C. Sibley, sub-agent and factor. From Atkinson's journal of the Yellowstone Expedition, Kennerly's diary and papers, the Tesson Papers, and many other collections useful information was culled. The usefulness of many other books is attested by the footnotes.

The frontier newspapers of the period deserve special mention. To the everlasting regret of historians, most newspaper editors were engrossed with European affairs, speeches in Congress, departmental reports, and territorial laws. Items that are of value and interest to students today did appear occasionally, however, and these little articles, admitted by grudging editors, constitute the great value of the early frontier newspapers. For the purposes of this study the *Detroit Gazette* is the most valuable. Photostatic copies of this paper for the years from 1817 to beyond the period of this study are in the library of the Missouri Historical Society. The two St. Louis papers, the *Gazette* and the *Enquirer,* also have great historical value. The file of the former is practically complete for the decade from 1815 to 1825, and that of the latter is fairly complete from the summer of 1819. Unfortunately the issues of 1818 and part of 1819 have not been preserved. Files of these two papers are the property of the Missouri Historical Society. The *Missouri Intelligencer*, published at old Franklin and edited by a man with considerable local pride, included many items of interest and value. A file of this paper is owned by the State Historical Society of Missouri, at Columbia. I did not use the *Arkansas Gazette*, but I had an almost complete check of its items. The *National Intelligencer* and *Niles' Weekly Register* were of great value for their original contributions and doubly valuable for what they quoted from numerous frontier papers. Unfortunately neither of them was scrupulous in making acknowledgments, and so the origin of many items is lost. Other newspapers, especially those of the South, are cited in the footnotes and are listed in the bibliography.

Chapter I clarifies the definition of a frontier by distinguishing the line of settlement, the cession line, the military line, and the international line. During a part of the decade under consideration the international line was unmarked on the north, west, and south and so constituted an integral part of the frontier. Chapter II gives a view of the tribes and their attitude toward the United States in 1815. Chapter III analyzes the work of Indian agents and shows how it was related to frontier defense. The activities of two agents afford specific illustrations of the agency system. Chapter IV is a history of the factory system. Chapter V summarizes the condition of the fur trade in 1815, indicates its development, and shows its connection with Indian and frontier policies. Chapter VI traces the development of the national military policy in regard to the size, employment, training, discipline, and cost of the army. Related phases, such as the militia and military roads, are also discussed. Chapter VII outlines the organization of the army and discusses its administration on the frontiers. The geographical units of administration are explained in the text and shown on two maps. Chapters VIII to XII deal with the application of the defense policy on the various frontiers.

I wish to indicate specifically what I believe are the salient features of this study. It represents what is perhaps the first attempt at a comprehensive definition of frontier defense and a critical evaluation of the factory system. The national military policy from 1815 to 1825 is treated in detail. The administration of the army in the early period has not heretofore been critically considered. The expedition up the Missouri River in 1819 has not received adequate treatment. Several minor points, such as Jackson's inconsistency in issuing his order of April 22, 1817, new facts concerning many forts, the permanent retention of Florida after 1818, and the farming policy of the army, have either been overlooked or have received only incidental attention. Lastly, three of the maps present hitherto uncharted facts.

I gladly acknowledge the assistance and cooperation of many persons who have contributed to this study. The officials in charge of the archives at Washington were courteous and obliging. To the late Mr. J. D. Parker, chief clerk of the Inspector General's Office; Colonel J. William DeGrange, clerk of archives in the Office of Engineers; Mr. Brent M. Morgan, clerk in the Indian Office; Dr. H. L. Street, clerk of the Old Files Section; and especially to Major John E. Brooks, chief clerk of the Record Division, I am indebted for permission to examine materials. Dr. Newton D. Mereness, dean of researchers, piloted, befriended, and encouraged me. Dr. Thomas P. Martin of the Manuscript Division of the Library of Congress and his assistants were courteous and helpful. The clerks in the newspaper room of the Library of Congress maintained their even tempers under repeated loads of newspapers. Attendants at libraries and historical societies were obliging. To the staffs of the Library of Congress, the St. Louis Public Library, the Lexington (Kentucky) Public Library, the State Historical Society of Missouri, the Washington University Library, the Missouri

Historical Society, and the University of Minnesota Library thanks are due. Mrs. Nettie Harney Beauregard, archivist, and Miss Stella M. Drumm, librarian, of the Missouri Historical Society, cheerfully furnished material and assistance. To Professor Frederic L. Paxson thanks are due for calling my attention to two theses on frontier defense. Dr. Solon J. Buck and Dr. Milo M. Quaife answered inquiries, and Mr. Fred Dustin of Saginaw, Michigan, furnished valuable material.

Acknowledgments are due the *North Dakota Historical Quarterly* for permission to reprint the major portions of Chapters V and X, which have previously appeared in that magazine, and to the *Journal of Business and Economic History* for permission to reprint the material contained in Chapter IV. I appreciate their courtesy.

I am under special obligations to Dr. Thomas M. Marshall for suggestions, criticisms, and encouragement, and to the staff of the University of Minnesota Press for its careful editing of the manuscript.

EDGAR BRUCE WESLEY

University of Minnesota
August 1, 1935

CONTENTS

MAPS

CHAPTER I

THE PROBLEMS OF FRONTIER DEFENSE

THE WESTWARD expansion of the American people involved a threefold struggle: the mastery of the difficulties of nature, the subjection of the Indians, and the contest with foreign powers, whose subtle machinations threatened to destroy American control of the West. After the War of 1812 the menace of foreign powers gradually lessened, but the Indian problem was ever present. Before the frontiersman could clear the forests or plow the fields, he had to safeguard himself against attack. Individual settlers could not overcome the opposition of determined tribes, and whole settlements were sometimes unable to do so. Under such circumstances the frontiersman naturally felt that his country owed him protection, and the United States government was not slow to acknowledge the obligation and to shoulder the task.

The national obligation of protecting the frontiersmen involved the power of designating frontier lines. After the government obtained a cession of land from a tribe, the tract was opened for settlement, and the Indians were left in possession of the areas beyond the treaty line. The United States assumed the obligation of protecting the settlers and guaranteeing the integrity of the lands in possession of the Indians. An Indian frontier was thus established, but the establishment of such lines was easier than their maintenance. Marauding Indians and intruding whites had little respect for treaty obligations, and the security and peace of the frontier required the presence of garrisons.

The frontier, as defined by the census of 1890,[1] was the edge of the region that had fewer than two persons to the square mile.

[1] *United States Census,* 1890, *Population,* p. xxi.

I

This frontier of settlement did not coincide with the military frontier, for some regions having a denser population needed protection, and others having fewer people did not. The frontier line of settlement was determined by the fertility and accessibility of the land, the military frontier by the location and attitude of the Indian tribes. It was thus possible for a frontier to have four parts, divided by the line of settlement, the cession line, the military line, and the international line. This terminology is by no means universally applicable, but in theory it represents the progressive steps in the advancement of the frontier.

The protection of the line of settlement was not the only aspect of frontier defense. While the United States was willing to respect the Indian lands to the extent of restraining its citizens from settling on them, it could not afford to lose sight of the national frontiers that lay beyond the tribes. Spain, England, and the United States were interested in various areas for various reasons and sought to control the Indians in those regions. In some instances conflicting policies resulted. The United States, in order to counteract this foreign influence and insure its complete control over the Indians, extended the military frontier far beyond the cession lines and the settled area. The protection of trade and the defense of boundary lines sometimes necessitated the erection of forts within the Indian country and the establishment of a line of defense near or along international boundaries. Frontier defense thus became far more than a local or domestic question.

But frontier defense against the Indians was not merely a military problem. The defeat of the combined forces of the tribes in ordinary warfare would have been easier, quicker, and cheaper than the variety of methods that were adopted. Defense against the Indians, who were nominally independent and in reality wards of the nation, who were sometimes enemies of the nation, generally enemies of each other, and always enemies of some frontiersmen, was a complicated problem. The humanitarian aspect could not be ignored, and the United States was in the paradoxical situation of opposing and protecting the Indians, of taking land from them and of guaranteeing their possession of land. The military alone could not solve so complex a problem. Even the purely military aspects were complicated. The defeat of a group of Indians, the erection of a chain of forts, or the negotiation of a treaty might temporarily insure peace and security to one part of the frontier, while disaffection continued in other parts. The typical line of settlement can scarcely be called a line, for occupied areas indented the Indian country in irregular tongues and often constituted isolated islands of settlement entirely surrounded by Indians, and the lingering line of retreat left tribes in the midst of white settlements.[2] The ideal situation would have been an orderly advance of settlers in sufficient numbers to constitute their own defense,[3] but differences in land values and individual ambition ran counter to such a development. The land office offered several tracts bordering the Indian country for sale at the same time, and the occupation of land yet unopened for settlement occurred so frequently that it was necessary to call for military force to remove the intruders. Indians surrounded by white settlers could hope for little justice or security, and isolated whites could scarcely expect the government to guarantee them protection in any and every place to which their fancy led them. Naturally the attempt to bring peace and security to all citizens on the frontier was unsuccessful.

Various methods of defense against the Indians were tried. Actual war against offending tribes was the simplest and, for the frontiersmen, the most desirable, but it seldom resulted in the extermination of the enemy. Purchase of the land and removal of the Indians, a natural expedient, was advocated and tried, but it was expensive and required time, tact, and sometimes force.[4]

[2] *Ibid.*, pp. xxi–xxiii. The frontier line of 1810 was 2,900 miles long, that of 1820 was 4,100 miles, and that of 1830 was 5,300 miles.

[3] These problems were recognized at the time, and the ideal situation was recommended. *American State Papers: Military Affairs,* 2:84, 124; Brown to Calhoun, February 5, 1818, Brown Letter Books.

[4] The policy of removals aroused the bitter opposition of the people of Missouri and Arkansas. For a particularly vehement utterance against the removal of the Kickapoo see the *St. Louis Enquirer* of September 19, 1820.

A chain of posts was the most widely applied method, but a sufficient number of posts to insure peace to all parts of the frontier could not be built or maintained. Impressive expeditions intended to overawe and humble the tribes were sent out, but their effects were short-lived. Factories, annuities, gifts, oratory, and treaties were tried, and perhaps each played its part in the eventual solution. One Indian agent [5] proposed that the Indians be fed to death. He declared that three or four months of full rations of bread and meat would bring on disease, and that six or eight months of such a regimen would bring on great mortality. He thought that a hundred thousand dollars worth of food would kill more Indians than an army on which a million dollars was expended.

Frontier defense may be divided into the Indian policy and the military policy. The Indian policy consisted of three aspects: diplomatic, humanitarian, and commercial. The diplomatic representatives were the Indian agents who furnished the medium of communication between the United States and the tribes. The humanitarian policy was carried out partly by agents and factors, and more fully by teachers and missionaries. The factory system was a combination of commercial and humanitarian aspects. The fur traders constituted no part of the national Indian policy, but their influence was important in the development of both Indian and military policy. The frontier policy was dependent upon the national military policy and army administration. The application of defense upon each of the frontiers was the result of a combination of all phases of the frontier policy.

At the close of the War of 1812 the northern boundary was settled along only a fraction of its length. The western boundary of the Louisiana Purchase was unsettled and unmarked;[6] the West Florida question was practically settled so far as the United States was concerned, in spite of the fact that Spain had

[5] Letter of Benjamin F. Stickney, October 1, 1818, *American State Papers: Indian Affairs*, 2:86.
[6] Marshall, *Western Boundary of the Louisiana Purchase*.

not consented to the alienation of the province;[7] East Florida was still debatable land. The Indians on the northern, western, and southern frontiers were restless and unpacified. Settlers by the thousands were eager to occupy the western lands. Frontier defense, domestic and international, was imperative.

The nation was equal to the occasion. The war had engendered a spirit of conscious nationalism which extended to the frontiers. Their defense became the defense of the nation itself. Their maintenance meant the preservation of national dignity, their extension the furthering of national aspirations. The history of frontier defense involves national and international aspects that make the subject of more than local interest and value.

[7] Cox, *The West Florida Controversy.*

CHAPTER II

THE PACIFICATION OF THE TRIBES

THE INDIAN situation in 1815 required immediate attention. The pacification and control of those who had been hostile in the War of 1812 and the maintenance of friendly relations with the loyal tribes were primary objects of the frontier policy of the government. The Indians who had fought against the United States included those on the northern frontier, those on the western frontier as far south as the Missouri River, and the Creeks on the southern frontier. The friendly and neutral Indians included those in the Southwest, many along the southern frontier, most of the tribes between the Missouri and the Mississippi, and scattered bands on all the frontiers. Naturally the War Department gave its first attention to the regions inhabited by those who had been hostile. The northern tribes were suspected of being unduly influenced by the English and the southern tribes by the Spanish. Military control of all the tribes was a necessity.

Frontier defense was primarily defense against the Indians. The attitude of the tribes was sometimes the result of foreign influence, but the military aspects of defense may be considered without reference to the causes that made it necessary. The disposition, location, and strength of the various tribes vitally affected frontier policy. Definite and reliable information about such matters was difficult to obtain in the decade when it was of considerable moment, and the lapse of time has increased the difficulties. Tribes shifted from one place to another, restrained only by the danger of attack from other tribes and by the limits of the food supply. The exact number of Indians in a given area can seldom be ascertained, and estimates vary greatly.[1] In spite

[1] For a discussion of the problem, with examples of various estimates, see Swanton, *Indian Tribes of the Lower Mississippi Valley and Adjacent Coast of the Gulf of Mexico,* pp. 39–45.

6

of the difficulties of obtaining accurate information, some conclusions, which will be approximately correct, may be reached. The northern frontier was inhabited by several fairly populous tribes.[2] The Chippewa, who lived along the Great Lakes from Saginaw Bay to the headwaters of the Mississippi, and who were considered to be brave and revengeful, probably numbered five or six thousand warriors, but they were too scattered to effect a united force. They came into contact with the posts at Detroit, Saginaw, Mackinac, Sault Ste. Marie, and Green Bay.[3] Northwest of Detroit and along the eastern shore of Lake Michigan north of Grand River were the Ottawa, who probably numbered eleven or twelve hundred warriors.[4] They were closely attached to the British cause and continued their visits into Canada long after the war was over. The Menominee, who lived around Green Bay and roamed over the region to the northwest, numbered five hundred warriors.[5] A small number of the same tribe lived on the Illinois River.[6] Scattered over what is now southern Wisconsin and northern Illinois were the Winnebago, whom Forsyth characterized as "a fierce, brave nation." They numbered from five to eight hundred warriors.[7] They sullenly

[2] The location of the principal tribes is shown on the map on page 8.
[3] The estimates of the various tribes are based chiefly upon contemporary materials. Thomas Forsyth, Indian agent, made a report to Governor William Clark of Missouri Territory, dated at St. Louis, December 23, 1812, which is now in the Forsyth Collection in the Missouri Historical Society. It is fairly detailed in its treatment of the Indians of the Old Northwest. In 1814 Forsyth made another report, which he submitted to Rufus Easton, delegate to Congress from Missouri Territory; this was published in the *Missouri Gazette* of January 21, 1815; it may also be found in Wisconsin Historical Collections, 11:331–36. Clark's Report to the Secretary of War, September 20, 1815, was printed in *American State Papers: Indian Affairs*, 2:76–77. His later and probably more reliable report of September 14, 1816, is in the Indian Office. Additional information may be found in Wisconsin Historical Collections, 19:470–72; 20:50; *Detroit Gazette*, January 4, 1822; Morse, *A Report to the Secretary of War on Indian Affairs;* and Blair, *Indian Tribes of the Upper Mississippi and the Great Lakes Regions,* vol. 2.
[4] Forsyth's Report to Clark, Missouri Historical Society, printed in Wisconsin Historical Collections, 20:50.
[5] John Bowyer, Indian agent at Green Bay, to Governor Cass, August 12, 1817, Wisconsin Historical Collections, 19:470–72.
[6] Wisconsin Historical Collections, 20:50.
[7] Forsyth's Report to Clark, Missouri Historical Society, printed in Wisconsin Historical Collections, 19:470–72; 20:50.

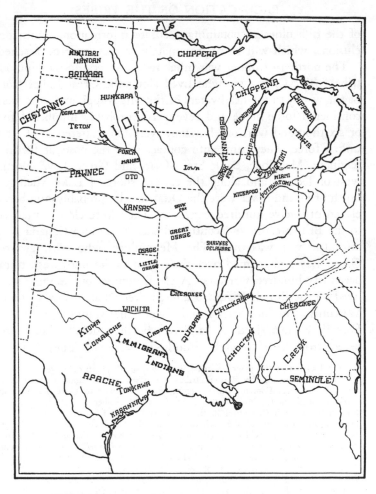

APPROXIMATE LOCATION OF THE INDIAN TRIBES THAT
AFFECTED FRONTIER POLICY, 1815–25

8

accepted peace, but their hostile disposition was one of the reasons for the establishment of Fort Crawford at Prairie du Chien. The Potawatomi and remnants of various tribes occupied the region south and southeast of Lake Michigan and occasioned the continued occupation of Forts Wayne and Harrison, but their power declined rapidly before the advancing tide of settlers.

The tribes on the northern frontier, with the exception of some of the bands, had fought against the Americans. By the Ninth Article of the Treaty of Ghent the United States agreed to restore the rights and privileges that the Indians had enjoyed in 1811.[8] The pacification of some of the northern tribes was effected by the Treaty of Spring Wells, negotiated near Detroit on September 8, 1815. The commissioners, Major General William Henry Harrison, Brigadier General Duncan McArthur, and John Graham,[9] met the chiefs and leaders of the Chippewa, Ottawa, Potawatomi, and certain bands of Wyandot, Delaware, Seneca, Shawnee, and Miami in August and early September and agreed upon terms of peace. The United States pardoned the tribes and bands that had been hostile and restored the privileges they had had before the war, and the Indians agreed "to place themselves under the protection of the United States, and of no other power whatsoever," and to confirm previous treaties.[10]

The Mississippi-Missouri frontier[11] was the scene of many engagements during the war,[12] and the restoration of peace was a slow process because of the attitude of the Indians. The most belligerent of the tribes were the Sauk and Fox, whose principal villages were near the mouth of the Rock River. They also had

---

[8] Malloy, *Treaties, Conventions, and Agreements*, 1:618.

[9] For a complete list of commissioners from 1815 to 1825 see Appendix C.

[10] The treaty and the report of the commissioners are given in *American State Papers: Indian Affairs*, 2:12–25. The treaty is also printed in Kappler, *Indian Affairs, Laws, and Treaties*, 2:117–19.

[11] The term is used to denote the region along the Mississippi from St. Louis to Prairie du Chien, the lower Missouri, and most of Illinois.

[12] For a list of the chief events see Wesley, "James Callaway in the War of 1812," *Missouri Historical Collections*, 5:44–45.

small settlements on the west side of the Mississippi and a village on Grand River in what is now north-central Missouri. Their warriors totaled about twelve hundred.[13] Fort Armstrong was erected at the mouth of the Rock River in 1816 because that location was a convenient one from which to control these Indians, whom Forsyth characterized as "dastardly, cowardly," and "full of duplicity." Around the southern end of Lake Michigan, on the Illinois River, and westward to the Mississippi lived the powerful Potawatomi. Forsyth, who knew them well, observed that they were, "as most Indians are, a deceitful, treacherous people and with very few exceptions cowardly" and "the greatest horse thieves of any Indians that exist." They were able to muster at least a thousand warriors.[14] Fort Clark was built at Peoria in 1813 for the purpose of controlling the tribe and was maintained for a few years after the war. Fort Edwards, on the site of the present town of Warsaw, Illinois, also afforded some security against the Potawatomi. The Kickapoo, who inhabited east-central Illinois, numbered about four hundred warriors.[15] Their lands were within easy reach of Fort Clark on the west and Fort Harrison on the southeast. The Iowa, who numbered about four hundred warriors, lived in two villages, one on the Des Moines River and the other on the Grand River in Missouri.[16]

The tribes between the Mississippi and the Missouri were only slightly affected by the war, and their attitude did not materially influence the policy of defense after the war. Their attitude later became a matter of importance, for, aside from the Seminole War, the most serious Indian disturbance of the decade occurred on the Missouri. Above Fort Osage on the west bank of the Missouri was the Kansa tribe, which numbered three or four

[13] Estimates by Edward Tanner (*Detroit Gazette,* January 8, 1819), who passed up the Mississippi in 1818, coincide with Clark's Report of 1816. Forsyth thought the number might be fifteen hundred.

[14] Forsyth's Report to Clark, Missouri Historical Society; Forsyth's Report to Easton, *Missouri Gazette,* January 21, 1815.

[15] Forsyth's Report to Easton, *Missouri Gazette,* January 21, 1815.

[16] Clark's Report of 1816, Indian Office; Tanner in *Detroit Gazette,* January 8, 1819.

hundred warriors.[17] They never caused any serious trouble but were important because of their interest in the fur trade. On the lower Platte were the friendly Oto, who numbered about three hundred warriors.[18] The Pawnee lived in three villages, two on the Platte and one on the Republican. Their warriors numbered about two thousand. The Maha lived on the Horn, a branch of the Platte, and numbered about five hundred and fifty. The Ponca, who lived on White Paint Creek, had about two hundred warriors. Scattered from the mouth of the Big Sioux northward beyond the forty-ninth parallel and from the Minnesota River westward to the Black Hills were several bands of Sioux: the Yankton, numbering six hundred; the Yanktonai, eight hundred; the Teton, six hundred; the Oglala, three hundred; the Hunkpapa, three hundred; and the Assiniboin, two thousand. Being largely dependent upon the buffalo, these bands lived a comparatively unsettled life. Their policy was one of peace toward the whites. The Cheyenne, occupying the region from the Cheyenne River to the Black Hills, numbered about six hundred warriors. The Arikara, numbering five hundred warriors, led a fairly stable life in their dirt villages on the Missouri; they raised corn and vegetables and hunted the buffalo. Above the Arikara were the Mandan and Minitari (Gros Ventres), who numbered five hundred warriors. On the headwaters of the Missouri and west of the Black Hills were the Crow, Blackfeet, and other tribes which had no official contact with the whites during the decade.[19] The southern part of the present state of Minnesota was occupied by various tribes of Sioux, chief of which were the Sisseton, Wahpeton, Wahpekute, and Mdewa-

[17] Clark's Report of 1816, Indian Office; Forsyth's Report to Easton, *Missouri Gazette*, January 21, 1815; George C. Sibley, factor at Fort Osage, in *Missouri Gazette*, May 16, 1812.

[18] Clark's reports of 1815 and 1816 and Forsyth's report to Easton deal with the Indians of the upper Missouri. It is probable that more reliable statistics for the area are contained in the report by General Henry Atkinson and Indian Agent Benjamin O'Fallon, who led the Yellowstone Expedition of 1825. *American State Papers: Indian Affairs*, 2:605–08. It may be added that the various estimates show no great divergence.

[19] *American State Papers: Indian Affairs*, 2:605–08.

kanton. In 1823 these tribes numbered about a thousand war-riors.[20]

The pacification of most of the tribes along the Mississippi and the Missouri was effected in the summer and fall of 1815. Great preparations were made for the assembling of the tribes at Portage des Sioux on the Mississippi, a few miles above the mouth of the Missouri. The commissioners, William Clark, Ninian Edwards, and Auguste Chouteau, held a preliminary meeting at St. Louis and sent out invitations to the tribes to assemble on July 6. The Indian agents were notified of the meeting and were asked to see that the tribes they represented sent delegations. Lieutenant George H. Kennerly was sent to bring the chiefs of the tribes from the Missouri River region. Twenty thousand dollars worth of presents for the Indians were furnished by the government, and ample supplies for visiting delegations were provided. The commissioners, accompanied by a secretary, Indian agents, interpreters, a detachment of troops, officers of the army, the witnesses, took up their quarters at the appointed place. In spite of the extensive preparations, the attendance of the Indians was unsatisfactory. In some instances unauthorized delegations and unimportant individuals pretended to speak for their tribes, and the commissioners sent them back to obtain more suitable representatives. Some tribes sent no delegations at all, and those that did come arrived many days after the appointed time. Several weeks were consumed in speech-making and negotiations, but by the end of October twelve treaties had been completed.

The Potawatomi, Piankashaw, Teton, Sioux of the Lakes, Sioux of St. Peter's, Yankton, Kickapoo, Osage, Sauk of the Missouri, Foxes, Iowa, and Kansa made peace and signed treaties. Acts of hostility were forgiven, privileges of both friends and former enemies were confirmed, and existing treaties were acknowledged. The Sauk of Rock River, the Winnebago, the Menominee, and the Chippewa sent no delegations. Their failure to do so, according to the commissioners, was due to the liberal

[20] Keating, *Long's Expedition*, 1:380.

distribution of presents among them by the British government and to intrigues of British traders.[21]

In 1816 the Sauk of Rock River, having learned of the fort that was to be established in their midst, sent a delegation to St. Louis and accepted the terms that had been offered other tribes. Shortly afterward the Winnebago and Ottawa, and early in 1817 the Menominee, accepted similar terms.[22]

In 1819 Calhoun very correctly observed that the Indians of the Southwest constituted no problem.[23] But his remark soon ceased to be true, for two reasons: the development of the policy of removals and the long struggle over the southwestern boundary. Thus the Indians became important in a region unaffected by the War of 1812. Bands of Indians from the east side began to move across the Mississippi during the Spanish régime,[24] and in 1815 there were Piankashaw, Shawnee, Delaware, and Peoria in southern Missouri, numbering, all told, about 835 warriors.[25] The Cherokee also had crossed the Mississippi in considerable numbers. In 1815 several bands of them, sufficient numbers to furnish six hundred warriors,[26] had settled on both sides of the Arkansas for two hundred miles above its mouth. By 1817 their total number had increased to thirty-seven hundred,[27] and by the end of the decade they numbered several thousand.[28] Their arrival started a series of contests with the Osage, who lived on the Osage, Verdigris, and Neosho rivers, and numbered fifteen hundred warriors. On the lower Arkansas were two bands of the friendly Quapaw with about 340 war-

[21] *American State Papers: Indian Affairs*, 2:1–12; Kappler, *Indian Affairs, Laws, and Treaties*, 2:110–24.

[22] Kappler, *Indian Affairs, Laws, and Treaties*, 2:128–33, 138.

[23] *American State Papers: Military Affairs*, 2:33.

[24] Houck, *Spanish Régime in Missouri*, 1:210; 2:169–81, 209–10.

[25] Clark's Report of 1816, Indian Office.

[26] Forsyth's Report to Easton, *Missouri Gazette*, January 21, 1815. Clark estimated the warriors at a thousand and the total at five thousand, but in 1816 he reduced his estimate to thirty-six hundred. The actual number in the latter year was about twenty-six hundred. Return J. Meigs to the Secretary of War, quoting William L. Lovely, Indian agent on the Arkansas, Territorial Papers, State Department.

[27] Bassett, *Correspondence of Andrew Jackson*, 2:289.

[28] Hodge estimated the Cherokee at six thousand in 1838. *Handbook of American Indians*, 1:247.

riors.[29] Southward, in Louisiana, were remnants of many tribes, some of whom had migrated from the east side of the Mississippi. Many Choctaw, Delaware, Cherokee, and Shawnee pushed westward across the Red and Sabine, a movement that brought them into contact with the Caddo, who inhabited that region. In 1820 the Caddo numbered about three hundred warriors.[30] The tribes of eastern Texas had no official contact with the Americans during the decade.[31] Thus the Indian situation in the Southwest began to become complicated and important in the very year in which Calhoun dismissed it as settled.

The Indian frontier on the south presented a problem, but one that constantly grew less serious. The policy of removals[32] slowly reduced the strength of the southern tribes, although the process required many years. The most northern and eastern tribe was the Cherokee, who were of no military significance east of the Mississippi during the decade. The Creek, inhabiting western Georgia and parts of Alabama, numbered several thousand, although their strength had been greatly reduced by the war. The Choctaw were numerous and powerful in western Alabama and various parts of Mississippi, and the Chickasaw of northern Mississippi and western Tennessee were also numerous, but both tribes were peaceably disposed toward the United States and gave no serious trouble during the decade. Across the border, in Florida, were the Seminole, who, because of their location and the nature of the land, were stronger than their number of warriors, a few thousand, would indicate.[33] They were allied with many dissatisfied Creek who crossed the border after Jackson's campaigns.[34]

[29] Clark's Report of 1816.

[30] *Niles' Weekly Register*, 19:133.

[31] For a concise summary of the Indian situation on the Sabine frontier at a little later date see Marshall, *Western Boundary of the Louisiana Purchase*, pp. 124–40.

[32] For a discussion of Indian removals see Abel, "The History of Events Resulting in Indian Consolidation West of the Mississippi," Annual Report of the *American Historical Association*, 1906, 1:233–450.

[33] See Hodge, *Handbook of American Indians*, under the various tribes, and Pickett, *History of Alabama*, 1:74–163.

[34] Bassett, *Correspondence of Andrew Jackson*, vol. 3, *passim*.

Of the tribes on the southwestern and southern frontiers only the Creek engaged in the War of 1812 against the United States. Their opposition was terminated by the signing of a treaty at Fort Jackson, near the junction of the Tallapoosa and the Coosa, on August 9, 1814. Major General Andrew Jackson, the sole commissioner, demanded and secured a large cession of land, the exact limits of which were to be marked by commissioners. It consisted approximately of the central and southern parts of the present state of Alabama and that part of Georgia south of a line running straight east from Fort Gaines.[35] The cession resulted in the opening of a large tract for settlement and in the virtual isolation of the Creek from other tribes. The Creek also agreed to refrain from communicating with foreigners and to allow the erection of forts and factories and the opening of roads.[36] The treaty cannot be properly called a pacification, because its hard terms aroused the bitter opposition of the Creek, and those who fled across the border had an opportunity for further resistance.

[35] Royce, *Indian Land Cessions*, pp. 678–79, and plates 1 and 15.
[36] Kappler, *Indian Affairs, Laws, and Treaties*, 2:107–10.

CHAPTER III

INDIAN AGENTS

As INTERNATIONAL relations call forth the diplomat, the commercial agent, and the soldier, so the problem of frontier defense produced the Indian agent, the factor, and the frontier soldier. The Indian policy of the United States was fourfold: diplomatic, commercial, humanitarian, and military. Each of these aspects constituted an integral part of the general plan of frontier defense. The making of treaties and the removal of tribes to more remote lands lessened friction and helped to insure peace on the frontier. The regulation of traders, the operation of the factory system, and the awarding of annuities and presents were means toward making the frontier safe. The establishment of a school, a mission, or a model farm tended to promote good will and preserve the peace. The presence of garrisons added the final assurance and guarantee of a workable defense policy. In the accomplishment of these plans the indispensable medium was the Indian agent.

The necessity of having special representatives among the Indians had been recognized even in colonial days. Several of the colonies had maintained agents, and when the Revolutionary War began, the united colonies were confronted with an Indian problem. The friendship and assistance of the Indians, or at least their neutrality, became highly important from a military as well as from a commercial standpoint. In 1775 the Continental Congress made an effort to solve the problem by establishing Indian departments under the supervision of commissioners authorized to expend money, make treaties, and appoint agents.[1] The commissioners for the Northern Department negotiated the treaty of Albany, by which they hoped to secure the assistance

[1] *Journals of the Continental Congress*, 2:174–77.

of the Iroquois, but the tribes were imperfectly represented and British influence was strong.[2] Other legislative and diplomatic attempts were made during the war,[3] but they produced no tangible results, and expenditures for the Indian department declined to almost nothing by the end of the war.[4]

The inauspicious beginning was not easily overcome, for the adoption of the Articles of Confederation gave rise to an interesting and important constitutional question, which handicapped the central government and paralyzed its Indian policy. Article IX provided that "the United States in Congress assembled have the sole and exclusive right and power of regulating the trade, and managing all affairs with the Indians not members of any of the states; provided that the legislative right of any state within its own limits be not infringed or violated." This statement apparently meant that Congress had power over the Indians in the national domain, and the states over those living within their respective boundaries.

This was the interpretation insisted upon by Georgia, North Carolina, and, to a lesser extent, other states. A vigorous committee in Congress opposed the claim of the states. It pointed out that the Indians were regarded as constituting independent communities to which the laws of the states did not apply; that they were the common friends or enemies of all the states; that the provisions would be reduced to an absurdity if the states controlled the Indians; that it would be folly to leave the power of peace and war for the whole country in the hands of one state; that the power of making treaties and wars and of purchasing lands was indivisible; and that the authors of the Articles intended to give such powers wholly to the states or to the Confederation.[5] Add to the arguments of the committee the simple fact that the Confederation owned no public lands at the time of the drafting of the Articles, and the conclusion is inescapable

[2] For an account of the treaty and many related documents see Stone, *Life of Brant*, 1:104–05, Appendixes IV and XXXI; *Journals of the Continental Congress*, 2:250–51; 3:350, 363–66.
[3] *Journals of the Continental Congress*, 3:366; 4:96–98, 318.
[4] *American State Papers: Indian Affairs*, 2:210.
[5] *Journals of Congress*, 4:766–67.

that the authors intended to give such powers to the Confederation, and that the states were acting illegally when they dealt with the Indians. Rightly or wrongly, legally or illegally, Georgia, North Carolina, and at various times Pennsylvania, Massachusetts, and New York, assumed the powers claimed by the committee to be the exclusive prerogatives of Congress. The divided powers and conflicting claims largely nullified the actions of both states and nation. Several treaties were made, but they were generally useless.

This state of affairs led to exploitation of the Indians, causing them to lose goods and lands. Washington warned Congress that land-grabbing and intrusions into the Indian country should be stopped. To insure fair dealing he suggested that the government conduct the Indian trade.[6] In accordance with this recommendation Congress issued a proclamation forbidding all settlements on Indian land and declaring purchases, cessions, or gifts of land from Indians null and void without the express sanction of Congress.[7] Shortly afterward a committee urged stricter laws for protecting the Indians,[8] but several years passed before any definite action was taken. In 1786 Congress passed a law dividing the western country into two districts, separated by the Ohio River, and providing for a superintendent for each and two deputies for the Northern District. The superintendents were to prevent foreigners from engaging in the trade and were to issue licenses to citizens of established character who paid an annual fee of fifty dollars and furnished a bond to the amount of three thousand dollars.[9]

The general debility of the government under the Articles and the constitutional question of the power of dealing with the Indians left such matters largely unsettled. The advent of the new

[6] Washington, *Writings*, 8:477–84. The letter was written on September 7, 1783. It is interesting to note that the ideas of Washington that caused him to recommend the establishment of the factory system when he became president were formulated as early as this.

[7] *Journals of the Continental Congress*, 25:602.

[8] *Journals of Congress*, 4:294–96. The report was dated October 15, 1783.

[9] *Ibid.*, 4:677–78; also printed, with a few minor changes and errors, in *American State Papers: Indian Affairs*, 1:14.

government in 1789 produced no immediate changes. In 1790 a law reaffirmed some of the provisions of former acts. Licenses were required of all traders under penalty of the forfeiture of one thousand dollars; trade permits were valid for two years only; sale of land by an Indian was declared to be invalid; and an offender against Indians was to be punished as though the offense were against whites. No license fee was required, and there was no prohibition against foreigners.[10] Early in 1793 the president was authorized to furnish the Indians with domestic animals, and he was empowered to appoint agents who were to be under bonds of a thousand dollars.[11]

In 1796 Congress passed a new law regulating Indian affairs. It specified the boundaries of Indian lands and provided for making treaties. No citizen was to trade with the Indians without a license, buy horses from them, contract for land, or settle among the tribes.[12] To facilitate trade with the Indians the general revenue act of 1799 provided that no duties should be charged on peltries coming from their lands.[13] The law of 1796 was renewed in 1799,[14] and an act of 1802 forbade the sale of liquor to the Indians.[15] The laws of 1796 and 1802 were the most important ones regulating Indian agents, and copies of them were usually sent to newly appointed agents.[16]

The laws of 1796 and 1802, with occasional renewals and alterations, formed the legal bases for the growth of the agency system. Regulations by the War Department frequently supplemented the laws, and the financial provisions for the Indian department varied from year to year. While the general nature of the duties was the same for all agencies, each agent had prob-

[10] United States Statutes at Large, 1:137–38. The law was passed on July 22, 1790.
[11] Ibid., 1:329–32. The law was passed on March 1, 1793.
[12] Ibid., 1:469–74. This law was signed on May 19 and was limited to two years plus the duration of Congress.
[13] Ibid., 1:702.
[14] Ibid., 1:743–49. It was approved on March 3.
[15] Ibid., 2:139–46. This prohibition was enacted in response to Jefferson's request; he said the Indians themselves desired such restrictions. American State Papers: Indian Affairs, 1:653.
[16] Secretary of War to Richard Graham, July 14, 1815, War Department Letter Book C, in Indian Office.

lems peculiar to his location, which he met in accordance with his ability and resources.

The variety of duties performed by the Indian agents indicates the importance of their services and shows how closely they were connected with the policy of frontier defense. They arranged and negotiated treaties; promoted peace on the frontier and among the tribes; persuaded Indians to move to new lands; assisted in running boundary lines; served as the media between the tribes and the government; arranged for delegations of Indians to visit Washington; assisted factors; licensed traders; filed claims; paid annuities; distributed presents; helped missionaries and teachers; provided blacksmiths; maintained farmers to instruct the Indians; inspected passes; restrained traders; ejected squatters; adjusted quarrels between whites and Indians; served as officers to bring offenders against Indians to trial; conferred with army officers; reported wars and rumors of wars; and tried in general to carry out the policy of the United States toward the Indians.[17]

Most agents had one or more assistants called sub-agents, who received their appointments from the secretary of war, from superintendents of Indian Affairs, or from agents.[18] They were under the supervision of the agents to whom they reported, and in many instances they did most of the work. Though their salary was only half that of the agent, there was no essential difference in their duties.

Another important assistant to the agent was the interpreter. Few men who had the influence to obtain an appointment as agent had ever been under the necessity of learning an Indian language, and so they had to employ, at government expense, interpreters, who were often humble and ignorant traders or half-breeds. The limited training of most of the interpreters enabled them to do little more than translate the simplest ideas. Some of them had an imperfect understanding of the Indian

    [17] Gallaher, "The Indian Agent in the United States before 1850," *Iowa Journal of History and Politics*, 14:3–32, has discussed some phases of the work of Indian agents.
    [18] *American State Papers: Indian Affairs*, 2:365.

language and others an inadequate command of English.[19] The agent thus often acquired a contempt for the intelligence of the Indians, and they in turn often obtained an unfavorable notion of the agent's intentions. Hence the services of the interpreter became a determining factor in the work of the agent. If the interpreter had the intelligence, tact, and courage to phrase properly the words of both Indians and agents, the negotiations were more likely to be successful. Had the agents themselves been versed in the language of the tribes to which they were sent, many misunderstandings would have been avoided.

An Indian agent was usually stationed at each frontier post. He had the assurance of governmental support and protection and in turn gave warning when disaffected tribes were likely to go on the warpath. His efforts to maintain peace, secure land cessions, effect removals, and restrain traders and intruders were strengthened by the implied threat of force. Officers were instructed, at his request, to eject squatters and destroy their establishments.[20] The army was thus the protector of the Indian as well as of the frontiersman, and the soldier's attitude toward one seems to have been about as cordial as toward the other. Hostilities against the Indians resulted when the efforts of the agent had failed, and his failure was sometimes due to his instructions, urging him to make untimely demands for land cessions and removals.[21]

In spite of their varied and important activities, the legal position of the agents was indefinite and unspecified. They were supposed to restrain undesirable traders, but they could not refuse a license if the applicant met the legal requirements of

[19] John Jamison, agent at Natchitoches, asked that he be furnished with an interpreter who could speak English. Jamison to Secretary of War, June 19, 1816, Letters Received, Old Records Division, Adjutant General's Office.

[20] Order of Crawford to Jackson, Macomb, Gaines, and Smith, January 27, 1816, Military Books, Old Records Division, Adjutant General's Office. Benjamin F. Stickney recommended that Indian agents be given military rank in order to simplify the problem of the relative powers of officers and agents. *American State Papers: Indian Affairs*, 2:85. The agents at some posts attained such complete domination over the military as to arouse the resentment of officers. Inspection Reports, Inspector General's Office, 1825–28, pp. 45–52.

[21] *American State Papers: Indian Affairs*, 2:83–84.

bond and fee.[22] They were instructed to arrest offenders, but
their power was no greater than that possessed by any other citizen, for they could merely be a witness against the offenders.[23]
They were instructed to settle cases of robbery, abuse, and quarrels between Indians and whites, but since Indians could take
no oath in a civil court, the agents could act only as arbitrators.
They questioned witnesses and submitted documents to the secretary of war, who made the final decision.[24] From a legal
standpoint, the agents were little more than individuals paid by
the government and charged with carrying out its Indian policy.

In addition to the legal handicaps that circumscribed the
powers of the agents, the measures they did try to effect were
often opposed by frontiersmen in general. Not only did the
agents try to promote peace between the Indians and the settlers,
but they also endeavored to prevent war among the tribes,[25] and
in at least one instance an agent helped to negotiate a treaty
between a foreign country and a tribe within the United States.[26]
The popular feeling toward intertribal wars was expressed by the
Missouri Gazette when it said that peace between whites and
Indians prevailed, but that the tribes were at war with each
other and always would be unless "a mistaken philanthropy"
caused them to turn their thirst for blood against the settlers.[27]
Agents tried to protect the lands of the Indians against exploitation by hunters, trappers, and miners. Their efforts ran counter to popular wishes and were usually defeated. Grants of

[22] *Ibid.*, 2:63, 70; Morse, *Report to the Secretary of War on Indian Affairs*,
p. 43. Governor Edwards of Illinois Territory was severely criticized by the *Missouri Gazette* (January 20, 1816), for granting a license to a questionable trader.
Edwards convinced the editor that the law compelled him to issue the license
even though he thought it inadvisable, and the editor retracted his criticisms.
February 3, 1816.

[23] One of several that could be cited is Jamison to the Secretary of War,
June 16, 1819, Old Records Division, Adjutant General's Office.

[24] *American State Papers: Indian Affairs*, 2:77, 86–87.

[25] Monroe emphasized the evil results of intertribal wars. Richardson, *Messages and Papers of the Presidents*, 2:256.

[26] The agent was Benjamin O'Fallon, who helped to negotiate a treaty between
the Mexicans and Pawnee at Council Bluffs in 1824. *St. Louis Enquirer*, May 24,
31, 1824; *Niles' Weekly Register*, 27:151; Santa Fé MS., Missouri Historical
Society.

[27] May 15, 1818; also in *Niles' Weekly Register*, 14:328.

land to migrating Indians aroused bitter opposition among Westerners.[28] The whole movement to civilize and Christianize the Indians was often jeered at.[29]

The system of Indian agencies was loosely organized. Agents were appointed by the president or by the secretary of war and were under the supervision of the latter. To insure a closer supervision of the agents on the frontier where the most important ones were located, the governors of territories were given the additional office of superintendent of Indian Affairs.[30] They had immediate control of the agents and were responsible for the Indian policy within their superintendencies. They issued licenses to traders, entertained visiting Indians, distributed presents, received reports from agents, transmitted annuities, and unified the work of the agencies.[31] When a territory became a state, the supervision of agents within its boundaries was transferred to the War Department or to a neighboring territorial governor.[32] The control of agents by the secretary of war was thus sometimes direct and sometimes indirect through the superintendents.

[28] The commissioners who negotiated a cession to the Cherokee were denounced as "wooden-headed favorites," performing tasks for which nature had never designed them. *Missouri Gazette*, October 5, 1816. For a similar article see the *St. Louis Enquirer*, September 19, 1820.

[29] *Missouri Gazette*, October 26, 1816. The project for sending missionaries among the Indians created much amusement at Prairie du Chien. *Ibid.*, January 25, 1817. Not all agents, however, loved Indians. One agent in writing to another expressed the wish to get away from the "cursed stinking Indians." John W. Johnson to George C. Sibley, April 28, 1817, Sibley Collection, Missouri Historical Society.

[30] The governor of Michigan Territory was given such authority on January 11, 1805 (United States Statutes at Large, 2:309); similarly, James Miller in Arkansas Territory on March 2, 1819 (*ibid.*, 3:494). Other territorial governors were given similar powers. For numerous instances of the control of agents and the Indian trade by a territorial governor see Marshall, *Life and Papers of Frederick Bates, passim*.

[31] Calhoun to James Miller, September 21, 1819, Territorial Papers, State Department.

[32] Cass exercised control over agents in Ohio and Indiana. *American State Papers: Indian Affairs*, 2:284. There were many instances of variations from the general plan. When Missouri became a state a special office was created in order to retain the services of Clark, who was given supervision of all agents west of the Mississippi and north of Arkansas. Calhoun to Clark, May 28, 1822, War Department Letter Book E, in Indian Office.

The territorial governors were well situated to supervise Indian affairs, and when they understood such matters the plan had certain advantages. It expedited correspondence, for they could give instructions to agents and answer inquiries without long delays. If, on the other hand, the governor had little knowledge or understanding of Indians, he often blundered. Some governors considered Indian affairs beneath their dignity and by their aloofness made an unfavorable impression on visiting chiefs.[33] The control of agents by governors was not provided for by law, but rested upon custom and regulation and was implied in their office as superintendents.[34] The secretary of war did not always act consistently in assigning agents to superintendents; sometimes he allowed the governor of one territory to control agents in another.[35] The system produced some confusion, and agents were sometimes uncertain as to which accounts and reports should be sent to the superintendent and which to the secretary of war.

Legal limitations, popular opposition, loose organization, and the varied nature of the duties made the agent's position a difficult one. The office required a man of ability and resourcefulness. An agent needed to know the manners and characteristics of Indians in general and particularly those of the tribe to which he was accredited. A knowledge of the language was of inestimable benefit, for it freed him from dependence upon an interpreter. Intelligence, tact, candor, understanding, sympathy, and courage were requisite qualities. Unlike an international diplomat who contends for the advantage of his own country only, the Indian agent was in the position of representing the tribe as well as the United States. If he was imbued with the spirit of gaining advantage for his country at the expense of the tribe, he soon lost his influence and his usefulness was gone. If he was

[33] *American State Papers: Indian Affairs,* 2:79, 83–84.
[34] Secretary of War to Edwards, March 26, 1817, in Edwards, *Life and Times of Ninian Edwards,* p. 543.
[35] *American State Papers: Indian Affairs,* 2:63–64. It is probable that the secretary of war made some variations in order to assign as many agents as possible to governors who had shown ability in the management of Indian affairs. Geography doubtless played a part also.

partisan in maintaining the interests of the Indians, or if he opposed traders too vigorously, he usually lost his position.[36]

In spite of the exacting nature of the duties, agencies were frequently occupied by untrained men. Since the salary was good[37] and the power, dignity, and influence were considerable, the office attracted many claimants. Retired army officers and disappointed politicians often secured appointments; many of them knew little about the nature of their duties.[38] Some agents regarded the position as a sinecure and delegated the work to sub-agents and interpreters. Agents were instructed to live at or near the principal village of the tribe to which they were accredited, but such regulations were ignored on various pretexts, and the secretary of war was often ignorant of the absence of agents.[39]

The nature of the agent's most important task was largely determined by the location of the tribe to which he was accredited. The Northern agents felt that much of their energy should be spent in repelling British influence and in trying to steer the fur trade to the Americans. Those east of the Mississippi gave much of their attention to persuading the tribes to accept lands west of the river, and agents on the west side were frequently engaged in trying to reconcile the native tribes, who naturally objected to sharing their lands with the newly arrived Indians. Southern agents suspected the Spaniards of meddling with the Indians and endeavored to counteract such influence. An agent near a factory was frequently very energetic in promoting or hindering its operation, depending upon his attitude

[36] An illustration of the latter kind was the case of George C. Sibley, sub-agent for the Osage. He so deeply resented the conduct of private traders and protested so vigorously that he was discharged. Calhoun to Clark, November 14, 1822, and Calhoun to Sibley, June 5, 1823, War Department Letter Book E, in Indian Office. Agents were bitter in their complaints against the influence of the fur companies upon the tenure of agents.

[37] The salaries ranged from six to eighteen hundred dollars in the decade after the War of 1812, one thousand or twelve hundred dollars being typical salaries. Rations were also allowed.

[38] For a severe indictment of Indian agents see Forsyth, "Narrative," Minnesota Historical Collections, 3:162–63. British Indian agents were required to know an Indian language. American State Papers: Indian Affairs, 2:79.

[39] Ibid., 2:449.

toward that establishment. Agents of tribes that were inclined to be hostile spent their energies in speeches, threats, and expostulations, and finally, when the troubles were adjusted, in arranging for treaties.

A brief statement of the activities of two agents [40] will illustrate specifically and also serve as a fair representation of the nature of the entire agency system. The agency of Richard Graham, which was first in Illinois and then in Missouri, and the Natchitoches agency near the Texas border have been chosen as examples.

§

Major Richard Graham of St. Louis was appointed an Indian agent for Illinois Territory on July 14, 1815. He was directed to establish his agency at Peoria or at any convenient place in Illinois and to engage a gunsmith and a wheelwright. If his choice of location met the approval of the army it was to become a military post, and if approved by the superintendent of Indian Trade it was to become the site of a factory also. In due time a school for the Indians was to be established. He was instructed to require passes of all who entered the Indian country, to arrest offenders, to report illegal settlers, to confiscate the goods of unlicensed traders, to admonish the Indians, to introduce useful arts, such as spinning, weaving, agriculture, and stock-raising, to keep a journal of occurrences, and to report agitators.[41]

Graham reported to Governor Edwards and began his duties soon after his appointment,[42] but considerable time elapsed before an agency site was selected, and not until early in 1817 did he take up his duties at Peoria, where a garrison was already located. In some way Graham obtained the notion that he had authority over other agents in Illinois.[43] He wrote to Calhoun, secretary of war, to learn the extent of his authority. Calhoun replied by asking Graham to name the tribes he represented.

[40] A list of Indian agents is given in Appendix A.
[41] Graham Collection, Missouri Historical Society; War Department Letter Book C, in Indian Office. In many cases the citations to either source could be duplicated in the other.
[42] War Department Letter Book C, in Indian Office, p. 377.
[43] The origin of Graham's idea is probably to be found in a letter from Thomas L. McKenney, in which he referred to Graham as "now the principal Indian agent for that Territory." Graham Collection, Missouri Historical Society.

He did, however, point out more specifically that the admission of Illinois placed Graham directly under his supervision, that his agency included whatever tribes were outside other agencies, and that his authority did not extend over other agents.[44] In answer to Graham's request to be allowed to send a delegation of Potawatomi to Washington, Calhoun answered, "Permit a few of the most distinguished among them (the fewer the better) with an Interpreter" to come.[45]

The rapid growth of Illinois accelerated the transfer of tribes to the west side of the Mississippi. Graham and other agents were so successful in effecting removals that some posts and garrisons became useless. In accordance with the recommendation of Stephen H. Long, the engineer who had charted the Illinois River, Fort Clark at Peoria was abandoned in 1818 and Fort Edwards, Fort Harrison, and Fort Wayne about the same time or shortly afterwards. The removal of the Indians required the erection of new posts west of the Mississippi, and Long proposed one on the Red River above the settlements.[46] Agencies east of the Mississippi were abolished, and Graham was transferred to the Osage agency in Missouri.[47] There his duties became more arduous, for not only had he to oversee the Osage but he continued for a time in charge of the sub-agencies in Illinois. His principal task, aside from routine duties, was the promotion of further removals. Some chiefs would agree to move and then for various reasons refuse to do so. Perhaps the chief reason for the Indians' desire to stay in Illinois was the ease with which they could obtain whiskey, which they feared would be less plentiful west of the Mississippi. An obstacle to their removal was the objection of traders who profited by the proximity of the tribes. Conferences were arranged between chiefs from the west side and

[44] Calhoun to Graham, September 13, 1819, War Department Letter Book D, in Indian Office.

[45] Ibid., pp. 330–31.

[46] Long's Report of May 12, 1818, in Reports of the Corps of Engineers, 1812–23; Brown Letter Books, 2:112, 119; Department Orders (Ninth Department), 1819–25, Old Records Division, Adjutant General's Office.

[47] War Department Letter Book E, in Indian Office, pp. 80–81, 107; Graham Collection, Missouri Historical Society.

some as far east as Ohio. Inspired by the agents, the former gave
glowing accounts of the new lands. In 1825 Graham made a tour
of inspection through Illinois and visited the remnants of tribes
he wished to transfer. He learned that few outrages had been
committed and that most of the Indians were willing to move.[48]

The transfer of tribes and parts of tribes caused great confusion. The proper division of the annuities among the scattered
bands of a tribe and their transmission through various agents became a complicated problem. Since Graham was connected with
so many tribes, he sometimes received the total annuity and sent
the proper amounts to the different agents. Nor was the purchase
of lands for immigrant Indians an easy task, either diplomatically
or financially. The arrival of new bands started feuds and wars
which the agents could not control. Graham played no incon-
siderable part in the removal of the Indians, and he deserves great
credit for lessening the friction over a considerable area.

§

The agency at Natchitoches was, because of its location, of
great importance throughout the decade after the War of 1812.
Early in 1816 John Jamison became the agent there. He began
with a barrage of questions as to his duties, powers, and salary.
Was the cutting of timber on public lands illegal? How could
he restrain insolent traders? Did he have authority to issue pass-
ports to aliens? Was he entitled to living quarters? The significance of the last question he emphasized by declaring, "If I have
to pay house rent the economy of a Franklin will not keep me
out of Jail in this country." [49]

Arriving Indians and contentious settlers caused confusion, and
rumors of an advancing Spanish force created some excitement.
Many citizens were ready to go to Nacogdoches to assist in
repelling the troops if they came.[50] A month later some Spanish

[48] The Graham Collection contains many papers on the removal of Indians.
[49] Jamison to the Secretary of War, June 8, 19, July 10, 1816, Letters Received,
Old Records Division, Adjutant General's Office; Jamison to the Secretary of
War, March 24, April 26, May 6, June 3, 1818, Old Records Division, Adjutant
General's Office.
[50] Letters Received, Old Records Division, Adjutant General's Office; Jamison
to the Secretary of War, April 26, September 30, 1818, Old Records Division,
Adjutant General's Office.

visitors reported that a severe storm had killed many people, and Jamison surmised that the hostile force had perished.[51] He was troubled not only by Indians and by Spanish threats but also by a "knot of the most abandoned exiles" who made their headquarters at Pecan Point on the Red River. They sold whiskey in every village on the river, incited the Indians, and disregarded all laws and regulations. Although some of them took the trouble to secure licenses to trade in Louisiana, they traded beyond its borders into Missouri Territory,[52] fearing nothing from the Spaniards, for whose laws also they had only contempt. The traders kept "the Indians constantly drunk and murders are frequent among them." They plundered the tribes of their stock and gave one Cherokee who reported their conduct to the factor a severe beating. Jamison suggested the extension of the Osage boundary line to the Red River and the stationing of a guard at some point on the river with authority and power to prevent the taking of whiskey into the Indian country. He also suggested that the agency be enlarged to include all the tribes on Red River, for his authority did not extend to those in Arkansas, and that it be removed to the Kiamichi, beyond which whites were not allowed to settle. Settlers were "flocking there like Doves to the window" and any place below the Kiamichi would mean a continued collision with state authorities such as he had experienced at Natchitoches, much to the lessening of his power and prestige. His functions had shrunk to the narrow sphere of giving advice and urging state authorities to punish offenders. Another reason for the removal to the Kiamichi was its proximity to the Indians west of the Sabine, "with whom I presume it will be good policy to maintain a good understanding."[53]

[51] Jamison to the Secretary of War, October 28, 1818, Old Records Division, Adjutant General's Office. The Spanish force had merely marched eastward in order to break up the settlement of the Napoleonic exiles on the Trinity River. Jameson, *Correspondence of John Caldwell Calhoun*, p. 150.

[52] Between the dates of Jamison's letters cited below, Arkansas Territory was formed.

[53] Jamison to the Secretary of War, May 25, 1818, May 26, 1819, and enclosure of John Fowler (factor) to Jamison, April 16, 1819; Jamison to Calhoun, June 16, 1819, and enclosure of Fowler to Jamison, June 1, 1819, Old Records Division, Adjutant General's Office.

Jamison's suggestion was accepted, and the agency was extended to cover all the Red River tribes,[54] but the removal was postponed on account of Jamison's death.

The problem of controlling the Indians was difficult. The principal Caddo chief represented ten tribes, eight of which lived west of the Sabine. His visits to the west side, where he received presents and advice from the Spaniards, naturally caused apprehension. The chief returned from such a visit to enter a protest against settlements above the Great Raft. It was suggested by the United States factor that another chief be appointed and that if the incumbent refused to acquiesce, all presents be discontinued.[55] George Gray, who succeeded Jamison, was instructed to treat the Indians from Texas with civility, but to give them no presents.[56] The lawless conduct of the traders and the international aspects of the situation called for a display of force, and the troops were moved from Natchitoches to the Sabine, where they erected Fort Ripley in 1819.[57]

The Indian agent was no small factor in the administration of the national frontier policy. His character, disposition, and ability were of great consequence to the tribe he represented, for its material welfare was largely in his hands. The realization of this dependence caused many sincere agents to be somewhat pro-Indian in their attitude, but the results show that the interests of the United States did not suffer materially at the hands of Indian agents. By securing cessions of vast tracts of land, by effecting the removal of tribes, by promoting good will, by assisting traders and factors in supplying the Indians with goods, by reducing friction between whites and Indians, and by cooperating with the army, the agent rendered a unifying service to the diverse phases of the general frontier policy.

[54] Calhoun to Jamison, July 15, 1819, War Department Letter Book D, in Indian Office.

[55] Jamison to the Secretary of War, May 26, 1819, and enclosure of Fowler to Jamison, April 16, 1819, Old Records Division, Adjutant General's Office.

[56] Calhoun to Gray, December 1, 1819, May 16, 1820, War Department Letter Book D, in Indian Office.

[57] Orderly Book, Company H, First Infantry, Old Records Division, Adjutant General's Office.

CHAPTER IV
THE FACTORY SYSTEM

The United States government developed an Indian policy that included annuities, presents, removals, agents, and frontier garrisons for restraining obstreperous braves and aggressive whites. In addition it undertook to protect the Indians against the exploitation of private traders by setting up government stores where the Indians could buy dependable goods at fair prices. These stores were called factories and the man in charge of each was called a factor.[1]

The factory system lasted from 1795 to 1822 and included a total of twenty-eight stores. Since the system exerted a great influence upon the Indians, frontier defense, the fur trade, and international relations on the frontier, a complete study of its various aspects would require a many-sided treatment. Thus far no such study has been attempted. Many writers have touched upon the subject and have indicated a realization of its importance,[2] but they have failed to portray its origin, scope, and extent.

[1] Since government documents, as well as other books, have used the terms "agent" and "factor" interchangeably, it seems best to clarify their use and to distinguish between "agency" and "factory." Agents issued licenses to traders, arranged treaties, distributed presents, paid annuities, furnished their superiors with information, and acted as the general diplomatic representative between the government and the tribes to which they were accredited. The word "agency" meant the functions of the agent, his place of residence, or the area of the Indian country over which he operated. Factors conducted the government stores, buying furs and selling goods to the Indians. Although their principal duties were commercial, they were supposed to further official plans as much as possible. "Factory" was the word applied to the store itself or to the post at which it was located. The term "agent" was sometimes, though inexactly, applied to factors, for the two were distinctly separate, in fact often hostile toward each other, the agent becoming the natural friend of the traders whom he licensed and who were competing with the factors. There are instances, however, in which factors and agents worked together in harmony, and in at least two instances a man was both an agent and a factor.

[2] Coman, "Government Factories: An Attempt to Control Competition in the Fur Trade," Papers and Discussions of the American Economic Association, 1911,

The factory system originated during the colonial period. The mere presence of the Indians gave rise to a variety of problems concerning land ownership, military control, and the regulation of trade. The European governments formulated rather beneficent policies, which were often nullified by exigencies of circumstances on the frontier. In the English colonies the principle that only the government could acquire land from the Indians was clearly and generally recognized at an early date,[3] but the most common relationship between the two races was that of trade, for it extended beyond the frontier and preceded the land question. Some of the colonies recognized the importance of trade in determining the conduct of the Indians, and for political and military as well as for economic reasons they took a definite part in the trade. Toward the middle of the eighteenth century Massachusetts conducted the Indian trade, supplying goods at cost, in order to secure and hold the friendship of the Indians. In 1753 Franklin recommended a similar system for Pennsylvania.[4] The official control of such trade by the French and Spanish offered further examples, so that the idea of governmental operation seems to have been firmly implanted in the minds of colonial Americans.

At the beginning of the Revolutionary War the colonists were forced to formulate an Indian policy. The control of the tribes was of importance from an economic standpoint, and their friendship and assistance, or at least their neutrality, became a military necessity. On July 12, 1775, the second Continental Congress appointed a committee to devise a plan for procuring goods

pp. 368–88; Quaife, *Chicago and the Old Northwest*, pp. 298–309; Chittenden, *The American Fur Trade of the Far West*, 1:12–16; Way, "The United States Factory System for Trading with the Indians, 1796–1822," *Mississippi Valley Historical Review*, 6:220–35. Other writers have made incidental references, but these are the principal accounts. Many documents relating to the subject may be found in Wisconsin Historical Collections, vols. 19 and 20. Attention should also be called to Griswold, *Fort Wayne, Gateway of the West*, which contains a mass of material, being the factory accounts at that place.

[3] A review of colonial land policy in dealing with the Indians is given in Royce, *Indian Land Cessions in the United States*, Introduction, and in Otis, *The Indian Question*, chapter 2.

[4] Franklin, *Writings*, 3:40, 43, 190, 191.

and carrying on the Indian trade.[5] Early in the following year Congress definitely decided upon a system of government trading posts "in order to preserve the friendship and confidence of the Indians." This latter provided for the importation of goods to the value of £40,000 and for the licensing of traders to handle them, but it allowed private traders to pursue their former course.[6] Thus the defect that later caused the downfall of the factory system was tolerated in these early plans. A congressional resolution forbade traders to enter the Indian country without a license and urged that prices be regulated to protect the Indians against exploitation.[7] These early enactments, which were little more than plans, indicate a realization of the importance and significance of the Indian trade and of the advisability of government operation or control. Nothing further toward a system of government trade was attempted until after the inauguration of Washington.[8]

The Indian wars on the Ohio frontier and the critical conditions on the Florida border provoked a serious consideration of the trade policy. In his fifth annual message to Congress, on December 2, 1793, Washington called attention to the need of formulating more definite plans for dealing with the Indians and suggested that a system of selling goods without profit would be a means of securing the good will and allegiance of the tribes. In his sixth annual message he repeated his recommendation.[9] In accord with these suggestions a bill for establishing government trading houses was introduced.

Congress took up the subject for debate on February 28, 1795. Josiah Parker of Virginia, William Vans Murray of Maryland, and others spoke in favor of the bill. Parker said that France, Britain, and Spain had adopted the policy, and he felt that the United States could well afford to imitate them. Murray said that the bill had three objects: (1) to protect the frontier; (2)

[5] *Journals of the Continental Congress*, 3:366.
[6] *Ibid.*, 4:96–98.
[7] *Ibid.*, p. 318.
[8] For a brief summary of the developing agency system see Chapter III.
[9] Richardson, *Messages and Papers of the Presidents*, 1:141, 167.

to restrain the frontiersmen and insure the Indians their rights; and (3) to gain the affection of the Indians by means of the factories, thus eliminating foreign influence. He declared that the frontier policy would be "unsystematic and despicable" without the establishment of the posts.

Jealousy of the incidental increase of presidential power seems to have been awakened, and the bill was defeated.[10] In spite of the defeat of the principal measure a substitute was introduced and passed in the closing days of the session. William Montgomery of Pennsylvania urged the passage of the substitute so as "to put the matter on a footing of experiment." "It is as clear as a sunbeam," he said, "that the establishment of trade must be the foundation of amity." [11] The law of March 3, 1795, appropriated fifty thousand dollars for the purchase of goods to be sold at such places as the president might direct.[12] In accordance with this law, two posts were established within the year, one at Coleraine, on the St. Mary's River in Georgia, and the other at Tellico, in what is now eastern Tennessee.[13]

The bill for extending the system and increasing the capital which was introduced in the following session of Congress brought forth debates that throw further light upon the objects of the factory system. During the debate Parker said that he favored the bill because Washington had recommended it from year to year and because it would save money by insuring peace among the Indians. James Hillhouse of Connecticut said that a beginning had been made and that it was best to extend the time of trial sufficiently to test the worth of the plan. John Swanwick of Pennsylvania urged that the civilizing influences of commerce upon the Indians should be tried out. He indicated that the small capital of the individual traders made it impossible for them to compete with the British. Murray said that the two

[10] *Annals of Congress,* 3d Congress, 2d Session, pp. 1262–63.
[11] *Ibid.,* 3d Congress, 2d Session, p. 1276.
[12] United States Statutes at Large, 1:443.
[13] *American State Papers: Indian Affairs,* 1:654, 768. Way, in *Mississippi Valley Historical Review,* 6:220–35, says these factories were established in 1800. He gives the date for the origin of the system as 1796. He also cites the wrong date for the abolition of the system, and there are other errors of detail.

objects of the bill were (1) to secure the friendship of the Indians
and (2) to supplant British traders, and that when the latter
object had been attained, the government would withdraw and
leave the field to private capital. A few days later Parker said
that the proposed appropriation would be added to the original
capital of fifty thousand dollars. He declared that a war with
the Indians had just ended, and he hoped that steps would be
taken to insure "perpetual tranquility." Robert Goodloe Harper
of South Carolina thought the government should lend money
to individuals to enable them to compete with the British. The
House passed the bill by a vote of 58 to 26,[14] and approval was
given on May 18, 1796.

The law of 1796 definitely established a system which had
been merely tried out under the law of the preceding year.[15]
The president was directed to appoint factors to reside at the
posts and sell goods to the Indians. They were to report twice
a year to the secretary of the treasury and account for all money,
furs, and supplies. They were to take oath for the faithful performance of their duties and to furnish bond as the president
directed. No factor was to be engaged in the trade on his own
account, and he was prohibited from receiving presents from
the Indians or any furs except in exchange for government
goods. The appropriation of $150,000 brought the total capital
to $200,000, and goods were to be sold at such prices as would
merely maintain the principal. The sum of $8,000 annually was
provided for maintenance. The act was limited to two years,
plus the duration of the Congress then in session.[16] The purpose
of the bill establishing the government factory system may be
summed up as (1) diplomatic, since its purpose was to destroy
British influence and secure the friendship of the Indians; (2)
economic, in that it sought incidentally to eliminate British
traders; and (3) military, as a system of controlling the Indians.[17]

[14] *Annals of Congress,* 4th Congress, 1st Session, pp. 229–32, 240, 283, 285.
[15] *American State Papers: Indian Affairs,* 1:583.
[16] United States Statutes at Large, 1:452–53.
[17] For a correct statement of the purposes of the factory system see Wisconsin
Historical Collections, 20:26–28. Although the statements were made by Ramsey

Before considering the establishment and operation of the factories, it is well to follow the course of the laws and renewals by which the system was kept alive. Such a review will clarify the effects of the various provisions on the Indian trade and will account for certain things that would otherwise be obscure. With the adjournment of Congress on March 4, 1799, the factory system lost its legal existence, for the law by which it had been established was limited to two years, plus the duration of Congress. But the mere lapse of the law could not extinguish the capital invested nor suddenly deprive factors of their postions; so the system was continued by sufferance. Early in 1802 Jefferson called attention to the lapse of the law,[18] and on April 30 Congress renewed the system and provided that it continue until March 4, 1803.[19] On February 28, 1803, it was extended for two years, plus the duration of Congress.[20] In 1805 no formal enactment was made in time to prevent the lapse of the legal provisions, but an act of March 3, 1804, appropriated $5,000 for exploring the Indian country and ascertaining the most suitable locations for new factories and $100,000 for establishing "additional trading houses."[21] The formal renewal of the law was made on April 21, 1806. It authorized the president to establish factories on both sides of the Mississippi and provided for a superintendent of Indian Trade, who was to make all purchases and distribute supplies among the factories. He was to receive an annual salary of $2,000. The president was to appoint factors, who, with the superintendent, were to be under the supervision of the secretary of the treasury, to whom they were to report quarterly. No factor was to receive presents from the Indians

Crooks and Robert Stuart, two great enemies of the factories, they are fair and reliable. The phraseology of the treaty with the Sauk and Fox in 1804 throws light on the objects of the system: "In order to put a stop to the abuses and impositions which are practised upon the said tribes by private traders" the United States will establish a factory where the Indians can secure "goods at a more reasonable rate than they have been accustomed to procure them." Kappler, *Indian Affairs, Laws, and Treaties,* 2:76.

[18] *American State Papers: Indian Affairs,* 1:653.
[19] United States Statutes at Large, 2:173.
[20] *Ibid.,* p. 207.
[21] *Ibid.,* p. 338.

or engage in the trade on his own account. The furs thus bought were to be sold at auction. The capital was set at $260,000,[22] and $10,000 annually was provided for clerks and factors and $3,000 annually for the salary and office expenses of the superintendent. The duration of the act was limited to three years.[23]

J. Mason, superintendent of Indian Trade, reported on January 16, 1809,[24] that the provision requiring him to sell the furs by auction was unwise, since the home market was oversupplied and prices were low. Accordingly, when the act was renewed on March 3, 1809, that provision was eliminated; the capital was increased by $40,000, and the act was extended for three years.[25]

On March 2, 1811, a year before the expiration of the existing law, a new act was passed. The Department of Indian Trade was transferred from the Treasury to the War Department, and the capital was increased to $300,000, with an annual fund of $14,750 for factors and clerks. The president was authorized to establish new factories, and the act was to remain in force for three years, plus the duration of the succeeding Congress, and all appointees were to hold office until removed.[26]

The uncertain hold which the system had is well illustrated by the number and brevity of the terms for which it was authorized. Renewals were passed on March 3, 1815, March 3, 1817, April 16, 1818, March 3, 1819, March 4, 1820, and March 3, 1821, the last extending it to June 3, 1822.[27]

While the legislative battles over the perpetuation of the factory system raged in Congress, the establishment of factories continued. The first two, Coleraine and Tellico, have already been mentioned. The former was located near the Spanish border, probably for the purpose of influencing the turbulent Indians of that section and securing them against foreign influence, but it was not well placed for trade. Consequently the factory was

[22] This was the total sum, for the remainder of former appropriations had been returned to the surplus fund.
[23] United States Statutes at Large, 2:402–04.
[24] American States Papers: Indian Affairs, 1:756.
[25] United States Statutes at Large, 2:544–45.
[26] Ibid., pp. 652–55.
[27] Ibid., 3:239–363, 428, 514, 544, 641, 679, 680.

moved to Fort Wilkinson in 1797, to Old Fields on October 16, 1806, to Fort Hawkins on December 31, 1808, and to Fort Mitchell in July, 1817,[28] and was finally discontinued after 1820. The shifting of this factory indicates the recession of the Indian frontier and the growth of the occupied area, for the factory was naturally so placed as to accommodate the greatest possible number of Indians. In 1807 the factory at Tellico was moved to Hiawassee, a few miles south of Tellico, and in 1811 it was discontinued.[29] In most cases the discontinuance of a factory indicates that the Indians had moved westward, and in some instances the factory was relocated so as to serve them in their new quarters.

In 1802 factories were established at Fort Wayne, Detroit, Chickasaw Bluffs, and Fort St. Stephens on the Tombigbee, just above the thirty-first degree of latitude.[30] The factory at Fort Wayne did a flourishing business until 1812, but in September of that year it was burned during an Indian attack.[31] The factory at Detroit was discontinued after 1805, and the one at Chickasaw Bluffs was removed to Arkansas in 1818.[32] The one at Fort St. Stephens was in charge of George S. Gaines of Virginia after 1807. Its trade was greatly hampered by the necessity of paying the Spanish officials a duty of 12 per cent on merchandise, even when it was destined for American markets. To escape this duty Gaines secured the consent of the Chickasaw to the opening of a route to Colbert's Ferry on the Ten-

[28] The various removals can be traced in general from the *American State Papers: Indian Affairs,* but the exact facts can be found only in the factory account books of the various factories kept in the Indian Office. Fort Wilkinson was on the Oconee near the site of Milledgeville; Fort Hawkins was on the Ocmulgee on the site of East Macon; Fort Mitchell was on the west side of the Chattahoochee a few miles below the site upon which Columbus, Georgia, is now located.

[29] *American State Papers: Indian Affairs,* 2:87.

[30] For the beginnings of the factories at Fort St. Stephens and Chickasaw Bluffs see *Claiborne Letter Books,* 1:150, 156, 181–83, 195, 222–24, 229–30, 260; 2:19–20, 38, 39, 108–10.

[31] McAfee, *A History of the Late War in the Western Country,* p. 126; Wesley, "A Letter from Colonel John Allen," *Ohio Archeological and Historical Society Quarterly,* 36:335.

[32] *American State Papers: Indian Affairs,* 1:768; 2:127, 208, 265.

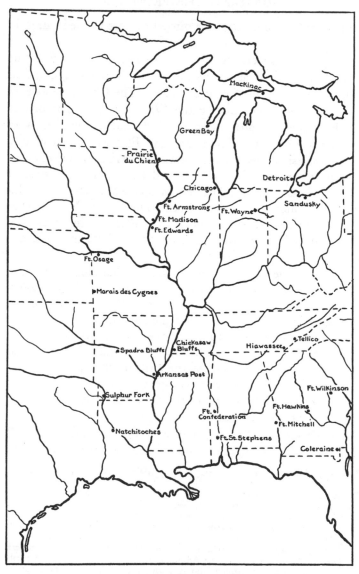

INDIAN FACTORIES IN THE UNITED STATES, 1795–1822

nessee River.[33] The factory was moved to Fort Confederation in 1817.[34]

In 1805 factories were established at Chicago, at Belle Fontaine on the Missouri just above its mouth, at Natchitoches, and at Arkansas Post, and in 1806 at Sandusky. The Chicago and Sandusky stores were lost during the War of 1812.[35] The one at Belle Fontaine was abandoned in 1808, and its supplies were distributed between the Fort Osage and Fort Madison factories, which were established in that year. The Arkansas factory was discontinued in 1810, but was revived in 1818 by the removal of the Chickasaw factory. The new factory was located at Spadra Bluffs, 140 miles above Little Rock. The one at Natchitoches had a continuous existence from 1805 to 1822, but in June, 1818, it was removed to Sulphur Fork on the Red River just above the Louisiana-Arkansas line.[36]

In 1808 factories were established at Fort Madison, in what is now southeastern Iowa, at Mackinac, and at Fort Osage (sometimes called Fort Clark) on the Missouri, just east of the site of Kansas City. The commander of the garrison at Fort Madison ordered the factory burned for fear the Indians would set it on fire and endanger the fort at a critical moment.[37] The stores at Mackinac fell into the hands of the British when that post was captured. The factory at Fort Osage was abandoned in June, 1813, and reopened in August of the same year [38] at Arrow Rock a few miles down the Missouri.

After the war, in 1815, factories were opened at Green Bay [39] and Prairie du Chien, and re-established at Fort Osage and

---

[33] Pickett, *History of Alabama*, 2:233-35; "Affairs at St. Stephens in 1810," *Gulf States Magazine*, 1:443.

[34] The site was secured in December, 1816. Military Books, 9:161, Old Records Division, Adjutant General's Office.

[35] Quaife in *Chicago and the Old Northwest* tells of the massacre at Chicago.

[36] *American State Papers: Indian Affairs*, 1:768, 784; 2:59, 68, 150, 208; Factory Account Books, Indian Office.

[37] A seven-page account of the history of Fort Madison was made by a clerk in the Officers' Record Division of the Adjutant General's Office. It is based partly upon the records of the department and is, perhaps, the fullest account extant of that post.

[38] Sibley Letter Books, Missouri Historical Society.

[39] Wisconsin Historical Collections, 19:380-81.

Chicago.[40] In 1818 a branch of the Prairie du Chien factory was established at Fort Edwards, which prospered so well that it was soon made a separate establishment.[41] It was moved from Fort Edwards to Fort Armstrong in the spring of 1822, shortly before the abolition of the factory system.[42] In 1821 a branch of the Osage factory was established at Marais des Cygnes on the upper waters of the Osage.[43] Thomas L. McKenney, superintendent of Indian Trade, was preparing to open eight additional factories at the time the system was abolished.

The general plan of operation was well established. The superintendent of Indian Trade [44] sent out order blanks, and the factors sent in their requisitions, basing their estimates upon past business, the condition of the market, the competition of traders, and future prospects. The superintendent endeavored to supply all goods ordered by the factors. He wrote numerous letters inquiring about quality and price and sometimes called for bids to supply the factories. Being limited to the domestic markets, he sometimes failed to secure goods of high quality. During the early years of the system the office of the superintendent was located at Philadelphia and most of the goods were purchased at that place. After the removal of the office to Georgetown, about 1808, that city became the principal supply market.

The transportation of goods to the factories was an expensive, time-consuming, and often wasteful process. Since most of the factories were located in remote places, goods had to be reshipped several times. The principal distributing centers were New Orleans, St. Louis,[45] and Detroit. A forwarding agent received

[40] *American State Papers: Indian Affairs*, 2:208.
[41] Wisconsin Historical Collections, 20:101–02.
[42] McKenney to the Secretary of War, October 27, 1817, Letters Received, Old Records Division, Adjutant General's Office; War Department Letter Book D, in Indian Office. The Fort Armstrong factory is also mentioned in *American State Papers: Indian Affairs*, 2:421, 532, 533, 534, 537.
[43] McKenney to Ballio and to Sibley, December 9, 1821, War Department Letter Book D, in Indian Office; *American State Papers: Indian Affairs*, 2:265, 371.
[44] John Mason held the office from 1808 until April 2, 1816, when he was succeeded by Thomas L. McKenney. Both men were sincerely interested in the welfare of the Indians and regarded their position as more than a financial opportunity. *American State Papers: Indian Affairs*, 2:422.
[45] The transport agent at St. Louis from 1813 to 1822 was James Kennerly, a brother-in-law of William Clark. The disheartening conditions of freight service

the goods and sent them on to the factories by boat, wagon, or pack horse as local conditions dictated. Under the circumstances freight charges were high. It cost from $4.00 to $9.00 to ship a hundred pounds of goods from Washington to St. Louis. In 1821 the cost was $4.24.[46] It cost almost as much to send a similar consignment on to the factories at Fort Madison, Fort Osage, and Fort Armstrong. It is thus apparent that the factory prices of heavy articles of little value would have to be greatly increased over their original cost if each article was to be sold at a price that would maintain the capital fund undiminished.

A typical shipment of factory goods consisted of blankets, strouds, guns, powder, lead, axes, knives, kettles, wampum, trinkets, coffee, and food supplies. The invoices contain numerous obsolete terms. As examples, consider siamoise, gorgets, mammoodies, callimanco, Bocking baise, pullicats, rumal, and shalloon. The developing civilization among the Indians is indicated by other items in the lists, such as tin cups, cowbells, maul rings, hoes, frying pans, arm bands, shirts, earbobs, silk socks, tinsel hatbands, jew's-harps, and sidesaddles.[47]

The factor sold his goods to various groups and by various methods. Indians were the principal customers, and for them the factory system was maintained, but the number of stores was hopelessly inadequate for supplying all tribes and villages. In order to reach those who lived at great distances from the factories and to offset the competition of private traders, the factors sent out their own traders supplied with factory goods. This practice was bitterly denounced by private traders, but had the approval of the superintendent of Indian Trade and was in

in that period are eloquently told in McKenney's letters to Kennerly. Sometimes they are severe on Kennerly, who seems to have been careless and indifferent. In 1821 he violated his instructions by selling furs at St. Louis and was charged with the difference between the amount received and what the furs would have brought at Georgetown. *American State Papers: Indian Affairs,* 2:419. Indian Trade Department Letter Books, *passim;* Wesley, "Diary of James Kennerly," Missouri Historical Collections, 6:41-97.

[46] *American State Papers: Indian Affairs,* 1:335.

[47] Griswold, *Fort Wayne, Gateway to the West, passim;* Wisconsin Historical Collections, 19:463–64; 20:62–64.

entire accord with the purposes that had led to the establishment of the system.[48] The Indians usually gave furs, skins, beeswax, tallow, bear oil, feathers, and other products in exchange for factory goods,[49] whereas soldiers, private traders, travelers, and other white customers usually paid cash. The factor shipped the furs, skins, and so forth that he had received to the forwarding agent at the nearest distributing center, who sometimes sold them locally but more frequently forwarded them to the superintendent, who sold them at auction.

Instructions were sent to factors to guide them in the details of their work. Those sent out in 1808 by John Mason, superintendent of Indian Trade, are condensed and summarized as follows: [50]

1. Bear in mind that the object of the factory system is to win and retain the friendship of the Indians.

2. The cost of goods should be figured as approximately 68 per cent advance over the marked cost. Watch carefully that the Indians do not sell you inferior furs, for they are likely to be made the instruments of unprincipled traders. On the other hand, do not sell any inferior goods without calling attention to the defect and making allowance for it.

3. Sell to Indians only. If it is necessary to sell to whites, do so by charging 10 per cent more than when selling to Indians. Give credit cautiously and mostly to chiefs.

4. You will be furnished with sufficient guards and with an interpreter if necessary.

5. You are forbidden to carry on any trade on your own account.

6. In no case will you sell or dispense liquors.

7. Send in your requisitions early and mark them explicitly.

8. Send your furs to Joseph Saul at New Orleans or General William Clark at St. Louis.

9. Invoices should be sent to the superintendent of Indian Trade.

10. Keep careful and correct records of all transactions.

[48] *American State Papers: Indian Affairs,* 2:329, 331–34, 357, 360; Tesson Collection, Missouri Historical Society; Wisconsin Historical Collections, 19:463–64, 20:62–64.

[49] *American State Papers: Indian Affairs,* 2:356.

[50] *Ibid.,* 2:520–21; Wisconsin Historical Collections, 19:326–30.

These instructions varied somewhat with the location of the factories. The instructions about selling only to Indians were often disregarded, for in many cases the factory was the only available store, and it would have been unjust to deny a white when he was willing to pay the price. The caution against credit was also often disregarded, for the factors soon learned that to deny an Indian credit was to lose his trade; so in practice the factors were forced to deal with the Indians very much as did the individual white traders.[51]

The financial operations of the factory system involved rather impressive sums. In December, 1809, the value of goods on hand ranged from \$1,134 [52] at Hiawassee to \$17,982 at Fort Osage, the total for the thirteen factories then in operation being \$74,311. The value of furs on hand was \$42,154, and accounts due amounted to \$19,554.[53] The amount of the debts, not an unusual sum, is conclusive evidence that the factors did sell on credit. It is rather curious that writers who have dealt with the factory system have insisted that it was bound to be unsatisfactory to the Indians because it sold only for cash or furs. It is still more curious that Ramsay Crooks, Ninian Edwards, and other frontiersmen made the same error. Up to this time the total losses amounted to \$44,538.[54] From 1809 to the close of the system in 1822 the trading fund amounted to \$290,000. In addition to the trade fund, annual appropriations were made for the salaries of all employees. The operations during 1810 and 1811 were more successful, for the superintendent estimated a gain of \$14,171.[55] The War of 1812, however, was a serious blow to the factories. Those at Chicago, Mackinac, Sandusky, Fort Wayne, and Fort Madison were captured or destroyed by the British, entailing a loss of \$43,369,[56] and the others suffered a diminution of business. An even more serious result, if one may judge by the number

[51] *American State Papers: Indian Affairs*, 2:66. The widespread practice of giving credit seems to have escaped comment by those who have written on the factory system.
[52] The odd cents are dropped from all sums given.
[53] *American State Papers: Indian Affairs*, 1:770–71.
[54] *Ibid.*, 2:127.   [55] *Ibid.*, 1:784.
[56] *Ibid.*, 2:59.

of times the superintendent used it as an excuse for the reduced trade fund, was the oversupply of inferior and unsalable goods which had accumulated during the war period. The losses were, however, overcome by 1817, if one can accept the report of a congressional committee which based its findings upon the superintendent's estimates.[57] The following table shows the total value of goods sent to the factories in the several years.[58]

1805....$71,530	1810....$45,287	1815....$68,283
1806....100,659	1811.... 42,811	1816.... 76,100
1807.... 39,513	1812.... 29,916	1817.... 69,709
1808.... 50,430	1813.... 28,494	1818.... 58,404
1809.... 46,354	1814.... 33,237	1819.... 29,666

The amount of business at the factories reflects the changes in the general economic situation. After the War of 1812 there was a steady rise in the volume of business until the panic year of 1819. The table below, which includes one southern factory (Fort Confederation), one western factory (Fort Osage), and one northern factory (Prairie du Chien), illustrates this fact. Green Bay is included to demonstrate the decline of business in that area coincident with the rising activities of the American Fur Company. The sums show the value of the total receipts, including cash, furs, and produce, which were received in the various years.[59]

Factory	1816	1817	1818	1819
Fort Confederation	$15,897	$16,917	$20,930	$ 4,761
Fort Osage	11,733	18,135	20,988	13,594
Prairie du Chien.......	4,910	13,564	27,642	6,390
Green Bay	374	4,536	3,444	2,640

The factors needed commercial sense and diplomatic skill. They were tested by wary Indians eager to sell their furs at high prices and secure goods at bargain rates. Dissatisfied groups required considerate treatment, and the laws of hospitality were

[57] *Ibid.*, pp. 127, 185.
[58] *Ibid.*, p. 214.
[59] *Ibid.*, p. 208.

subject to great strains. Rival traders often misrepresented the purposes of the factors and incited worthless Indians to buy goods on credit at the factories. Some of the factors took their families with them and lived the life typical of the frontier. Lost goods, spoiled skins, bad debts, commercial rivalries, and Indian alarms occasioned much worry and prevented the factors from leading an idyllic life.

The connection between the factory system and the army was close. Factories were usually located at fortified posts, occasionally occupying one of the rooms within the fort.[60] The soldiers were ordered to assist the factors in transporting goods, beating and packing furs, and erecting buildings, for which extra-military services they were rewarded with a gill of whiskey and fifteen cents a day.[61] For the most part soldiers were not well disposed toward the system because they disliked the performance of such tasks.[62] Nor could officers have enthusiasm for a system under which they were sometimes subject to the orders of a government storekeeper.[63] Protection, however, was the chief service of the army to the factories, and in most cases the mere presence of the troops was all that was needed.

The position of factor was considered a desirable one. The pay was sometimes as much as thirteen hundred dollars a year and rations, and the opportunities for influence and advancement were considerable. George C. Sibley, who was factor at Fort Osage from 1808 to 1822, probably holds the record for length

[60] The factory at Fort Edwards was so located in 1819. Atkinson's Order, July 30, 1819, Department Orders, Old Records Division, Adjutant General's Office.

[61] Mason asked Crawford on August 7, 1815, to instruct officers to furnish men to erect factory buildings, since there was no other supply of labor. He promised ten cents a day and the whiskey. Wisconsin Historical Collections, 19:389–90. On August 9, 1816, the secretary of war ordered Macomb and Smith to furnish help for the factors. The soldiers were to be paid fifteen cents a day. War Department Letter Book C, in Indian Office. According to McKenney, however, the troops did only a small part of the work of erecting factories. American State Papers: Indian Affairs, 2:355.

[62] Ibid., p. 82.

[63] Secretary of War to Brigadier General Bissell, August 4, 1815, War Department Letter Book C, in Indian Office, pp. 255, 410–11; Adjutant General to Brigadier General Smith, May 16, 1818, Letters Sent, Old Files Section, Adjutant General's Office.

of tenure. He was widely known on the frontier and served as sub-agent as well as factor. Thomas M. Linnard served as factor at Natchitoches for about eleven years. Matthew Lyon, an ex-congressman who had been fined and imprisoned under the Sedition Act, was factor on the Arkansas during the closing years of the system. Matthew Irwin was factor at Chicago, and Jacob B. Varnum served for a time at Mackinac and then at Chicago. John B. Treat also served at two different posts, Arkansas and Chickasaw Bluffs. George S. Gaines was factor for a number of years at Fort St. Stephens, and Jonathan Halstead at the Georgia factories.[64] A full knowledge of the activity of any factor would throw additional light on the history of the frontier.[65] In spite of able factors and the beneficent intentions of the government, many people and circumstances combined to discredit and eventually destroy the system.

The opponents of the factory system were the fur companies, individual traders, and many disinterested persons who really believed it to be a failure. The system had its defects, and its enemies took delight in pointing them out; often they added misrepresentation to honest criticism. In one instance the Indians were told that the purpose of the factory system was to induce them to run into debt so that the United States could seize their lands.[66] Traders told Indians that the factors *sold* goods that were intended by the government as *presents,* and that the agents stole half the presents.[67] The factors were sometimes the objects of personal slander.[68] They were accused of being inattentive to the Indians and of seeking only their own preferment and safety.[69] John Johnston, who had been a factor, denounced the

[64] For a complete list of factors see Appendix B.

[65] *American State Papers: Indian Affairs,* 1:769; 2:57, 371. Fortunately extensive correspondence of George C. Sibley has been preserved by the Missouri Historical Society. Some accounts of John Johnston, factor at Fort Wayne, were published in Indiana Historical Collections, vol. 15. Several of the factors are fairly well known.

[66] *American State Papers: Indian Affairs,* 2:85.

[67] Forsyth Collection, Missouri Historical Society.

[68] Jamison to the Secretary of War, May 26, 1819, referring to factor John Fowler, Old Records Division, Adjutant General's Office.

[69] *St. Louis Enquirer,* April 20, 27, 1822.

system as expensive and inefficient.[70] In 1819 St. Louis citizens presented to Congress a petition, which became known as the Missouri Scroll, in which they asked for many favors, one of which was the abolition of the factories.[71] Frontier newspapers were generally hostile.[72] Another opponent of the system was the Reverend Jedidiah Morse, who made a tour of the Indian country in 1820 and rendered a careful report in which he recommended the abolition of the system.[73] Governors Edwards and Cass condemned the factories, and Edwards was even more emphatic in his criticisms of private traders, who corrupted the Indians with liquor, misrepresented the intentions of the government, and robbed each other by inducing Indians to leave their former debts unpaid in order to deal with a trader who happened to be at hand.[74] Cass submitted a severe arraignment of the factories to John C. Calhoun, secretary of war. He said that they had little effect, since they sold so small a percentage of the goods used by the Indians. He argued that a more stringent regulation of licenses was the remedy.[75] The fur companies added their condemnation and influence. For a number of years the St. Louis Missouri Fur Company, whose principal field of operation was the upper Missouri, where there were no factories, manifested no special hostility toward the system, but the American Fur Company, which carried on its early operations around the Great Lakes, felt the competition of the factories and inaugurated a campaign to have them abolished.[76] After the War

[70] *American State Papers: Indian Affairs,* 2:82.

[71] *St. Louis Enquirer,* June 16, 1819; *National Intelligencer,* August 4, 1819.

[72] *St. Louis Enquirer,* October 2, 1819; *Detroit Gazette,* May 24, 1822.

[73] Morse, *Report to the Secretary of War on Indian Affairs,* pp. 60–64.

[74] *American State Papers: Indian Affairs,* 2:62–67.

[75] Wisconsin Historical Collections, 20:82–86. Cass's argument about the extent of the factory trade is not convincing. The undying enmity of the fur companies is eloquent evidence of the fact that the system was of considerable proportions. See Wisconsin Historical Collections, 19:395; 20:1–12, 12–16, 26, 31, 37–41, 82, 204, 242; Chittenden, *American Fur Trade,* 1:9–16; and Lewis' "Essay on Indian Policy" in Coues, *History of the Lewis and Clark Expedition,* 3:1215.

[76] For a partisan statement of the plan see *American State Papers: Indian Affairs,* 2:360. McKenney's feelings are well shown in the phrases "the American Fur Company, now so called," "as its title denotes it," and "as it is denominated." *Ibid.,* pp. 355, 356.

of 1812 the company planned to defeat the British traders, but at the same time make use of British *engagés*. American traders were aided by the law of 1816 forbidding foreigners to trade within the United States,[77] and the factory system was the remaining competitor which they feared. The fur traders at St. Louis soon joined in the attack on the system.[78]

The opponents of the factory system were divided as to what system should supplant it. The most frequently mentioned plans were those for the establishment of a large factory at St. Louis, which would sell to traders only, and the formation of a company guaranteed and regulated by the government. The first plan was advocated in 1816 by John Mason, superintendent of Indian Trade. He proposed that $150,000 worth of goods be allotted to private traders who would carry them to the Indians.[79] Morse advocated a modified form of this plan.[80] The second plan was modestly suggested by Clark in 1815,[81] indorsed by Calhoun two years later,[82] and vehemently advocated in the Missouri Scroll. The plan was ridiculed by the *National Intelligencer*[83] and denounced by Niles.[84]

The supporters of the factory system included many who were well disposed toward the Indians, most public officials, and the factors themselves. They upheld it because of its supposed benefits to the Indians. It was repeatedly sustained by committees of Congress and by Congress itself in the face of opposition,[85] and was upheld by Crawford and Calhoun.[86] Clark thought factories "extremely useful" when well located and properly man-

---

[77] United States Statutes at Large, 3:332–33.

[78] *American State Papers: Indian Affairs*, 2:66–67. Factor George C. Sibley wrote a severe arraignment of the Chouteaus for their opposition to the factory system. *National Intelligencer*, April 18, 1822.

[79] *American State Papers: Indian Affairs*, 2:70.

[80] Morse, *Report to the Secretary of War on Indian Affairs*, pp. 40–60.

[81] Rufus Easton, delegate from Missouri Territory, presented a petition to the House in 1816 asking for the formation of a company to trade with the Indians. *Annals of Congress*, 14th Congress, 1st Session, p. 1301.

[82] *United State Papers: Indian Affairs*, 2:78, 184.

[83] August 4, 1819.

[84] *Niles' Weekly Register*, 16:408–09.

[85] *American State Papers: Indian Affairs*, 2:183, 205–06.

[86] *Ibid.*, pp. 28, 182.

aged. One Indian agent stated that the factories were rallying centers where the Indians felt at home and that they considered them "as their father's houses." Another advocated the monopoly of Indian trade by the government.[87] Niles argued that though the factory system had its defects, it was to be preferred to the unrestrained activity of private traders.[88] The supporters blamed the enemies of the system for many of its faults. Factor George C. Sibley, one of the most vehement critics of the fur traders and fur companies, asserted that the practices of the fur companies rendered the factories useless. He aroused the ire of more than one by hinting that the American Fur Company smuggled its goods into the country.[89]

Early in 1822 a Senate committee, with Thomas H. Benton as chairman, began to gather evidence against the factory system. Benton claimed that, being from a frontier state, he understood the operations of the factories. In his account he observed, "It cost me a strenuous exertion"[90] to accomplish their downfall. It is difficult, however, to escape the suspicion that Benton was serving Clark, Hempstead, Chouteau, and other influential fur dealers who were his constituents. The committee's inquiries brought forth various objections. Benjamin O'Fallon, Indian agent on the Missouri, wrote that the Indians entertained a mean opinion of a government that would compete with individuals and that consequently the system tended to lower the dignity of the government. He said that the Indians were good judges of the quality of goods and of the value of their furs, so they naturally resented receiving goods of such poor quality as those sold by the factors. John Biddle, Indian agent at Green Bay, also believed that government participation was unwise. He said that factors sold to whites as well as to Indians, charged high prices, and engaged in the trade on their own account. John R. Bell,

[87] *Ibid.*, pp. 78, 87, 203–04.
[88] *Niles' Weekly Register*, 22:129.
[89] *American State Papers: Indian Affairs*, 2:362–63; *National Intelligencer*, April 18, 1822. For an answer to the charge of smuggling see the *Detroit Gazette* for May 24, 1822.
[90] Benton, *Thirty Years' View*, 1:21.

a journalist who accompanied Long on his expedition, said that the Indians on the Missouri thought that British goods were superior to those sold at factories. The Cherokee in Arkansas said that blankets were cheaper by a dollar at private stores, and that they received just as much for their furs at such stores. Bell cited Hugh Glenn's store at the mouth of the Verdigris as one that answered the needs of the Indians. Ramsay Crooks of the American Fur Company emphasized all that had been said by the others and commented at some length upon the inefficiency of factors. He cited George C. Sibley, factor at Fort Osage, as one who had engaged in the trade on his own account.[91]

Thomas L. McKenney, superintendent of Indian Trade, presented an able defense. He asserted that the unscrupulous conduct of traders and the open competition had prevented the factories from proving their worth. He submitted many letters and tables to prove that he secured the best quality of goods to be had in the United States, and that they were similar to those the traders sold. Such goods as were of inferior quality or high in price were those remaining from the period following the War of 1812. His report was accompanied by letters from the factors complaining of the lawless conduct of the traders. Sibley, in speaking of the conduct of the traders, exclaimed, "What is the bleeding scalp of an infant compared with the rich fur of a beaver skin?" He said the hostility of traders caused disrespect for the government. He also complained of the instability of the system. "We are left for another year, powerless, and unprotected from the malice and galling insults of every renegade trader."

Conditions favored the opponents of the factory system. The steady rise of the American Fur Company was a menace to the success of the factories. In its early years the company chose to concentrate its efforts in the region of the Great Lakes, and the

[91] The letters referred to may be found in Senate Document No. 60, Senate Documents, 17th Congress, 1st Session, vol. 1; also in *American State Papers: Indian Affairs*, 2:326, 364.

declining volume of business of the government factories at Mackinac, Green Bay, and Chicago is evidence of its success. About 1815 the fur traders of St. Louis became conscious of the part the factories were playing in the fur trade. Consequently they became hostile and began agitation for the abolition of the system. They were fortunate in securing the services of Benton when he entered the Senate in 1821. In addition to the combined efforts of the great fur traders the opposition was supported also by the state of the financial affairs of the system.

The trade fund was fairly large, the salaries of the employees were paid by annual appropriations, and the factory buildings were erected by soldiers. Thus it appears that the system had enormous advantages over private traders. With even tolerable management it should have been possible to operate without diminishing the capital. The superintendent claimed that the losses incurred during the War of 1812 could not justly be charged against the factories. The military neecssity of abandoning certain posts naturally resulted in considerable loss. Such losses did not indicate mismanagement of the trade fund. In any case, these losses, being less than one-sixth of the capital fund, should not have permanently handicapped operations. The vague and contradictory reports were too complex for congressional committees to understand. Bad debts amounted to nearly $29,000, and unsalable goods further depleted the capital fund.

From the inception of the system the opposition had been sufficiently strong to limit the continuation of the laws to one, two, or three years. The new nationalism, so pronounced in the period following the war, favored the laissez faire policy. Thus the specific opposition was aided by a widespread feeling that private business should not be injured by official undertakings. The fiery and astute Benton was able to unify the opposing forces and to secure the passage of an act on May 6, 1822,[92] repealing the entire system.

The closing of the factories and the sale of goods and property naturally resulted in severe losses. The trade fund was $290,000.

[92] United States Statutes at Large, 3:679–80.

Theoretically the value of goods and equipment should have equaled that sum. Early returns showed a paper value of $269,673, but the committee report of May 25, 1824,[93] shows that only $38,178 had actually been paid into the treasury. A further sum of $52,951 was due from factors and agents who disposed of the goods, and some additional sums were received at later dates. Approximately half the capital fund was lost.

The factory system lasted twenty-seven years. It failed to justify the sanguine expectations of its friends and afforded many just grounds for the criticism of its enemies. The factories were inaugurated during a period when private capital was unable to meet the situation and when traders were powerless before the stronger organization and greater experience of the British. During the period of their existence the War of 1812 enabled the United States to shake off British influence and thus open a more unhindered field to native traders. The system was probably unnecessary after that event, but its abolition led to unrestrained competition, and the *engagés* of great companies fought each other in more than commercial ways. After the abolition of the factory system, the government made little effort to protect the Indians against the outrages of the trader, and the rapid development of the fur-gathering industry almost eliminated the need of the Indian altogether. Within a decade after the abolition of the factories the fur region east of the Rockies was rapidly being depleted. Perhaps Calhoun's summary is an adequate estimate of the value of the system:

It was commenced, and has been continued, from motives both of prudence and humanity; and though it may not have fully realized the expectations of its friends, it has no doubt produced beneficial effects. If wars have not been entirely prevented by it, they probably, without it, would have been more frequent; and if the Indians have made but little advances in civilization, they probably, without it, would have made less.[93]

A similar summary was made by a House committee which reported in 1819:

[93] *American State Papers: Indian Affairs,* 2:182.

Although these establishments have been a pecuniary loss to the United States, in some respects, yet no doubt is entertained that, on the whole, they have been of great advantage, not only on the score of humanity to the Indian tribes, but also in preserving the lives and property of our frontier inhabitants, which would otherwise, under the influence of foreign traders, have been in hostile array against us; and, no doubt, this policy has much weakened the power and force of those nations that have been at war with us.[94]

[94] *Ibid.*, p. 185.

CHAPTER V

THE FUR TRADE

ONE OF THE most important factors in the development of the frontier was the fur trade.[1] The term in its broad sense includes the trade not only in furs but in hides, skins, buffalo robes, tallow, beeswax, maple sugar, and all the products of the forest that the Indians could exchange for the commodities of the trader. But the Indians were not skilled enough in hunting and trapping to be able to supply the demand for furs. The trader's efforts were quickly supplemented by the trapper and hunter, who in many cases made it unnecessary to depend upon the Indian at all. The South and Southwest supplied vast quantities of skins, hides, and buffalo robes, which were obtained by hunters as well as by trappers and traders. The North and Northwest were lucrative fields for all types of fur traders. The trade vitally affected all frontiers. It promoted exploration; it led to contact with the Indians; it promoted the growth of other kinds of trade and industry; it paved the way for settlers; and it was in itself a great industry. The fur trader was the forerunner of an oncoming civilization which was to push the frontier ever farther and farther to the west.

The northern trade was the most lucrative. The high prices received for the furs from that region led to the formation of great companies and to rapid exploitation. The business became so extensive that in one way or another it affected nearly all

---

[1] The bibliography of the fur trade is extensive. Chittenden, Dale, and Lippincott have dealt with the Missouri trade; Willson, Bryce, and Davidson with Canadian companies; Johnson with the Michigan area; Stevens with the Northwest up to 1800; and there are numerous articles on special phases of the trade. There are, however, three great gaps in the history of the fur trade: the activity of the American Fur Company, the southern, and the southwestern fur trade have not yet received adequate treatment. Porter in his life of Astor has contributed much valuable information concerning the American Fur Company.

frontiersmen. The fur merchants were men of influence and standing who were able to secure the attention of Congress and the War Department. Yet the northern trade during the American period was of comparatively brief duration. Its very efficiency caused its early decline. The trade of the Great Lakes and upper Mississippi Valley passed its zenith within the decade after the War of 1812,[2] and by the end of the decade the upper Missouri trade had reached its greatest development.[3]

Southern furs, being lighter than those of the North, did not command so high a price.[4] In contrast with the northern trade, the southern was carried on mostly by individuals or small companies. The predominance of hides and skins over furs proper also made the trade somewhat different, for the greater bulk and weight in proportion to the value made the question of transportation important. The trade was of relatively longer duration than that of the North, for it was considered a side issue which engaged the frontiersmen in the winter months only.[5] The fur traders were the settlers, whereas in the North the great bulk of the furs had been gathered before widespread settlements were made.

The control of the fur trade in the decade from 1815 to 1825 was a matter of national importance. The close of the War of 1812 ushered in a period of conscious nationalism, which found expression in a larger standing army, a tariff for protection, a new Bank of the United States, internal improvements, and a general increase of interest in national affairs. The development of American trade and industries became a patriotic as well as an economic purpose. The British fur companies operating in the United States were a challenge to this new spirit of nationalism. The close relationship between the fur trade and Indian policy made the success of American fur traders a matter of governmental concern.

[2] Johnson, *The Michigan Fur Trade,* chapter 8.
[3] Senate Document No. 90, Senate Documents, 22d Congress, 1st Session.
[4] They were worth from 40 to 60 per cent as much as northern furs. Senate Document No. 60, Senate Documents, 17th Congress, 1st Session.
[5] Schoolcraft, *Journal of a Tour into the Interior of Missouri and Arkansas,* pp. 26, 30, 37, 40, 41, 60, 63, 67, 68, 73, 77.

The condition of the fur trade in 1815 was not satisfactory to the United States government. The Hudson's Bay and the Northwest Company, both British concerns, were operating along the northern frontier and in the far Northwest. The formation of the American Fur Company in 1808 [6] had given rise to hopes that the trade would be won by Americans, but the results had been disappointing for two reasons. Astor was interested in the fur trade rather than in forwarding patriotic aspirations. Before 1817 his interests in the Canadian trade were probably more extensive than those in the United States. In the second place, Astor's ventures in the United States had not been very successful. The Astoria enterprise of the Pacific Fur Company, a branch of the American Fur Company, had resulted disastrously.[7] Another Astor concern, the Southwest Company, which had bought an interest in the Mackinaw Company shortly before the War of 1812, had had no opportunity to succeed.[8] The only sphere in which the valuable northern fur trade was completely in the hands of Americans was that which centered at St. Louis. Since the St. Louis traders did not operate around the Great Lakes, where it was considered so important to establish American supremacy at the close of the war, their success was of less concern to the government than that of Astor, whose operations were in the region of the Great Lakes.

From the official viewpoint the situation in the fur trade began to improve shortly after the war. Some of the factories that had been closed or destroyed during the war were reopened, and new ones were established. Naturally the government could trust its own system to further official policy. The St. Louis traders, who controlled the valuable trade of the Missouri River, showed renewed energy and gave promise of preventing any considerable encroachment of the British companies on the headwaters of that river. The passage of the act of 1816, which was

[6] Chittenden, *American Fur Trade*, 1:167; Wisconsin Historical Collections, 19:291, 337.
[7] Irving tells the story in his *Astoria*.
[8] Wisconsin Historical Collections, 19:451.

designed to prevent foreigners from engaging in the fur trade,[9] gave legal support to the American traders in their fight to gain control of the trade.[10] In 1817 Astor bought the Canadian interests in the Southwest Company,[11] and the American Fur Company soon gained undisputed control of the American trade along the Great Lakes. National law and governmental jealousy slowly forced the company to become American in reality as well as in name.

The St. Louis companies pursued their course for a few years undisturbed by the growing American Fur Company. The St. Louis Missouri Fur Company, which had been organized in 1809 and reorganized in 1812 and in 1813, was the dominating ,firm. Its personnel changed, but it was easily foremost in the business of collecting furs from the Missouri River area.[12] It did not, however, enjoy a monopoly of the field. Independent companies and enterprising individuals were sufficiently numerous and powerful to prevent the company from securing the capital and support that the situation demanded. In 1822 William H. Ashley formed a company, later called the Rocky Mountain Fur Company, and sent an expedition into the mountain regions, which had previously been unworked.[13] His spectacular success was the envy of his rivals and probably encouraged a spirit of competition. Less successful but no less persevering traders

[9] United States Statutes at Large, 3:332–33.

[10] It has been stated (see Chittenden, *American Fur Trade,* 1:310) that the law excluding foreigners was passed at the suggestion of Astor. The situation seems to support such a statement, for the law would free Astor from the keen competition of the vigorous Northwest Company. Chittenden's statement, however, is open to doubt. In the first place, Astor's partners and *engagés* were Canadians, and the law certainly put him to great inconvenience in securing the admission of his assistants. In the second place, the temporary suspension of the law by the president was primarily for Astor's benefit. Some proof tending to show Astor's surprise and regret because the law was passed is recorded in Wisconsin Historical Collections, 19:423. It is clear, however, that he knew of the proposed law before its passage and gave it verbal approval either from motives of policy or because he actually believed it a wise provision. Porter, *John Jacob Astor,* 2:1144–45.

[11] Wisconsin Historical Collections, 19:451; Chittenden, *American Fur Trade,* 1:311.

[12] Chittenden, *American Fur Trade,* 1:138, 146, 148, 262.

[13] Dale, *The Ashley-Smith Explorations,* pp. 11–112.

divided the field and by their rivalries invited the entry of the American Fur Company.

The St. Louis traders and the American Fur Company worked together to effect the overthrow of the factory system in 1822. This year also marks the opening of the Western Department of the American Fur Company at St. Louis. Pursuing its policy of establishing or operating through subsidiary companies, the American Fur Company employed Stone, Bostwick, and Company to manage its Western Department. Other subsidiaries were employed, and within a decade the company secured a virtual monopoly of the trade centering at St. Louis.[14]

The success of American fur traders was not the only concern of the government. Their success was soon assured, but the problem of supervising them was not so easily solved. In their eagerness to succeed, traders and companies often disregarded the rights of Indians, exploiting their lands and depriving them of their prior claims to the game. Several laws designed to regulate and restrain the traders and trappers were passed. The laws of 1799 and 1802 establishing the system of agencies prescribed the conditions under which traders were to operate. Licenses and bonds were required, and the sale of liquor to the Indians was forbidden. Purchase of land or horses from the natives was also prohibited, and no trader was to reside among them. The act of April 29, 1816, subjected the right of foreigners to engage in the trade to the discretion of the president.[15] In 1824 a law was passed restricting traders to certain posts designated by the agents who issued the licenses.[16]

The execution of the laws was a difficult task. Liquor was constantly being taken into the Indian country by traders, and no officer was successful in stopping the practice. The system of issuing licenses was not uniform. The law specified no fee, but it was customary to charge two dollars, and one agent charged fifty dollars.[17] Some agents required one license for a group of

[14] Chittenden, *American Fur Trade*, 1:320–23.
[15] United States Statutes at Large, 3:332–33.
[16] *Ibid.*, 4:35.
[17] Wisconsin Historical Collections, 7:271; vol. 19, *passim*.

traders who worked together; others required a license for each member. It was sometimes presumed that the license gave the holder the right to hunt and trap, but in reality it authorized him to trade only.[18] Another unsettled question was the extent of territory covered by a license. Was it valid only for the purpose of trading with a certain tribe, was its extent geographical, or did it extend to all Indians? In many cases the license specified the tribes and localities for which it was valid, but that did not answer the question of the extent of the agent's powers. In 1817 the officer at Fort Armstrong arrested some foreign traders on the Mississippi, although they carried licenses from the Indian agent at Mackinac.[19] A partial answer to the question of the extent of the agent's power is found in Cass's regulation of 1818 for the Northwest. He divided the region into agencies and restricted the issuance of licenses beyond those boundaries, but he refrained from delimiting the agencies that bordered other superintendencies, and so the question was still unanswered.[20] In 1819 the War Department ruled that any license was valid in all sections of the country.[21] This ruling clarified the situation, but it destroyed what little power the agents had over traders, for they could secure licenses elsewhere if the local agent refused to issue them.

The act of 1816 had no immediate effect, for the president temporarily suspended its operation and allowed foreigners to continue their activity. This action was taken because the American traders were unable to supply all the tribes with

---

[18] *American State Papers: Indian Affairs*, 2:455.

[19] Wisconsin Historical Collections, 19:477–79, 485–86. Chittenden (*American Fur Trade*, 1:312) and all who have followed him have erred as to why these traders were arrested. The explanation is clear. The law of 1816 excluded foreigners, but they could be admitted at the discretion of the president. Authority to license foreigners was given *only* to the agents of the Northwest. Wisconsin Historical Collections, 19:443. Naturally the agents and officials on the Mississippi, who knew nothing of the exception, were merely performing their duty in arresting the foreigners. The problem was thus one of the extent of a license as well as of the rights of foreign traders. The fact that Astor obtained a judgment against the officer who tried to restrain his agents in no wise invalidates the above explanation. Incidentally, the judgment was never paid.

[20] Wisconsin Historical Collections, 20:47–49.

[21] Chittenden, *American Fur Trade*, 1:314.

necessaries at the close of the war.[22] In 1817, however, the president decided to enforce the exclusion rigidly, and Indian agents were notified to issue no licenses to foreigners. Early in the following year orders were given to allow foreigners to serve as *engagés* and interpreters on the condition that the trader gave bond for five hundred dollars for each foreigner employed. An additional bond of half the value of the goods was required to insure that they belonged to American citizens. At least half of the interpreters must be Americans.[23] The law of 1824 was also difficult to enforce. It restricted the operation of traders to certain designated posts and was designed to protect the Indians against unprincipled traders, but it caused great inconvenience and aroused bitter opposition.[24]

Although many of the fur traders were honest, fair, and considerate, and succeeded in maintaining the most amicable relations with the tribes, they were the forerunners of settlers and so frequently aroused the enmity of the Indians. This was particularly true of the hunters and trappers, whose activities resulted in no advantage whatever to the natives. The fur trader was not the intentional promoter of settlements, and the great Canadian companies effectively opposed for a time all settlements in some regions. The trade in the United States was never so well organized as the Canadian trade, and no concerted effort was made to discourage settlers.[25] Hence the Indians, although they required the services of the traders, came to regard them as enemies. Though not personally responsible for the border troubles, the trader, because he was the first of the advancing tide, bore more than his share of the blame.

The fur trade was the first step in the development of a frontier and was largely responsible for creating a condition that

[22] Wisconsin Historical Collections, 19:405–07.
[23] Graham Collection, Missouri Historical Society. The letter to Graham consists of a copy of a letter from Calhoun to Cass, March 25, 1818, amending the instructions of November 26, 1817. See Wisconsin Historical Collections, 20:16–17, 42–47.
[24] *American State Papers: Indian Affairs*, 2:658.
[25] The slow settlement of Michigan is sometimes attributed to the maliciously discouraging reports of fur traders. Johnson, *Michigan Fur Trade*, pp. 148–49.

made defense necessary. It was also instrumental in securing the defense it required for its own existence, thus incidentally assisting in the general protection of the frontier. The trader was welcomed by the tribes, but when the trapper and hunter came, their welcome turned to resentment, which soon grew to chronic hostility against fur traders in general. The dwindling supply of game, the approach of settlers, and the activities of Indian agents aroused the tribes to a realization of their dangers. The interests of the fur trader conflicted with those of the Indians, and his activities required the support of troops.

Traders were often vehement in their demands for government protection. In 1816 the citizens of St. Louis petitioned Congress for the formation of a company guaranteed by the nation.[26] In the same year a proposal for the erection of thirteen posts between the mouth of the Kansas and the Pacific was seriously discussed. The proposed locations were selected, and an army of two thousand men was to garrison them.[27] An even more ambitious project was launched in 1819 by a petition, among the many objects of which were the development of post roads and canals, the adjustment of land titles, and the protection of the fur traders. The last was to be accomplished by the establishment of posts at the Mandan villages on the Missouri and at the mouth of the St. Peter's, by the abolition of the factory system, and by the formation of an American fur company that would have a monopoly of the trade.[28] One of the staunchest supporters of protection for the fur traders was Thomas H. Benton's paper, the *St. Louis Enquirer*.[29] It demanded that the

[26] *Annals of Congress,* 14th Congress, 1st Session, p. 1301.

[27] *Missouri Gazette,* November 9, 1816.

[28] *St. Louis Enquirer,* June 16, 1819; copied by the *National Intelligencer,* August 4, 1819; and in part by *Niles' Weekly Register,* 16:408–09. Niles waxed vehement in his opposition to "exclusive privileges" and the plan to "build forts, and make war and peace, as the British corporations do." The *Intelligencer* was sarcastic. "We delight in enlarged views of national policy, and have more than once admired the magnificence of the anticipations of the Missouri writers. There is a freshness and vigor about their conceptions, which relieve the dull sameness of everyday occurrences and which we indulge in contemplating with much the same feeling as one revels in the fairy land of reverie."

[29] In 1820, three years before the Arikara War, it demanded the occupation of the upper Missouri. See the issue of June 7, 1820.

government stop intertribal wars that interfered with the activities of fur traders.[30] It exulted in the abolition of the factories and noted a decided improvement in the fur trade because of the removal of official competition. It estimated the number of employees on the Missouri at one thousand and those on the Mississippi at five hundred.[31] It protested against the charge of unfairness lodged against the fur traders in their relations to the Indians. It criticized the Convention of 1818, which allowed the British to use the Columbia, and declared that fur traders were entitled to protection as much as Cape Cod fishermen, Nantucket whalers, and New York and Boston China merchants.[32] It ridiculed the denial of protection because the fur trade paid no direct revenue.[33] It recounted the loss in men and property suffered by a fur company and sarcastically remarked that Americans ran to Europe to help the Greeks while it allowed the fur traders to face dangers unprotected.[34]

The fur traders may have been justified in their complaints of the lack of protection, but they had no grounds for complaining of the national policy, for protection of the fur trade was one of the constant aims of the government after the close of the war. On February 22, 1815, Monroe, then secretary of war, proposed the erection of forts on the upper Mississippi and near the northern boundary for the purpose of securing the Indian trade.[35] Calhoun made persistent efforts to repel British interests and protect the fur trade. The purpose of the Missouri Expedition was to extend and protect the trade.[36] Northern posts were established and maintained as much for the support and protection they gave it as for military reasons.[37] The Arikara War, however one interprets it, was essentially a fur trade

[30] October 13, 1821.
[31] June 3, 1822; also in Niles' Weekly Register, 19:53.
[32] February 9, 1824.
[33] February 16, 1824.
[34] March 29, 1824. For a discussion of the need of protection for the fur traders, see American State Papers: Indian Affairs, 2:455–57.
[35] Monroe, Writings, 5:325.
[36] Jameson, Correspondence of John Caldwell Calhoun, pp. 134–36, 138, 147–48. For further discussion of this point see Chapter IX.
[37] See Chapter VIII.

struggle.[38] The purpose of erecting posts in the Southwest was
to protect the fur traders, and the survey of the main Santa Fé
trail in 1825 was, in part at least, the result of their petitions and
agitation.[39] The fur trade thus received its full share of official
attention and protection.

[38] See Chapter X.
[39] The fur trade of the Far Southwest was, of course, outside the United States,
but its effects were the same as though that region had been a part of the
country. Wesley, "The Fur Trade of the Southwest," master's thesis, Washington
University, 1925.

CHAPTER VI
THE NATIONAL MILITARY POLICY

For almost a century the defense of the frontier was the chief consideration in the military policy of the United States. Some theorists opposed any standing army whatever, and the militarists, ignoring actual requirements, advocated a large one. Neither group had its way. The defense of the frontiers necessitated the maintenance of an army of moderate size. The resulting policy slowly weakened, but did not destroy, the long-standing prejudices against a standing army. While international dangers occasionally threatened the peace and safety of the country, their effects were temporary. Such crises called forth volunteers from the entire nation, whereas the necessity of guarding the frontier was constant and could be performed by a relatively small permanent force. Each international crisis served to reassure the nation that its policy of relying upon enlistments was wise, but the never-ending task of guarding the frontier weakened the prejudice against a standing army and caused the nation to tolerate the growth of a policy it never deliberately adopted. This change is especially noticeable in the decade after the War of 1812, when a standing army was avowedly accepted for the first time.

The frontier defense policy of any period is naturally dependent upon the national military policy of that period. The size, location, and coordination of frontier garrisons were subject to the general policy. The proportion of the army that could serve on the frontier and in coast fortifications and the administration of the scattered units were dependent upon the national provision for the army. The whole policy determined the operation of its parts. Although the frontier received more attention in the decade after the War of 1812 than any other phase of national defense, it was only a part, and it. relative position will be clarified by a consideration of the natio ral military policy.

In 1815 two problems confronted the nation, the disbandment of the army and the determination of the size and functions of the standing army. Motives of economy resulted in the speedy discharge of the militia and the volunteers who had enlisted for the duration of the war and in a return to the pay schedule of a peace establishment for those in the regular army.[1] The reduction of the regular army and the determination of its size also received immediate attention. President Madison submitted the Treaty of Ghent to the Senate on February 15 and three days later sent a special message _ Congress. He warned Congress that the desire for economy should not lead to an immediate and radical reduction in the size of the army and asked for the maintenance of "an adequate regular force."[2]

Congress had begun the consideration of the reduction of the army even before the receipt of Madison's general message. On February 17, two days after the receipt of the treaty, Samuel Smith of Maryland introduced a resolution in the Senate that the Committee on Military Affairs be instructed to consider the propriety of reducing the army, and a resolution to that effect was passed on the following day.[3] The leadership in reducing the army, however, was assumed by the House, where George M. Troup of Georgia introduced a bill embodying the principal features of the law that was subsequently passed.[4] The question before the House, he said, was the extent and mode of redu tion. The extent should be determined by a consideration three things: the security of the country, the interests of the country, and the just claims of the army. He pointed out the presence of the armies and fleets of the late enemy, and declared that a

[1] Orders of D. Parker, adjutant and inspector general, February 18, 21, March 4, 1815. *National Intelligencer*, February 23, March 11, 1815; *Niles' Weekly Register*, 8:12.
[2] Richardson, *Messages and Papers of the Presidents*, 1:552–53.
[3] *Annals of Congress*, 13th Congress, 3d Session, pp. 244, 252.
[4] *Ibid.*, pp. 1177–78. The bill was introduced on February 22.

respectable army would be a safer guarantee that the late enemy would restore the posts and return property than a mere reliance upon their good faith. The interest of the country demanded "the exhibition of a respectable military force." The sudden reduction of the army would rob many men of their profession, and justice demanded a liberal provision for the disbanded officers. In regard to the mode of reduction Troup suggested three possible ways. The first was to reduce the number of men and officers, but to retain all regiments as a skeleton army that could be restored in case of need. The second plan suggested was to reduce the number of regiments to one-half or one-third, with a corresponding reduction of men, but to retain a sufficient number of officers so that the disbanded regiments could be restored when occasion required. The third plan was the consolidation and reduction proposed by the bill. Troup urged that the army not be reduced below the proposed ten thousand.[5] Timothy Pickering of Massachusetts wondered why so large an army should be maintained and asked the committee if it had any detailed statement of a plan for the use of so many men. Troup replied that no such statement was available, but he supposed that the posts, garrisons, and service would employ the total force. Joseph Desha of Kentucky moved to substitute six thousand for the ten thousand proposed by the bill.[6]

The debate on this amendment brought forth some new arguments as well as the timeworn platitudes about standing armies in time of peace. Desha said that in peacetime an army was needed only for the garrisoning of the frontier posts, which then numbered about twenty-five or thirty. Since one hundred men for each post were ample, he thought three thousand would be enough, and so the six thousand proposed by his amendment would be more than ample. He said that regulars were unsuited to Indian warfare, and he praised the militia and volunteers, declaring that they had won the war. Solomon P. Sharp of Kentucky was opposed to an army for any purpose except frontier

[5] *Ibid.*, pp. 1196–99.
[6] *Ibid.*, pp. 1190–1200.

garrisons. Unless it could be shown that ten thousand were necessary for that service, he favored five thousand. He declared that no gentleman would employ the soldiers in opening roads or making canals. Elisha R. Potter of Rhode Island wished that Desha had moved to reduce the army to two thousand. He thought that the consequent saving would raise the financial standing of the United States and secure more respect from other nations than a large army. The opponents of the amendment were equally emphatic. Robert Wright of Maryland considered it unwise to disband the army at a time when the nation was surrounded by enemies. He said that the Congress of Vienna might break up and another war ensue. The amendment was carried, and six thousand was substituted for ten thousand.

The House then engaged in a debate as to the time of disbanding the army, and whether to leave it to the discretion of the president. Pickering again showed his anti-preparedness attitude by saying that to leave it to the president might mean prolonging the event. William H. Lowndes of South Carolina thought it would be folly to bind the president to disband the army regardless of what circumstances might arise. Philip P. Barbour of Virginia argued that the president should be given the right to exercise his judgment. He called attention to the hasty disbandment of 1783 [7] and the resultant retention of the Northwest posts by England. John W. Eppes of Virginia declared that he was unwilling to allow the executive to decide so important a matter, and that financial considerations demanded an immediate disbandment. John G. Jackson of Virginia agreed with Eppes and said that he trusted the militia rather than the regulars, "enervated by the inactivity of a camp," constituting "a moth on the public Treasury, eating out the substance of the people." [8]

Before the House reached a decision it learned of the recommen-

---

[7] For an account of this see Wesley, "The Military Policy of the Critical Period," *Coast Artillery Journal*, 68:281–90.

[8] *Annals of Congress*, 13th Congress, 3d Session, pp. 1205–06.

dations of Monroe, acting secretary of war,[9] who wrote to the Senate Military Committee on February 22. Monroe said that the size of the army should be determined by the policy of Great Britain, which had thirty-five thousand men on the Continent. Affairs with Spain were unsettled, the seaports needed fortifications, frontier posts needed garrisons, and new posts higher up the Mississippi and along the boundary should be established in order to secure the friendship and "exclusive commerce" of the Indians. He concluded that twenty thousand men were needed to accomplish these objects and to maintain military knowledge and skill.[10]

On February 27 the House considered the report of the Committee of the Whole, which proposed to reduce the army to six thousand. Samuel Hopkins of Kentucky opposed the report, saying that the lack of an army in 1783 had caused "rivers of blood" to flow. He considered ten thousand men a small force for "this vast continent." "Is the possession of Fort Erie nothing? Of Michilmackinac the Gibralter of America, nothing?" He urged the retention of at least ten thousand until the following session.[11] John Forsyth of Georgia opposed the reduction to ten thousand, arguing that that number was needed in the West alone and that the unsettled condition of Spanish affairs made the proposed reduction unwise. The secretary of war had recommended twenty thousand, and he thought that the recommendation should carry weight.[12] Daniel Sheffey of Virginia refused to yield to executive recommendations and favored the reduction on account of expense.[13] James Fisk of Vermont said that the proposal was unwise, that he feared that similar circumstances would produce similar results, and that Indian wars would again follow.

John C. Calhoun said that the House was acting in the dark, since it had neither estimates nor facts. He thought that three

[9] For the exact tenure of the various secretaries of war see Appendix D.
[10] Monroe, *Writings*, 5:321–27.
[11] *Annals of Congress*, 13th Congress, 3d Session, pp. 1210–12.
[12] *Ibid.*, pp. 1212–14.
[13] *Ibid.*, pp. 1214–16.

objects should be kept in view: the maintenance of posts and garrisons, the preservation of military knowledge, and a consideration of the policy of the enemy. Since no facts were available, it was best not to act. He thought that the third point was the most important, that a reduction by the United States while England kept a large force in Canada was very foolish. He advised delay. Charles Goldsborough of Maryland felt that the retention of a large force might cause England to act similarly. He thought that England's retention of the posts in 1783 was no parallel to the present situation. Pickering again took the floor to remark sarcastically that he held a treaty of peace in his hand which he had supposed was an authentic document, but that the remarks of the House led him to doubt its authenticity. He had such confidence in England that he was willing to raze the frontier posts, and he regarded Spain as too feeble to excite any apprehensions. Thomas P. Grosvenor of New York said that disbandment was foolish while the enemy retained posts. He regarded the trifling expense of maintaining the army as cheap insurance against a calamity. Thomas Gholson of Virginia called attention to the extended frontier, the unexecuted treaty, Indian hostility, and Spanish affairs. John Rhea of Tennessee thought that the disbandment of the army would be as foolish as to discard one's coat when the first warm day arrives. Richard Stockton of New Jersey was alarmed that a secretary of war would recommend an army of twenty thousand. The most fundamental principle in America, as he saw it, was that a standing army was not to be tolerated in time of peace. Nathaniel Macon of North Carolina thought that no large army would be needed since the number of forts would not be increased. He declared that the British traders had caused all the Indian troubles and that peace would see an end of them.

The arguments over the peace establishment turned on the nature of the peace and the probability of its stability. When the vote was taken, the House stood seventy-five to sixty-five in favor of an army of six thousand.[14] The Senate amended the

[14] *Ibid.*, pp. 1251–52. The entire debate covers pages 1196–1253.

bill by changing six to fifteen,[15] but a conference effected a compromise on ten thousand,[16] and the president approved the bill on March 3.[17]

The law provided for artillery, infantry, riflemen, and engineers, the total not to exceed ten thousand men, and required the president to effect the disbandment of the excess number by May 1 if circumstances permitted. The organization of artillery was the same as that provided by the act of March 30, 1814. Each company thus consisted of one hundred privates and a total of one hundred and twenty-two men.[18] Each company of light artillery (riflemen) was to have the number provided by the act of April 12, 1808, which was fifty-eight privates and a total of eighty-one.[19] The act itself specified that each infantry company should consist of sixty-eight privates and a total of eighty-one.[20] It failed to provide for some staff officers whom Madison found it wise to retain temporarily in spite of the letter of the law.[21]

The reduction of the army was not a popular measure. While the debates were in progress the newspapers published many letters opposing any radical reduction.[22] Niles sarcastically remarked, "In the late proceedings of the House of Representatives, on a *military peace establishment,* we see that that body was determined, to the last, to let the minority govern." He observed that the policy of weakening the army would make employment in it "too contemptible for the high-souled men that now have command."[23] The *Missouri Gazette* complained that while the East rejoiced on account of peace, the West was the victim of "savage brutality." It declared that the reduction of the army to six thousand, as was proposed by the House, would

---

[15] *Ibid.,* p. 286.
[16] *Ibid.,* p. 1272.
[17] United States Statutes at Large, 3:224–25.
[18] *Ibid.,* pp. 113–16.
[19] *Ibid.,* 2:481–83.
[20] *Ibid.,* 3:224–25.
[21] The strength of the army in each year from 1815 to 1825 is shown in Appendix E.
[22] *National Intelligencer,* February 24, 28, March 3, 14, 1815.
[23] *Niles' Weekly Register,* 8:2.

be false economy, and would scarcely afford a "sergeant's guard."
It referred to the act as "the law for annihilating the army." [24]
Naturally the reduction was unpopular with the army. Elaborate
plans for a meeting of discharged officers to protest and petition
Congress for a reconsideration of their claims were alternately
praised and criticized.[25] One officer addressed a series of letters
to Henry Clay in which he deplored the false economy of Congress. He said that the soldiers could build roads and forts and
relieve the country of a great financial burden.[26]

The act of March 3 marks a distinct advance in the development of military policy. It is the first example of a frank acceptance and acknowledgment of the wisdom and intention of
maintaining a standing army in time of peace. The speeches of
the pro-militia, anti-army group indicate a genuine alarm, for no
peace establishment had ever before approached such numbers.[27]
Naturally, to Monroe and the men who had advocated one of
twenty thousand, it was disappointingly small, but the law was
interpreted as providing for ten thousand exclusive of officers,
and so the army under the act of March 3 actually numbered
nearly twelve thousand men.

When Congress met in December, 1815, Madison reported
that circumstances had made it inadvisable to discharge as many
officers as had been contemplated by the law of March 3. He
asked that the staff, which had been provisionally retained,
should be made permanent, and urged the continuation of
fortifications, the enlargement of the military academy, and the
classification of the militia.[28] Only the recommendation in regard
to the staff evoked any response from Congress. On December 21, 1815, the House Committee on Military Affairs asked
William H. Crawford, secretary of war, for a recommendation
as to the desired staff. Crawford replied that the peace organiza-

[24] General laments in the issues of April 1, 15, 22, July 22, 1815.
[25] *National Intelligencer*, June 14, 23, July 15, 24, August 1, 1815.
[26] *Niles' Weekly Register*, 9:214, quoting the *Boston Patriot*.
[27] The army consisted of 6,744 men in 1812, but it was unusually large in
anticipation of war. Upton, *Military Policy of the United States*, p. 95 and *passim*.
[28] Richardson, *Messages and Papers of the Presidents*, 1:564, 566.

tion of the staff should be as full and as well organized as in time of war. He recommended a list of offices whose occupants would constitute a general staff.[29] Richard M. Johnson of Kentucky introduced a bill in the House embodying Crawford's suggestions, and said that the proposed staff was no larger in proportion to the size of the army than it had been during the war.[30] The bill became a law on April 24, 1816.[31] It was a frank recognition that the act of March 3, 1815, was defective, and it gave legal sanction, with slight changes, to the staff that Madison had established by order.

While the bill for the reorganization of the staff was in progress, desultory criticisms were made, not on any specific motion to reduce the army but whenever occasion offered and particularly when the subject of taxes was raised. Benjamin Hardin of Kentucky sarcastically observed that officers were so numerous that he had heard a proposal that they be reduced in rank and organized to fill the ranks. He opposed an army of more than six thousand; in fact, he was against any standing army at all, preferring to trust to the militia. He said that garrisons were unnecessary and cited the one at Prairie du Chien as an example. He asserted that Rome's victory over Carthage had been due to the fact that Carthage had a standing army and Rome a militia, and added that Rome fell when it developed a standing army.[32] Clay made a long speech in which he praised the army, and Calhoun added his approval to Clay's remarks. Many speakers wandered from the subject of tax bills to talk about patriotism, heroes, the army, and the militia,[33] but the one feeble effort to alter the army received scant attention.[34]

[29] *American State Papers: Indian Affairs,* 1:636. Crawford's proposal was written on December 27 and was given to the House on February 6, 1816.
[30] The progress of the bill is noted in *Annals of Congress,* 14th Congress, 1st Session, pp. 235, 249, 253, 333–34, 336, 898, 1234–36, 1236–37, 1239, 1250, 1410–11.
[31] United States Statutes at Large, 3:297–99.
[32] *Annals of Congress,* 14th Congress, 1st Session, pp. 753, 755.
[33] *Ibid.,* pp. 721–22, 759–62, 786–92, 805–11, 823–24, 831–32, 835–36, 859–62.
[34] John Randolph, speaking on January 10, 1817 (*ibid.,* p. 460), said that he had tried to reduce the army in the preceding session. His effort provoked no recorded debate. *Ibid.,* p. 803. The resolution was introduced on January 29, 1816.

The session that began in December, 1816, produced some opposition to administrative practices. Ironically enough, one of the most persistent and successful critics was John C. Calhoun, who later, as secretary of war, bitterly resented the criticisms and requests for information that came so frequently from Congress. Early in the session he moved to curb the president's power to transfer appropriations.[35] In debating the general appropriation bill, he vigorously assailed the illegal transfer of appropriations. He cited the stone barracks at Sackett's Harbor, the military road from Detroit to Ohio, and the repairing of arms as examples of such transfers. He did not question the wisdom or necessity of these objects, but he did criticize a practice that did not have the express approval of Congress.[36] Calhoun's efforts resulted in the act of March 3, which curbed the president's power of transferring appropriations.[37]

The usual effort to reduce the army was made. On February 17, 1817, Jeremiah Mason of New Hampshire introduced a resolution in the Senate to instruct the military committee to report a bill reducing the army to five thousand. "A deliberate examination" had convinced him that the army was too large. It rendered general military training useless and was an unbearable expense. The only use for an army was to guard the western frontier and to protect the fortifications. The army and fortifications, however, were useless in guarding the coast, which could only be done by a navy. The army, scattered and unstandardized, was useless as a training school. Peace reigned, and there was no sign of a recurrence of the old troubles with Spain. Even when all Europe was engaged in war, the United States needed only a small force, and with universal peace prevailing there surely was no occasion for a large army.[38]

James Barbour of Virginia criticized Mason for beginning a fight on the question of the army so late in the session, and pointed out that the House had refused to consider such a

[35] *Annals of Congress*, 14th Congress, 2d Session, p. 374.
[36] *Ibid.*, pp. 956–60.
[37] United States Statutes at Large, 3:390.
[38] *Annals of Congress*, 14th Congress, 2d Session, pp. 124–30.

motion. He declared that a growing country needed a growing army; that the nation was surrounded by hostile Indians, threatening Spaniards, and British, who would help Spain in the event of war. The cost of arsenals, arms, munitions, and fortifications, he said, should not be charged against the army. The army was a valuable nucleus. "The history of the last war contains a volume of wisdom" upon the subject of keeping an army. He then made one of the most valid criticisms of the anti-army policy, when he said that the militia would be of value if it were "disciplined and armed," but that the nation could not use it unless the governors of the states gave their consent. Thus it was foolish to strip the nation of an army, which it could command, and to rely upon the militia, which it could not command.

James Brown of Louisiana approved of Barbour's remarks and said that the matter of reducing the army had been carefully debated two years before, and the size of the army had been fixed at ten thousand.[39] No one had objected; no citizen had said that the army was too large. It was folly to fear an army made up of good citizens, who were, moreover, widely scattered. From a financial standpoint he viewed the army as almost profitable, for the soldiers were working on roads and fortifications at five dollars a month, doing work that would cost thirty dollars a month if done by anyone else.[40]

The inauguration of James Monroe on March 4, 1817, marked a decided quickening of interest in military affairs. His course in favor of a large army during his short tenure as secretary of war assured those who believed in adequate defense that their cause had gained a powerful ally. On May 31 he set out on a tour of the country for the purpose of inspecting the defenses, reviewing the troops, and determining the expenditures on fortifications. In his own words, "I took that trip to draw the public attention to the great object of public defence."[41] He visited

[39] The army numbered 10,024, including officers, on January 1, 1817. *American State Papers: Military Affairs*, 1:662.

[40] *Annals of Congress*, 14th Congress, 2d Session, pp. 152–62.

[41] Monroe to Madison, May 10, 1822, in Monroe, *Writings*, 6:290. An earlier statement of his purpose is found *ibid.*, 6:22.

the eastern cities and went as far west as Detroit, returning to Washington on September 17. His movements were recorded in great detail, and his tour undoubtedly awakened a great interest in national affairs.[42]

One of the most important tasks confronting Monroe was the selection of a secretary of war. The numerous changes in that office had lessened its dignity and prevented continuity of policy.[43] Monroe offered the position to Clay, who, disappointed that he had not been chosen secretary of state, refused it. Monroe next thought of appointing Jackson, but the latter signified his unwillingness to accept.[44] Isaac Shelby of Kentucky declined because of advanced age.[45] In the meantime George Graham, chief clerk, continued to fill the post. Monroe next tendered the position to William H. Lowndes, who also declined. On October 10, 1817, the appointment was offered to Calhoun, who accepted it [46] and assumed the office on December 8, 1817.[47]

Calhoun took office under exceedingly unfavorable circumstances. Unbalanced and unsettled accounts had accumulated; questions of policy had to be studied and solved; no plans for coast fortifications had matured, although a survey had been ordered. No comprehensive frontier policy had been evolved, and the American fur traders were complaining loudly against the British and Indians. The method of supplying the army was chaotic, depending upon the selfish interests of irresponsible contractors. Worst of all, from the standpoint of administration,

---

[42] Waldo, *Tour of Monroe*. The faithful Niles also recorded "for posterity" many of the speeches and details of the tour. See *Niles' Weekly Register*, vol. 12, *passim*.

[43] The *Missouri Gazette* (September 27, 1817) lamented the long intervals of secretaries *ad interim*.

[44] Monroe to Jackson, March 1, 1817, in Parton, *Life of Jackson*, 2:368.

[45] Monroe to Shelby, February 20, 1817, in Monroe, *Writings*, 6:1–2.

[46] Monroe, *Writings*, 6:4–5; Jameson, *Correspondence of John Caldwell Calhoun*, pp. 131, 251–54. Calhoun's acceptance is dated November 1.

[47] Meigs, *Life of Calhoun*, 1:229. The official appointment is dated October 8. "A Foreigner" (*Letters from Washington*, p. 56), writing in the winter of 1817–18, said: "But the situation to which he has recently been elevated, has, I fear, abridged his sphere of usefulness, and as secretary of war, Mr. Calhoun, who occupied every tongue during the sessions of the national legislature, may dwindle into obscurity, but will never be forgotten."

there was no unity or system in the army; there were no heads of military departments to whom all inferior officers were accountable, and no general staff in the correct sense of the term. The army had no uniform system of discipline and no generally recognized regulations; various commands could not even drill together creditably. The War of 1812 had demonstrated the weakness of the policy of relying upon the militia, and some reforms seemed imperative. Besides these problems, the new secretary had the unenviable task of trying to maintain the size of the army and securing the necessary appropriations in the face of persistent hostility from a growing number of critics in Congress. It was no easy task which the young and inexperienced South Carolinian had assumed. The account of the national military policy for the remainder of the decade ending in 1825 is almost equivalent to an account of his efforts to solve the problems enumerated.

Before attempting reforms Calhoun labored patiently to learn the routine duties of his office, but his public duties began at once. On December 11 the House called on Monroe for a statement of the strength of the army,[48] and on the twenty-second Calhoun submitted his report to the president. He said that the army was large enough to maintain the fortifications but wholly inadequate for war. It was employed in arsenals, in cutting roads, and in building posts. A board of officers was engaged in examining the "whole line of our frontier." He declared defense was "among the most sacred duties of the Government." [49] The report is not a very elaborate affair, and it shows that the new secretary was proceeding cautiously. The returns show that the army had decreased in size, numbering only 8,221.[50]

On December 9, 1817, the day after Calhoun assumed charge of the department, he was subjected to one of the annoying experiences that the secretaries of war in the early period had to face. Almost every time Congress met, some member made

---

[48] *Annals of Congress*, 15th Congress, 1st Session, p. 432.
[49] *American State Papers: Military Affairs*, 1:669.
[50] *Ibid.*, p. 670.

an effort to reduce the army or cut down the military appropriations, or both. Although such efforts usually failed, they were a source of irritation to the officer who was largely responsible for the safety of the nation. In this session Richard M. Johnson of Kentucky introduced a series of resolutions, one of which proposed a reduction of the army to eight thousand.[51] This particular effort, however, received scant attention, and there was no definite movement toward reduction until the spring of 1818.

Some of the difficulties confronting Calhoun when he assumed office have been mentioned. Two of these, the supplying of the army and the coordination and administration of military departments, were overcome within the first year of his service. The solution of these two widely dissimilar problems was made possible by the passage of one law, and that law was planned, if not actually written, by Calhoun himself.[52]

The supplying of the army had always been a difficult problem. The War of 1812 had shown the defects of having each command look after its own supplies. The contractors fulfilled their agreements when it was to their advantage to do so, and when it was not, they were fertile in excuses. Since they were not under military law, they were practically free to furnish or not to furnish the supplies for which they had received the contract. If an army advanced into new country destitute of roads, and the contractor found his task difficult, he could plead that there was no means of transporting the supplies. If defective goods were furnished, he could blame the sub-contractor. In an emergency the commanding general could take the matter into his own hands, and in several instances this was done, but the expense was enormous. The officers felt that to prevent such failures the contractor should be under military law, since the existence of the army depended upon the fulfillment of his obligations.

As early as November 10, 1814, Calhoun, who was then in

<hr/>

[51] *Annals of Congress,* 15th Congress, 1st Session, pp. 420–21.
[52] *Congressional Globe,* 25th Congress, 2d Session, Appendix, p. 181. His complete knowledge of the administration of the War Department is shown by another speech. *Ibid.,* 30th Congress, 1st Session, p. 697.

Congress, offered resolutions to direct an inquiry into the expediency of changing the mode of supplying the army. He pointed out the prevalence of speculation and the shortcomings of the contractors.[53] Calhoun's resolution was adopted, and the committee received Secretary Monroe's reply, which embodied severe denunciations of the contract method by Generals Scott and Gaines and Colonel John R. Fenwick.[54] A bill providing for the establishment of a commissariat was introduced in and passed by the House and was in its last stages of enactment in the Senate when the news of the Treaty of Ghent caused its indefinite postponement,[55] and the matter rested for over two years.[56]

On December 9, 1816, the House directed the Committee on Military Affairs to report on the best method of supplying the army.[57] John Williams of Tennessee, chairman of the committee, made inquiries of General Gaines, who strongly indorsed the establishment of a commissariat. He said that the contractor supplied the cheapest and coarsest goods, and that any rejections by officers were attended with great inconvenience to the troops. He thought that the commissariat would be cheaper, for it would eliminate the profits of the contractor.[58] Nothing was done at this time, and the badly needed reform awaited the spur of necessity, which was soon supplied by the Seminole War.

In the fall of 1817 the contractors failed to fulfill their agree-

[53] *Annals of Congress,* 13th Congress, 3d Session, pp. 550–51.
[54] *American State Papers: Military Affairs,* 1:599–601.
[55] *Annals of Congress,* 13th Congress, 3d Session, pp. 228, 229, 230, 232, 234, 236, 1101, 1131.
[56] Food, as well as clothing and general supplies, was, prior to 1818, provided through the quartermaster's department. The changes in that department made by the statute of April 24, 1816, have not been overlooked, but they merely changed the organization and number of employees, and did not affect the contract system of supplying rations. United States Statutes at Large, 3:297–99.
[57] *Annals of Congress,* 14th Congress, 2d Session, p. 253.
[58] *Ibid.,* pp. 1255–58. Crawford's opinion is interesting as a contrast. Writing to Macomb on January 5, 1816, he rebuked him severely for buying supplies, saying it was illegal. "Universal experience has proven, that a commissariat is the most expensive mode of subsisting an army; whilst that of contractors, has been found to be the most economical." Military Books, Old Records Division, Adjutant General's Office.

ments on the southern frontier. This condition forced the generals in charge of the army to take over the supplying of the army. On January 21, 1818, John Williams introduced a resolution in the Senate requesting a report on the supplying of the army.[59] Calhoun's report to President Monroe showed that special precautions had been taken to insure delivery, by advancing money to contractors and by giving them ample notice. Nevertheless, the supplies were not furnished, and the utter failure and consequent inconvenience aroused Congress to action. On February 18 James Barbour of Virginia introduced a resolution instructing the Committee on Military Affairs to devise a better system for supplying the army.[60] The bill embodying Barbour's plans was called an act to regulate the staff, and was combined with the proposals of some members to reduce the number and expense of the military departments. The only recorded objection to the establishment of a commissariat was made by Joseph Desha of Kentucky, who said that each of the seventy-five posts would require an issuing commissary, which was not exactly a reduction of the staff. He declared that "young, high-minded military men" were not the ones to replace a hoop on a flour barrel or prevent the leakage of brine from a barrel of pork. He estimated that the proposed method would double the cost of supplies. Commanders desired the new system merely because they could not court-martial contractors. "The gentleman from Ohio [Harrison] brings in the little Seminole War, to aid in shoving this bill through the House." Desha ended his appeal by asking for delay. In spite of his objections, the bill was passed and on April 14 became a law.[61]

The new law abolished the contract system of supplying rations and established a commissary general and the necessary assistants, who were to purchase food supplies for the army, by contract whenever possible, after public notice had been given.[62]

[59] *Annals of Congress*, 15th Congress, 1st Session, pp. 119, 129.
[60] *Ibid.*, pp. 211–13. The resolution was adopted on February 20.
[61] *Annals of Congress*, 15th Congress, 1st Session, pp. 268, 273, 289–90, 293, 350, 1568–69, 1656, 1687–90, 1692.
[62] United States Statutes at Large, 3:426–27.

Soldiers were no longer dependent upon uncertain contractors who might fail them in emergencies, for the supplying of the army had become a military function. Officers of the army bought, forwarded, and distributed supplies, and uncertainties and delays were largely eliminated.

The first commissary general was Colonel George Gibson, who was appointed on April 18, 1818,[63] and the new system, according to the provisions of Section 6, went into effect on June 1, 1819. Its success was immediate and constant. A report of February 24, 1820, shows that it had reduced the cost per ration from about nineteen to about sixteen cents.[64] The reorganization of 1821, which so materially altered the army, left the commissary department practically unchanged. Further proof of its efficacy is found in Monroe's message of December 3, 1822, in which he spoke of "its great utility" and advised Congress to re-enact the law,[65] the original enactment having been for five years only. Congress complied with the president's suggestion, and on January 23, 1823, re-enacted the law for another five years.[66]

In connection with the supplying of the army it is interesting to note the efforts to make the army partially self-sustaining. By the general orders of September 11, 1818,[67] the garrisons at all permanent posts were required to cultivate gardens. Extensive plans were made for stock-raising and general farming at many of the western posts. The products were to be bought by the commissary, and the money was to be divided among the soldiers.[68] Considerable success attended these plans, and frequent mention of livestock and food supplies at the various posts was made by inspectors and newspapers. The "turnip patches at Council Bluffs" were dignified by mention in Congress.[69]

[63] Rodenbough and Haskin, *The Army of the United States*, p. 75.
[64] *American State Papers: Military Affairs*, 2:72–74.
[65] Richardson, *Messages and Papers of the Presidents*, 2:190.
[66] United States Statutes at Large, 3:721.
[67] General Orders, 1815–21, pp. 135, 141, Old Records Division, Adjutant General's Office. A little later the adjutant and inspector general sent copies of *The American Gardener*, containing directions for working gardens, to the various posts.
[68] *Missouri Gazette*, October 30, 1818; *Niles' Weekly Register*, 15:91.
[69] *St. Louis Enquirer*, December 8, 1819, July 15, 1820; *Annals of Congress*, 16th Congress, 2d Session, p. 769; *National Intelligencer*, May 18, 1822, quoting

Calhoun was unable to devote his whole attention to solving problems; much of it was consumed in maintaining the ground that had been won.[70] On April 7, 1818, David Trimble of Kentucky introduced a resolution in the House calling for a report as to the advisability of reducing the army. Samuel Smith of Maryland opposed the resolution, asserting that the extended frontiers and fortifications made reduction of the army absurd. Lewis Williams of North Carolina supported Trimble and declared that the army was too large and too expensive. The resolution was adopted on April 17.[71]

In answer to this resolution Calhoun submitted his report to the House on December 11, 1818. It first considered the advisability of reduction. "On the lakes, the Mississippi, Arkansas, and Red River, our posts are now, or will be shortly, extended, for the protection of our trade and the preservation of the peace of the frontiers, to Green Bay, the mouths of the St. Peter's and the Yellow Stone rivers, Bellepoint, and Natchitoches." He ridiculed the idea that so scattered an army could be dangerous to the liberties of the people, and concluded that it would be unwise to reduce it. He then considered the reduction of officers; some posts, he said, had to be held and officered even if the army were reduced by half, and since the organization should be perfect even in time of peace, he opposed any reduction of officers. He gave the House no reason to suppose that expenses could be reduced, but he did point out that the garrisons were helping to support themselves and that the commissariat would in time reduce the cost.[72]

The report was convincing and was probably of considerable weight in preventing a reduction, but it did not prevent further attempts to effect that object. On February 12, 1819, Lewis Wil-

---

the *Arkansas Gazette*, April 2; Doty, "Official Journal, 1820," Wisconsin Historical Collections, 13:168; Inspection Reports, Inspector General's Office, 1814–23, pp. 138, 179.

[70] The spring of 1818 also witnessed the formulation of an aggressive frontier policy. This is considered in Chapters VIII to XII, dealing with the different frontiers.

[71] *Annals of Congress*, 15th Congress, 1st Session, pp. 1766, 1767.

[72] *American State Papers: Military Affairs*, pp. 779–82.

liams introduced a resolution in the House to reduce the army to six thousand men. He spoke for two hours and was answered by William Henry Harrison, who also consumed much time. The bill was amended to abolish the office of major general and reduce the staff by one-half. Eldred Simkins of South Carolina opposed the reduction. He said that there were seventy-three posts, and more were to be established, that the army was necessary as a teacher for the militia, and that any reduction would be attended with unfortunate results. Reduction was postponed indefinitely.[73]

The next session brought forth the customary efforts to reduce the army. On January 5, 1820, Tunstall Quarles of Kentucky introduced a resolution in the House to reorganize the army in such a way as to reduce the staff; according to his statement, the army consisted almost exclusively of officers. Newton Cannon of Tennessee, a persistent opponent of the army, made an attempt to reduce the military forces to five thousand and supported it by a long speech containing the customary arguments. On the same day, March 8, 1820, Arthur Livermore, in speaking on the appropriation bill, recited the evils of a large army. He called on its opponents to unite in opposing the appropriations. He declared the army to be so widely scattered that a new one could be raised more quickly than the scattered garrisons could be brought from the Yellowstone and other remote corners of the earth. He made the customary objection to the size of the staff. In the following month [74] John Floyd of Virginia endeavored to have the army reduced to six thousand. Finally, on May 11, at the instance of Henry Clay, the House passed a resolution asking the secretary of war to prepare plans for reducing the army to six thousand. The resolutions requested that his report be ready for the opening of the next session.[75]

It was generally believed that in its next session Congress would reduce the army. The new principle of a real standing

[73] *Annals of Congress,* 15th Congress, 2d Session, 1:1155, 1156–66.
[74] April 29, 1820.
[75] *Annals of Congress,* 16th Congress, 1st Session, pp. 859, 1597–1602, 1607, 2145, 2233–34.

army had aroused the powerful objections of a numerous group of congressmen, who had repeatedly tried in vain to restore things as they were before the War of 1812. Success was at last to crown their efforts, though not a complete nor satisfying success, for the nation had learned by experience and had grown in size and numbers. The opening speech was made by John Cocke of Tennessee, even before the receipt of Calhoun's report.[76]

Calhoun's report, submitted on December 12, 1820, is one of the ablest of American state papers, and it secured the respect of even the anti-army group.[77] Calhoun ingeniously began by saying that the question of a standing army was not involved, for its necessity was so apparent that its bitterest opponents had never tried to abolish it. The question then was merely the extent of reduction. Of the two objects of an army, defense in peacetime and preparation for war, he regarded the latter as by far the more important. Since the mere existence of an army presupposed the possibility of war, it was apparent that the army should be ready for such an emergency. To be ready it should be so modeled as to meet the test. No new creation nor reorganization should be necessary. The skeleton should be intact, and the only thing necessary should be the enlargement of the body of the army. The bureau organization, in which every distinct branch terminated in a chief, should remain unimpaired, for it had proved its efficiency and economy. The number of officers should be proportionately greater in peace than in war, for otherwise the increase would really be the creation of a new army rather than the augmentation of one already in existence. The report was accompanied by many documents in which were worked out the details of the new organization.[78]

Since the army reorganization of 1821 remained unchanged for seventeen years, the ideas of the congressmen who framed the measure are worthy of attention. Realizing that a reduction would be made, the proponents of a large army took the lead

[76] *Ibid.*, 16th Congress, 2d Session, p. 444 (November 20, 1820).
[77] Brown's advice in regard to reducing the line rather than the staff was accepted by Calhoun. Brown Letter Books, 2:192–96.
[78] *American State Papers: Military Affairs*, 2:188–91, 191–98.

in order to save the staff organization and restrict the reduction as much as possible. The two leaders whose views will be noted were Alexander Smyth of Virginia and Eldred Simkins of South Carolina. The leaders of the movement for a large reduction were Thomas W. Cobb of Georgia, Lewis Williams and Charles Fisher of North Carolina, Newton Cannon and John Cocke of Tennessee, David Trimble of Kentucky, and John Floyd of Virginia. The debate was long and vigorous, and the trite arguments were repeated, amplified, and explained. Even when other subjects were nominally before the House, the army seems to have been the center of attention. On January 3, 1821, the House debated a resolution to reduce appropriations for the army, navy, fortifications, and the departments.[79] Cobb said that Calhoun's report was "the ablest, most ingenious, and upon the whole, the best defense of a standing army in time of peace which I have seen in print," but it did not propose to reduce the staff. "I can see no utility in an army of officers." He cited, as did many others, Jefferson and his message in favor of reducing the army.[80]

Smyth, speaking on January 5, made out an able case for an adequate standing army. He said that the army, being a portion of the people, would be no source of danger to the country. The militia as organized did not deserve the confidence of the nation as a force for carrying on war. Its record in the Revolution was discreditable according to Washington himself.[81] Its record in the War of 1812 was even worse, for nine thousand of the militia in New York refused to answer when called, and the United States had no control over them until they were in its service. Militia fled at Camden, Guilford Courthouse, Sackett's Harbor, Buffalo, and Bladensburg. In the second place, the militia was the most expensive type of army, for it wasted supplies and arms, and the short terms and numerous officers swelled the pay rolls. In the third place, the maintenance of the militia in

[79] *Annals of Congress,* 16th Congress, 2d Session, pp. 715–16.
[80] *Ibid.,* pp. 728–29.
[81] Upton in *Military Policy of the United States, passim,* gives the significant portions of Washington's letters which bear upon this point.

the field was most distressing to the people, for it was made up of conscripted men, whereas the regular army was made up of willing men. In the fourth place, the militia laws operated unequally and unjustly. States near the scene of war had to bear a disproportionate burden, while those farther removed were exempted. The payment of a bounty to escape service constituted a tax paid in particular districts, while thousands of the wealthy escaped service and taxation. In some cases the boards went only halfway through the militia rolls, and so discrimination resulted. Militia service was a capitation tax. The militia belonged to the states and could not be relied upon by the nation. Since there was no other means of national defense, it would be folly to destroy or cripple the army seriously.[82]

On January 8 Simkins said that the nation had "loudly and universally" approved Monroe's military policy. Not a word against the army had been uttered by the people; not a petition had been presented. The only opposition was in Congress, where the cry was, "Stop your fortifications, diminish the progress of your navy, lessen all your salaries, dismiss your staff and cut down your little army to the command of a single Brigadier General." Jefferson had been ill advised in reducing the army, as his own course showed, for in the beginning of his administration the army consisted of 3,300, but in 1808 it had an authorized strength of 10,000. Its weakness was explained by the fact that it had no adequate staff to discipline and organize it.[83]

Williams answered Simkins' arguments. He said that all American constitutional history bore witness to the truth that "standing armies are dangerous to liberty." Military life made officers feel superior, and even in civilian life they would not associate with former privates on terms of equality. The army developed two attitudes, one "domineering and intolerant" and the other "servile and dependent." The army was a "necessary evil," and the question before the House should be, "With how much of the evil can we dispense?" and not, "With what quan-

[82] *Annals of Congress*, 16th Congress, 2d Session, pp. 744–55.
[83] *Ibid.*, pp. 758–61.

tity of it can we be able to subsist?" The secretary of war knew that it was the officers who caused the expense, yet he advised the retention of the full number. There were only four men to each officer, counting noncommissioned officers and musicians. The secretary's reports were "more like speeches addressed to the army, than communications made to this House." He argued that the regiments and companies needed the officers, whereas he should have shown that there were men who needed the officers. Fifty posts were more than enough, for the frontier line had not been extended in proportion to the increased area. The acquisition of Louisiana really decreased the frontier because it took in Indians who were hostile. As the navy increased, the army on the coast ought to be reduced.[84]

Fisher said, "Sir, I have always thought, that one of the best features in our Government is its unfitness for war."[85] Cannon said that however large the army was in time of peace, it would be inadequate for war. Trimble said the frontiers were increased only slightly by the acquisition of Louisiana. He cited the number of troops that had held the frontier in 1802, 1806, and 1809, and stated that the number of Indian warriors had decreased. The doubling of population was no argument for doubling the army. The number of posts had not doubled, for there were only fifty-four, which were occupied by more than ten men each. Trimble then proposed a substitute plan. Defense, he said, consisted of many things—moral energy, money, credit, roads and canals, labor, and economy. If there was no desire to save the million that could be saved, then the wisest way to expend it for defense purposes was to establish training camps for the militia for one month in each year. He estimated the number of men in the country between twenty-one and twenty-eight years of age at 290,000. The training could be given by officers and graduates of West Point.[86]

Floyd derided Calhoun's list of posts, saying that he thought

[84] *Ibid.*, p. 818.
[85] *Ibid.*, p. 824.
[86] *Ibid.*, pp. 876–78, 885–86.

a post was a fortified place. On the list was Fort Mims, which had been burned; Fort Stoddart, which had not been occupied for ten years unless an alligator had chosen it as a place to bask in the sun undisturbed. "Some posts startle us with their warlike preparations." Belle Fontaine had three men. Fort Strother was not at the junction of any stream with the Coosa. Fort Plaquemine and Fort St. Philip were the same spot; Fort Bowyer and Fort Mobile Point were the same spot; and Fort Toulouse and Fort Jackson were the same spot. Floyd succeeded in reducing Calhoun's list of 126 posts to 58, and asserted that only 30 were necessary.[87] The debates occupied the major portion of the attention of the House until January 23, when the bill was passed by a vote of 109 to 48.[88]

The debates in the Senate, where the bill was amended in several particulars, brought forth no new arguments, but Mahlon Dickerson of New Jersey, a bitter opponent of a standing army, made a speech that throws light on the cause of the reduction. "I should wish to see the army reduced to five thousand men in time of peace, when no enemy threatens to molest us, even if our finances were in the most prosperous train. But a reduction which principle would render proper, our empty Treasury will render necessary; and but for this necessity no reduction would take place. If our country was not in distress—if our finances were not embarrassed, the army, as at present established, would be permanently fixed upon us. No efforts of those who think such a force unnecessary for our defense, or dangerous to our liberties, would have the least avail." He complained that there was no public interest in reducing the army. "The apathy of the people upon this subject, to judge from their silence, would indicate that their former jealousies of permanently standing armies, by some strange influence, had been put to rest forever. . . . The presses, once the guardians of our liberties, are now silent upon this subject, or advocate the present

[87] *Ibid.*, pp. 896–98.
[88] The debates are reported with considerable fullness. *Ibid.*, pp. 902–07, 932–34, 936–37, 1242–43.

establishment of the army; and not a breath is heard against it except upon the floor of Congress." [89]

The act to reduce and fix the military establishment was approved on March 2, 1821. It provided for an army of 6,183, under the command of a major general and two brigadier generals. Since the army was to be reduced, the number of privates in each company was reduced from that established by the act of 1815—the artillery company from one hundred to forty-two; the infantry from sixty-eight to forty-two.[90] Congress ignored many of Calhoun's recommendations. It failed to provide for an increase in an emergency, and so the nation was still dependent upon the militia. Had the skeleton organization been adopted, new recruits could have been absorbed without delay. An even worse defect was the provision for filling the staff with men from the line, for it meant a dearth of officers on duty; Calhoun had planned for a full staff and an ample number of officers. The failure to provide the better plan was in no way due to prejudice against the army but solely to financial considerations. Experience, painful and costly, was eventually to show the wisdom of Calhoun and the shortsightedness of Congress.

Public opinion, so far as it was articulate upon the subject, seems to have been opposed to the reduction of 1821—or, if not opposed, entirely indifferent, for, as Senator Dickerson pointed out, the public had lost its prejudices on the subject. Only on the frontier was sentiment expressed in favor of a large army. The *Detroit Gazette* hoped there would be no reduction, for force alone had any effect upon the Indians.[91] The *National Intelligencer* regretted that the bill had been treated entirely as a matter of economy.[92] A correspondent of the same paper said that the reduction of the number of posts meant the abandonment of any hope of extending American influence.[93]

[89] *Ibid.*, pp. 367–68. The progress of the bill through the Senate is found *ibid.*, pp. 238, 261, 364–65, 367–74, 377–78, 379, 389.
[90] United States Statutes at Large, 3:615.
[91] September 15, 1820.
[92] January 25, 1821.
[93] January 16, 1821.

No further reduction in the army and no important change in its organization was made during the remainder of Calhoun's tenure as secretary of war, but another effort was made in 1822, when Newton Cannon, a steadfast opponent of a large army, tried to reduce the staff [94] and restore the companies to their former size. He stressed the saving that would be made by the elimination of supernumerary officers and estimated that 784, who had nothing to do, could be discharged.[95] William Eustis of Massachusetts made a similar effort, but he was ably answered by Edward F. Tatnall of Georgia, who characterized the bill as one for disorganizing the army, and by Joel R. Poinsett of South Carolina, who said that the plan would make any increase impossible, since each regiment would already be filled. He also pointed out one of the great defects of the existing organization when he declared that the seeming surplus of officers was more than absorbed by being detailed to act as quartermasters, assistants, teachers, and other staff officers, a practice made necessary by the defective staff. He thus answered Cannon's arguments and pointed out that many posts had only one or two officers. All these proposals were, after considerable debate, either defeated or laid on the table.[96]

The act of 1821 marked the close of congressional reorganizations in this period, and so Calhoun had a better opportunity to complete some of the plans that had been projected, one of which was the establishment of a uniform discipline. He had tried to accomplish this in 1814 when he was a member of Congress. He pointed out the lack of a uniform system of regulations and the impossibility of different divisions drilling together when five or six different systems were used.[97] In 1815 General Swift had drawn up a set of uniform infantry tactics, which were adopted by general orders.[98] In 1818 Scott conceived the idea of writing a system of general regulations, and proposed the matter

[94] *Annals of Congress*, 17th Congress, 1st Session, p. 535.
[95] *Ibid.*, pp. 785–87.
[96] *Ibid.*, pp. 896, 1565–74, 1580–90, 1591–1612, 1615–16, 1618.
[97] *Ibid.*, 13th Congress, 3d Session, pp. 550–51. Brown praised Calhoun's "enlightened movement." Brown Letter Books, 1:270–71.
[98] Brown Letter Books, 1:397–98.

to Calhoun, who consulted Monroe and secured his approval.[99]
The sanction of Congress was given in a resolution of December 22, 1819, and Scott completed his general regulations and Judge Advocate Major Samuel A. Storrow wrote a system of martial law. The systems were submitted to Congress and were enacted into law, forming Section 14 of the act of March 2, 1821.[1]

Scott says, "This was the first time that the subjects embraced were ever reduced, in any army, to a regular analysis and systematized into institutes."[2] They gave detailed rules concerning the conduct of officers and men, compliments, honors, dress, arrests, care of arms, sutlers, marches, prisoners, and numerous details of military life in peace and war.[3] Complete and useful as they were, an unfortunate incident caused their immediate repeal, though not their abandonment. Some minor differences were detected between the original copy submitted to Congress and the final published edition. Scott explained the points to the entire satisfaction of some congressmen, but the majority insisted upon the repeal of the regulations.[4] An inquiry by Congress in 1824 elicited the information from Calhoun that Scott's regulations had been continued in force by the president's orders in so far as they did not conflict with positive legislation by Congress.[5]

Calhoun's efforts in another direction were less successful. The military academy at West Point, originally founded in 1802 merely as a training school for engineers, had grown to have a far wider usefulness, and its graduates entered all branches of the service, where their training soon demonstrated the great value of the school. Calhoun was an enthusiastic supporter of

[99] Scott, *Memoirs*, 1:205–06; Scott to Calhoun, September 2, 1818; *American State Papers: Military Affairs*, 2:199–200; Jameson, *Correspondence of John Caldwell Calhoun*, p. 140.

[1] Submitted to Congress on December 22, 1820. *American State Papers: Military Affairs*, 2:199; United States Statutes at Large, 3:615–16.

[2] Scott, *Memoirs*, 1:206.

[3] *American State Papers: Military Affairs*, 2:199–274.

[4] *Annals of Congress*, 17th Congress, 1st Session, pp. 297, 307, 380, 383, 1591, 1613, 1694, 1730–34, 1753–58, 1868. Repealed May 7, 1822. United States Statutes at Large, 3:686.

[5] *Annals of Congress*, 18th Congress, 1st Session, pp. 1470, 1486, 1620; *American State Papers: Military Affairs*, 2:623.

military training schools, but he felt that more than one was needed. While in Congress he had spoken in favor of a bill to establish three additional academies,[6] and in 1819 he recommended the establishment of an academy to serve the South and the West, and a school for practice near Washington.[7] On February 23, 1821, he called attention to the fact that the principal engineers, as well as other staff officers, were stationed at Washington, and the West Point academy was thus only nominally under the control of engineers. Since its graduates entered all branches of the service and since it had ceased to be a school for engineers only, he recommended its separation from that corps.[8] The academy received its share of criticism. Newton Cannon of Tennessee tried to defeat the appropriation for it in 1820. He characterized it as a school for the sons of wealthy men and as an aristocratic class school for training a "privileged military order." [9] Two years later he urged that the number of cadets be reduced, since there could be no use for so large a number.[10]

In the establishment of a training school Calhoun was more successful, although the institution existed for several years before receiving legislative sanction. The scattered condition of the artillery corps made practice difficult and maneuvers on a large scale impossible. In the spring of 1824 [11] eleven companies of artillery were gathered at Fort Monroe, Virginia, and were instructed in their art. A system of rotation was devised, so that eventually all artillery regiments attended the school. Calhoun

[6] *Annals of Congress*, 14th Congress, 1st Session, pp. 430, 431, 1235.

[7] *American State Papers: Military Affairs*, 1:834.

[8] *Ibid.*, 2:75. No action was taken to recognize this separation legally until 1866.

[9] *Annals of Congress*, 16th Congress, 1st Session, pp. 1603–06, 1629–32.

[10] *Ibid.*, 17th Congress, 1st Session, pp. 535, 877–78. The cadets numbered 250 at this time.

[11] Calhoun's plans were formed by the early part of 1823, for Brown, in answer to Calhoun, March 21, 1823, approved the idea. Brown Letter Books. There is little doubt that Calhoun's ideas were derived, in part at least, from Inspector General Samuel B. Archer, whose able report of 1822 gave cogent reasons for the establishment of such a school. Inspection Reports, Inspector General's Office, 1814–23, pp. 172–249.

asked Congress for an appropriation for purchasing horses.[12] The school demonstrated its usefulness and soon received legal sanction and congressional support.[13]

Intimately connected with the national military policy, but almost beyond national control, was the militia of the various states. The provisions of the Constitution are plain and understandable when viewed in the light of the intention of the framers, but the manner of securing their actual service by the nation is not so clear. During the War of 1812 the problem became acute when the governors of Massachusetts, Rhode Island, and Connecticut objected to, and partially prevented, the transference of their militia to national control. They took the captious position that they were the judges of whether conditions warranted such transference and the still more unreasonable position of objecting to the militia serving under army officers or anyone else but the president personally.[14] Monroe in 1815, while serving as secretary of war, analyzed these pretentions and showed their absurd reasoning,[15] but he did not solve the problem. It remained to perplex succeeding generations, and may be said to have been solved only by the recent recognition of the justice and necessity of conscription.

The Constitution [16] gives Congress the power "to provide for calling forth the militia to execute the laws of the Union, suppress insurrections, and repel invasions." The next clause gives it power "to provide for organizing, arming, and disciplining the militia, and for governing such part of them as may be employed in the service of the United States, reserving to the States respectively, the appointment of the officers, and the authority of training the militia according to the discipline prescribed by Con-

---

[12] *Niles' Weekly Register*, 26:99; *American State Papers: Military Affairs*, 2: 699.

[13] For a careful treatment of the artillery school see Arthur, *The Coast Artillery School, 1824–1927*.

[14] *American State Papers: Military Affairs*, 1:604–23. Also see Marshall, "Remnants of the Letter Files of the Dearborn Family," *Mississippi Valley Historical Review*, 2:407–24.

[15] Monroe, *Writings*, 5:308–09, 309–21.

[16] Article I, Section 8, Clause 15.

gress." The Constitution [17] also provides that "The President shall be commander-in-chief of the army and navy of the United States, and of the militia of the several States, when called into the actual service of the United States." In the provision that the disciplining of the militia shall be done by state officers lies the weakness. The laws and regulations may be written by Congress, but the nation is powerless to insure any definite standard. The returns of the militia illustrate the laxity of control. The report of 1825 shows that Delaware had made no returns for eleven years, Mississippi none for thirteen years, and Maryland none for fourteen years. Similar delays may be noted in other reports, and only about a third of the states made their reports on time.[18] It is thus apparent that the main dependence of the nation was upon uncorrelated groups of untrained citizens. This confusion and lack of power on the part of the national government were in no small measure the cause of the development of a standing army. The nation could not run the risk of being totally unprepared for emergencies that would leave it a helpless supplicant before the states.

The experience of the War of 1812 had shown the folly of relying upon the militia, and several efforts were made to increase the national control. William Henry Harrison of Ohio, who entered Congress in 1816, took the lead. In the preceding session Congress had called for a report on the militia, and on December 13, 1816, George Graham, acting secretary of war, submitted his report,[19] which was referred to the Committee on Reorganization of Militia, of which Harrison was chairman. The committee reported on January 17, 1817,[20] and introduced a bill for organizing, classifying, and arming the militia, but it was allowed to lie on the table.[21] Harrison's report proposed a system of military instruction in the schools. Such a proposal was naturally treated with indifference, for it promised no tan-

[17] Article II, Section 2, Clause 1.
[18] *American State Papers: Military Affairs,* 1:677–80; 2:135, 321, 362, 823.
[19] *Ibid.,* 1:642–44.
[20] *Ibid.,* pp. 663–66.
[21] *Annals of Congress,* 14th Congress, 2d Session, pp. 270–75, 567.

gible results. Refusing to accept defeat, he proposed the appointment of a committee to draw up an amendment to the Constitution that would enable the government to adopt a system of
discipline. He said that Congress had no power to call out the
militia for training and no power to grant money for that
object, and that unless some such plan was adopted, they must
give up the idea of relying upon the militia. Timothy Pickering
of Massachusetts said that the militia could not be disciplined
by the nation without placing them on a footing with the regular army. The plan was defeated.[22]

On January 9, 1818, Harrison made another report, in which
he proposed a less radical plan, leaving the training to the
states,[23] but it failed to attract favorable attention. The only law
of the session that affected the militia was the act of April 20,
which provided for paying the expenses of the men to the place
of rendezvous when they were called into the service of the
United States.[24] In the following session Eldred Simkins of
South Carolina tried to effect some changes in the militia. He
rebuked Congress for its lack of interest in the subject. Congressmen paid close attention when Jackson, the bank, or private
bills were debated, but scurried from their places when the
subject of the militia was brought forward. The indifference
toward the subject and the loss of military knowledge had caused
many casualties in the recent war. The secretary of war was
unable to learn even the number of militia in the various states.
The members who opposed an adequate army were absent and
unwilling to provide a well-trained militia. The bill tried to
clarify the constitutional confusion by granting to the president
power to call the militia and compel it to cross border lines in
case of necessity.[25] Simkins' efforts also failed.

Further efforts were made in 1823.[26] Newton Cannon of
Tennessee stated that Harrison had labored in vain, that not

[22] *Ibid.*, pp. 845–46.
[23] *American State Papers: Military Affairs*, 1:675. The exact plan, together with
Knox's plan of 1790, was again submitted on January 22, 1819. *Ibid.*, pp. 824–27.
[24] United States Statutes at Large, 3:444.
[25] *Annals of Congress*, 15th Congress, 2d Session, pp. 548–51.
[26] *Ibid.*, 17th Congress, 2d Session, pp. 330–31, 333–34, 338, 341, 357, 425, 471.

a dollar had been expended. He favored the bill, which provided for an annual encampment of from four to six days. Elias Keyes of Vermont, an old Revolutionary soldier, said that the militia untrained was better than any regular army in the world. Romulus Saunders of North Carolina said that the proposed encampment of militia officers would be a waste of time and money and a humiliating experience. "The science of military tactics is studied by the pusillanimous, as that of medicine is by the sick." He declared that the committee itself was not in earnest about the bill. It also failed.[27] The militia remained the strength of the nation in name, but in time of war it was necessary to call for volunteers.

Another phase of the military policy of the period received much attention. The hopeless condition of the roads had materially hindered and in some cases completely stopped the progress of armies and the transportation of supplies during the War of 1812. The condition of the roads is illustrated by a story that went the rounds of the newspapers.

A traveler on a muddy road in Ohio saw a hat lying in the road. As he stooped to pick it up, he was surprised to hear a voice bawling out, "What ye doin?"

"Oh, I didn't know anyone was underneath it."

"Ya. I am sitting on my horse, resting, for this is the first solid bit of ground I've found in several miles."

The military importance of roads was only one reason for the great demand for internal improvements, but it was an important one and gave a technical basis for national aid that would have been denied on other grounds. The national spirit, which grew so rapidly in the post-war period, expressed itself in many ways, one of which was a desire for better communications. The constitutional problem of the power of the national government to construct roads had never been solved. John Quincy Adams claimed to have been the first to propose national improvements,[28] and Albert Gallatin, while secretary of the treasury,

---

[27] *Ibid.*, pp. 553–60, 562–66, 566–76.
[28] *Memoirs*, 8:444; *Annals of Congress*, 9th Congress, 2d Session, pp. 77–78.

had made a similar proposal in 1818.[29] Calhoun's Bonus Bill of 1816 was only one of several attempts to supply national aid for roads and canals.[30] All these efforts, however, were concerned primarily with the economic, commercial, and social value of improvements. Madison's constitutional scruples and Monroe's objections delayed and prevented action on any extensive scale, but in the meantime military necessity demanded the construction of some roads and the maintenance of others.

The impassable roads from the Ohio River to Detroit had caused disaster during the War of 1812. Late in 1815 Brown recommended that roads to Detroit and along the border be constructed. Work by the soldiers, who received fifteen cents a day extra, was in progress near Detroit from June to November, 1816.[31] The progress was evidently not satisfactory, for Cass, writing to the secretary of war late in 1817, asked that a road be built from Detroit to Sandusky.[32] It is certain that some progress had already been made.[33] By 1819 seventy miles, eighty feet wide, had been completed,[34] and an act of Congress in 1824 appropriated twenty thousand dollars for completing the Detroit-Maumee road.[35]

The soldiers stationed at Plattsburg were engaged in a similar task. Two hundred and thirty men under Colonel Josiah Snelling worked during September and October, 1817, on the road to Chateaugay and resumed their task in the following May, completing thirteen miles of graveled road toward French Mills by autumn.[36] The criticisms in Congress caused Calhoun to ask for suspension of the building of a road at Niagara in 1819 unless the military features predominated.[37] In 1823 General

[29] *American State Papers: Miscellaneous*, 1:724–921; *Niles' Weekly Register*, 15:10–24, 44–58.
[30] *Ibid.*, 2:421–23; Stephen H. Long's Report of 1817 on the Illinois and Lake Michigan Canal, *ibid.*, pp. 555–57.
[31] Brown Letter Books, 1:399, 401; 2:25, 36–37, 60.
[32] *Annals of Congress*, 16th Congress, 1st Session, pp. 2477–80.
[33] *Detroit Gazette*, November 28, 1817.
[34] *Annals of Congress*, 15th Congress, 2d Session, p. 2454.
[35] United States Statutes at Large, 4:71.
[36] *Niles' Weekly Register*, 13:64, 207; 14:424; 15:267.
[37] Brown Letter Books, 2:159.

Brown reported the completion of twenty miles of road toward
French Mills and one of equal length from Sackett's Harbor
toward Morristown.[38]

Roads regarded as necessary for military purposes were also
constructed in the South. Jackson pointed out the close connection between roads and defense and was advised to use the
troops in constructing them.[39] In 1817 Gaines caused ninety
miles of road to be constructed between Forts Scott and Montgomery,[40] and in the same year engineers under Jackson's order
surveyed a route from Nashville to Madisonville, opposite New
Orleans.[41] Returns from the Southern Division for June, 1818,
show that a detachment of ninety-seven men was engaged in
cutting a road,[42] and the Nashville–New Orleans road was almost
completed by December, 1819.[43] A memorial of the Louisiana
legislature asked for the construction of a road from New Orleans
to Fort St. Philip and suggested that the troops be employed in
the task.[44]

Military necessity had thus established the custom of using
the soldiers for building roads. They were paid fifteen cents a
day extra, an expenditure that brought on a considerable debate
in Congress. Henry Clay called attention to the fact that the
president had denied the right of Congress to appropriate money
for building roads, yet had spent money for the same purpose
by a mere executive order. Philip P. Barbour of Virginia said
that the proposed military appropriation bill included a section
granting a million dollars for paying the soldiers and asked if

[38] *American State Papers: Miscellaneous*, 2:987–88.
[39] Bassett, *Correspondence of Andrew Jackson*, 2:222–23, 235.
[40] Mitchell to Graham, December 14, 1817, Old Records Division, Adjutant
General's Office.
[41] Young to Jackson, March 14, 1817, Old Records Division, Adjutant General's
Office.
[42] Officers' Record Division, Adjutant General's Office.
[43] Bassett, *Correspondence of Andrew Jackson*, 2:439; *Alabama Reporter*,
December 17, 1819; *Niles' Weekly Register*, 17:376.
[44] *American State Papers: Military Affairs*, 2:6–7. Other roads in the South are
mentioned in *American State Papers: Miscellaneous*, 2:273, 402, and a complete
list of military roads constructed before 1830 may be found in *American State
Papers: Military Affairs*, 4:626–27. For a brief discussion see MacGill, *History of
Transportation in the United States before 1860*, pp. 31–37.

the sum was going to be used for that purpose only. Other speakers raised the question as to whether there was any such thing as a military road and pointed out the president's inconsistency in spending money for building roads while denying Congress the right to appropriate funds for the same purpose. To force the president to recognize that right, Congress made a special appropriation of ten thousand dollars for paying soldiers for work on the roads. [45]

In the preceding session [46] Congress had directed Calhoun to prepare a constitutional plan for congressional aid in constructing roads and canals, "with a view to military operations in time of war." The disguise was thin, for it was apparent that the plan was adopted in the hope that Congress would thus be able to overcome Monroe's constitutional scruples. Calhoun submitted a lengthy report, outlining plans for roads and canals,[47] but no action was taken until April 30, 1824, when Congress authorized a survey of such roads and canals as were "of national importance in a commercial or military point of view, or necessary to the transportation of the mails." [48] The subject of roads had become of economic and political importance and had ceased to be primarily military.

[45] *Annals of Congress,* 15th Congress, 2d Session, pp. 451–52 (January 6, 1819), 453, 480–88, 488–514.
[46] April 4, 1818.
[47] *American State Papers: Miscellaneous,* 2:533–37; Calhoun, *Works,* 5:40–54; *Annals of Congress,* 15th Congress, 2d Session, pp. 2443–54.
[48] United States Statutes at Large, 4:22–23.

CHAPTER VII

ARMY ADMINISTRATION

THE NATIONAL military policy was determined by Congress and the president, who had the advice of the secretary of war. The laws prescribed limits to the size and cost of the army, but the numerous details of administration were worked out by the War Department, and the task of carrying out the policy fell upon the officers and the rank and file. The reduction of the army, the selection of officers, the organization of military units, the formation of defense plans, the location and erection of forts, the allocation of troops, the establishment of rules of procedure, and the supplying and transportation of troops were among the details that had to be planned after the reorganization act of March 3, 1815.

The principal agency in settling many of these questions was a board of officers. On March 27 the acting secretary of war, A. J. Dallas, asked Generals Andrew Jackson, Jacob Brown, Winfield H. Scott, Edmund P. Gaines, Alexander Macomb, and Eleazer W. Ripley to constitute a board to advise the president.[1] They were invited to Washington, but Jackson received the invitation too late to comply, Gaines also failed to attend, and Brown did not arrive until April 25.[2] Scott presided, and the board began its deliberations on April 8.[3] Dallas asked the board for advice as to the organization of the army, the selection of officers, the division of the country into military units, and the location of garrisons. The reduction of the army was an embarrassing task, for it involved the discharge of more than

[1] Bassett, *Correspondence of Andrew Jackson*, 2:204.
[2] *National Intelligencer*, April 26, 1815.
[3] Military Books, 8:79, Old Records Division, Adjutant General's Office. Scott (*Memoirs*, 1:155) says that the board first met in May, but he is in error. See *Niles' Weekly Register*, 8:146, 221–24.

two-thirds of the men[4] and the reduction in rank of many officers who were retained. Only 39 of 216 field officers and only 450 of 2,055 regimental officers could be retained. Dallas said that Madison was deeply sensible of the delicate nature of the duty of discharging officers and had asked that the omission of a name should in no wise be considered as a reflection upon the conduct or standing of the officer. Conduct and character were to determine the selection, but ability to pursue a civil career and financial standing might be considered in settling doubtful cases. If decisions could be made in no other way, a lottery was recommended.[5]

The board was unable to conclude its work in time to effect the reorganization by May 1, the date recommended by the law, but it rendered its report to Dallas, who approved it on May 12,[6] and Madison added his approval on the fifteenth. The reorganization was effected through four general orders, the first of which divided the country into two military divisions and into nine subdivisions called departments. The Division of the North consisted of the region north of Virginia and the Ohio and east of the Mississippi, with the exception of Illinois Territory. The remainder constituted the Division of the South. The departments numbered 1 to 5 were in the Northern Division and the other four in the Southern Division.[7] The first order also specified the number of troops for each department. Ten companies of infantry and four of riflemen, including a total of 1,154 men, were assigned to Detroit and its dependent posts in the Fifth Department. The same number was assigned to the Ninth Department with headquarters at Belle Fontaine near St. Louis. Other departments received similar assignments, and the greater part of the artillery was sent to garrison the coast fortifications.

The second general order announced the army register. Major

---

[4] The returns of September, 1814, show that the regular army numbered 38,186. Upton, *Military Policy of the United States*, p. 137.

[5] *Niles' Weekly Register*, 8:222–23.

[6] *Ibid.*, p. 224; *National Intelligencer*, May 1, 13, 1815.

[7] See the map on page 103.

General Jacob Brown was directed to assume command of the Division of the North and Major General Andrew Jackson that of the South.[8] The third general order provided for the discharge of the surplus troops, and the fourth directed the new officers to assume charge.[9] Although the law left no leeway in the matter of the number of units, it did leave open the selection of officers, the organization of military districts, the selection of sites for posts, and the assignment of troops. It would be logical to assume that Brown, considering his rank and the absence of Jackson, was the dominating member of the board. But such an assumption would be incorrect. In the first place, he did not arrive until exactly half the sessions were over, and he left Washington on May 11, a day sooner than the other members.[10] In the second place, his letter books indicate no particular interest in the subject. On March 6 he wrote to Monroe soliciting the command of what was then the Ninth District. On the fourteenth Dallas informed Brown that he had been chosen as one of the two major generals to be retained and advised him to maintain silence on the subject.[11] Brown's only recorded recommendations were the breveting of certain officers and the proper recognition for Ripley.[12] If there was any outstanding leadership in the work of reorganization it was taken by Scott, who has modestly implied as much.[13]

[8] It is well to note that there was no commander-in-chief. Brown and Jackson were equal in rank and power. Correctly speaking, there was no commander-in-chief from 1783 to 1821 except during the short period in 1798–99 when Washington was commander. Commands were geographical. It is incorrect to speak of Wilkinson as commander-in-chief and equally incorrect to refer to Brown as such before 1821.

[9] Thian, "Notes Illustrating the Military Geography of the United States" (MS. in Officers' Record Division, Adjutant General's Office); Army Register of 1815, in Gordon, *Compilation of Registers of the Army, 1815–1837*; *National Intelligencer*, May 22, 1815; *Niles' Weekly Register*, 8:221–31. The general orders and army register of May 17 are not given in the *American State Papers*, although the register and organization of January 1, 1816, which differ very little from the former, are given in *American State Papers: Military Affairs*, 1:626–35. An additional list of men retained in 1815 is in *Niles' Weekly Register*, 8:310.

[10] *National Intelligencer*, May 13, 1815.

[11] Brown Letter Books, 1:319, 320. Jackson received a similar notification. Bassett, *Correspondence of Andrew Jackson*, 2:204.

[12] Brown Letter Books, 1:310, 322, 330, 332, 333.

[13] *Memoirs*, 1:155.

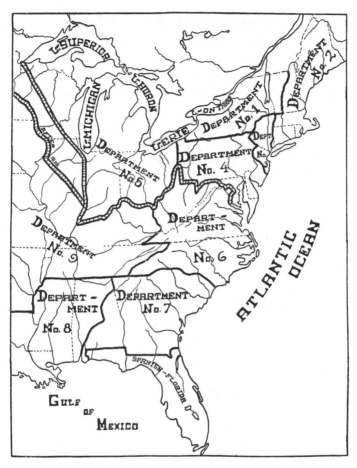

UNITS OF MILITARY ADMINISTRATION IN THE UNITED STATES,
1815–21

Departments 1 to 5 were in the Northern Division,
6 to 9 in the Southern Division.

The reorganized army found ample tasks to engage its time and attention. The frontier measurements of the country as computed by Major Stephen H. Long totaled 9,250 miles or, counting the indented lines of the seacoast, 11,955 miles.[14] The geographical aspects alone were impressive. The British forces in Canada caused uneasiness; the Florida frontier was a scene of uncertainty; and the western Indians were slow to accept the outcome of the war. The supervision and standardization of scattered units and the introduction of recognized rules of procedure required time and patience. The erection of forts and the construction of military roads were tasks of indefinite duration.

Next to the secretary of war the most important officers in the administration of the army were the two major generals, each of whom was in charge of a division. They supervised the department commanders, who in turn had charge of garrison and post commanders. General Brown established his headquarters for the Northern Division at Brownsville, New York, from which point he also administered the affairs of the First Department. The officers in charge of the other departments were: Ripley, the Second, with headquarters at Boston; Macomb, the Third, with headquarters at New York; Lieutenant Colonel George E. Mitchell, the Fourth, with headquarters at Philadelphia; and Colonel John Miller, the Fifth, with headquarters at Detroit. In the Southern Division Jackson established headquarters at Nashville and assigned Gaines to the Sixth and Seventh departments, with headquarters at Augusta, and Scott to the Eighth and Ninth, with headquarters at St. Louis.[15]

These arrangements were subject to variations. The Seventh Department was immediately extended westward to include Fort Montgomery and all the region east of the Alabama,[16] and the Fifth Department was extended to include Green Bay, Chicago, and all posts on the Great Lakes that could best be supplied

[14] *American State Papers: Military Affairs*, 1:791–92.
[15] Army Register of 1815, in Gordon, *Compilation of Registers of the Army, 1815–1837*; *National Intelligencer*, June 13, July 1, 1815.
[16] *National Intelligencer*, July 1, 1815.

from Detroit.[17] In 1818 the Eighth Department, which embraced Alabama, Mississippi, and Louisiana, was divided into Eastern and Western sections.[18] In the same year Fort Armstrong[19] and all posts on the Mississippi above that point were transferred from the Southern to the Northern Division.[20] Early in 1816 Ripley, who had had a disagreement with Brown, was transferred to Jackson's division,[21] and Macomb replaced Miller in the command of the Fifth Department. In the same year the rifle regiment was transferred to the Southern Division.[22]

The major generals were busily occupied in inaugurating the new system. In the late summer of 1815 General Brown made a trip to Detroit to supervise the distribution of troops and to plan new posts.[23] Troops were ordered to the Mississippi to insure the safety of the frontiers.[24] Repeated rumors of an intended attack by the Sauk and Foxes caused Jackson to take the precaution of calling on the Missouri militia to be in readiness to move.[25] Reassignment of troops and the shifting of commanders required frequent orders, and the new arrangements entailed much correspondence with the adjutant and inspector general.

Public opinion was all-important in determining the general military policy, and it was not without its effects upon army administration also. Each locality sought to obtain a fort or garrison, and the political advantage of pleasing some congressman was not overlooked. In 1815 Brown ordered the withdrawal of troops from Annapolis, but the protests of the citizens caused

[17] Brown to Macomb, April 27, 1816, Brown Letter Books.

[18] *American State Papers: Military Affairs*, 1:813.

[19] See the map on page 112 for the location of forts.

[20] Jameson, *Correspondence of John Caldwell Calhoun*, pp. 138, 148; *Missouri Gazette*, October 2, 1818.

[21] Military Books, 8:472–73, Old Records Division, Adjutant General's Office.

[22] Brown Letter Books, 2:26–27; Letters Received, 10:204, Old Records Division, Adjutant General's Office.

[23] Military Books, 8:96, Old Records Division, Adjutant General's Office; Brown Letter Books, 1:308–09; *Niles' Weekly Register*, 8:402; 9:75.

[24] Secretary of War to Clark, March 10, 1815, Territorial Papers, State Department; *National Intelligencer*, May 16, 1815.

[25] Military Books, 8:291–92, Old Records Division, Adjutant General's Office; *Missouri Gazette*, July 22, 1815.

Crawford to countermand Brown's order.[26] The proposal to remove the depot for military supplies from Newport, Kentucky, brought forth protests from that state.[27] In 1820 Brown observed that congressmen from Maine were unfavorably disposed toward the army, and he proposed to station more troops along the seacoast of that state in order to change their attitude.[28]

One of the unsolved problems of the army after its reorganization was the procedure to be followed in the transmission of orders. The lack of a coherent organization had prevented the evolution of a recognized etiquette of procedure. The first incident in which the question became an issue occurred in 1814. An order from the secretary of war directed that certain officers at Mobile report for recruiting service. Realizing the danger of an attack by the British, the officers refused to leave their posts and were vigorously upheld by Jackson, who wrote a remonstrance to Secretary Monroe in which he pointed out the dangers of issuing orders affecting his command without his knowledge and consent.[29]

The second incident that led to a crisis was the irregular issuance of an order by Jackson himself. Early in February, 1816, Colonel Thomas A. Smith, stationed at St. Louis, reported to Jackson that an Indian war was about to begin. He urged the necessity of immediate assistance and suggested that the troops at Fort Harrison were the nearest re-enforcements available, although they were in the Northern Division and thus outside Jackson's command. Nevertheless Jackson, thinking the occasion demanded action, ordered Major Willoughby Morgan, commander at Fort Harrison, to report to Smith at St. Louis. Realizing that he was trespassing upon Brown's prerogatives, Jackson notified the secretary of war of his action and the reason

[26] Crawford to Brown, December 9, 1815, Military Books, Old Records Division, Adjutant General's Office.

[27] R. M. Johnson to Secretary of War, July 20, August 16, 1816, Old Records Division, Adjutant General's Office.

[28] Brown to Calhoun, November 14, 1820, Brown Letter Books.

[29] Bassett, Correspondence of Andrew Jackson, 2:103–04; Upton, Military Policy of the United States, p. 145.

for it.[30] Crawford explained Jackson's reasons to Morgan and ordered him to obey if he could safely leave his post.[31] Macomb, who was in charge of the Fifth Department, in which Fort Harrison was located, remonstrated to Brown against Jackson's order.[32] Brown in turn complained to Secretary Crawford, who answered that Jackson had been under the mistaken impression that the situation was serious, and assured Brown that "Genl. Jackson will be instructed not to interfere again under any possible circumstances." [33] Brown answered Crawford in part as follows:

I was much gratified to learn from yourself that Genl. Jackson would be instructed not to interfere again, within the limits of the command assigned to me, under any possible circumstances. This distinguished man no doubt, was influenced by the purest intentions, when he issued his orders to Major Morgan but the example if not corrected by the War Department, would be most unfortunate for the army.[34]

Other instances of the irregular transmission of orders and reports occurred. In 1816 the secretary of war issued an order directly to Macomb, commander of a department, instead of sending it through the division commander, Brown, who resented the irregularity.[35] Gaines made the mistake of forwarding a report to the secretary of war and was rebuked by Brown, who said that it had been passed on to him "unopened." [36] The best-known instance was that connected with the Jackson-Long order.

In the summer of 1816 Major Stephen H. Long of the Corps of Engineers was engaged in making a survey of the Illinois River.[37] Without Jackson's knowledge Long applied for and re-

[80] Smith to Jackson, February, 1816, and Jackson to Crawford, March 25, 1816, Old Records Division, Adjutant General's Office.
[81] May 3, 1816, War Department Letter Book C, in Indian Office.
[82] May 10, 1816, Brown Letter Books.
[83] Crawford to Brown, June 19, 1816, Brown Letter Books.
[84] July 8, 1816, Brown Letter Books.
[85] Brown Letter Books, 2:36, 37.
[86] Brown to Gaines, February 7, 1825, Brown Letter Books.
[87] Reports of the Corps of Engineers, 1812–23, pp. 138–39; Order of June 7, 1816, Letters Sent, Old Files Section, Adjutant General's Office.

ceived permission to go to New York to complete his report and attend to some business. When Jackson learned of Long's absence from the assigned duty, he wrote a vigorous letter to the acting secretary of war, George Graham, protesting against the detachment of an officer from his command without his knowledge. He contended that "it is inconsistent with all military rule and subversive of the first principle of that subordination which ought, and must be maintained." [38] Graham explained that Long had not been transferred to the Northern Division and would return to Jackson's command when he had made his report, and added, "It is distinctly to be understood, that this department at all times exercises the right of assigning officers to the performance of special duties, at its discression." [39] This rebuke had no effect upon Jackson. On March 4, 1817, he wrote a long letter to Monroe and urged him to correct the irregularity before it became a precedent. "Such a doctrine [the power of the secretary of war to detach officers without the knowledge of the commanding general], is a violation of all military etiquette, and a subversion of every principle of subordination, and could only originate in an inexperienced head, perfectly unskilled in military matters." [40] Monroe deliberated, but on April 22 Jackson issued his well-known announcement explicitly and sternly forbidding his officers to receive orders from anyone but himself. [41]

The test of the matter soon came. Ripley, stationed at New Orleans, refused, in accordance with Jackson's order, to obey an order from the secretary of war. Jackson assumed responsibility, and in writing to Monroe on August 12 asked for Monroe's decision. He repeated his willingness to resign and contended with his accustomed vigor that his course was right. [42] Finally, on October 5, Monroe penned his decision. He pointed out that inconvenience and delay would sometimes result if orders were

[38] Bassett, *Correspondence of Andrew Jackson*, 2:274.
[39] *Ibid.*, p. 275.   [40] *Ibid.*, p. 281.
[41] *Ibid.*, pp. 291–92; also in *Niles' Weekly Register*, 12:320; Parton, *Life of Jackson*, 2:373; Upton, *Military Policy of the United States*, p. 146.
[42] Bassett, *Correspondence of Andrew Jackson*, 2:320–21.

sent through the commanding general. The extent of the country and the slow communication made Jackson's plan untenable, but Monroe agreed that in ordinary situations the orders should be issued through the commanding general, and that he would be notified if that procedure were departed from. On October 22 Jackson wrote his acceptance of Monroe's decision.[43]

Jackson's order provoked a storm of comment, favorable and unfavorable. Sticklers for military etiquette have commonly viewed his course with approval, but in view of his own conduct it is difficult to escape the suspicion that he was actuated somewhat by pride and vanity.

The official aspect was not the only side of Jackson's order. It provoked one of the most widely publicized controversies of the period, that between Jackson and Scott. The latter made some criticisms of Jackson's order of April 22. These criticisms, together with a garbled version of them in a New York newspaper, reached Jackson through an anonymous correspondent. Ignoring the slender basis of his right to do so, Jackson demanded an explanation from Scott,[44] who did not hesitate to render a full statement of his ideas. He characterized Jackson's order as "mutinous" and "a reprimand of the Commander-in-chief, the President of the U. States."[45] Jackson's insolent and bantering reply reveals him in a poor light. He characterized Scott's criticisms as "base and inexcusable conduct," and ended by a half invitation to duel.[46] Scott's reply of January 2, 1818, makes no new point, and the correspondence degenerated into a contest of billingsgate.[47] The whole correspondence was published in pamphlet form and widely circulated in the political campaign of 1824.[48]

[43] *Ibid.*, pp. 329–33. The decision was made official by Calhoun's letter to Jackson of December 29, 1817, given in Parton, *Life of Jackson*, 2:374–76.

[44] Jackson's first letter to Scott was dated September 8, 1817. Bassett, *Correspondence of Andrew Jackson*, 2:325.

[45] October 4, 1817. *Ibid.*, p. 327.

[46] December 3, 1817. *Ibid.*, pp. 338–39.

[47] *Ibid.*, pp. 344–45.

[48] It was also published in part in *Niles' Weekly Register*, 14:295, *passim*. John Quincy Adams' poor opinion of Scott's side of the controversy is found in

These irregularities in the transmission of orders were a symptom of fundamental defects in the administrative machinery of the army. The division and department commanders determined questions of discipline, procedure, and defense plans that should have been determined by a general staff. Each unit made its purchases and kept its accounts in accordance with the varying notions of the commanders. The accounts were sent directly to the Treasury Department without the unifying supervision or approval of a staff officer. In spite of the so-called general staff, there was little coordination. When Calhoun became secretary of war, he determined to systematize the administration of the army. He thought "that every distinct branch of the staff should terminate in a chief, to be stationed, at least in time of peace, near the seat of Government, and to be made responsible for its condition." [49] In accordance with Calhoun's plans and wishes a bill was introduced and became a law on April 14, 1818.[50]

This act authorized the secretary of war to coordinate administrative offices and supervise expenditures. The chief staff officers of each department of the army were called to Washington, where they, with their assistants, formed sub-departments or bureaus through which plans could be efficiently carried out.[51] Definite accountability was thus secured,[52] and the reorganization of 1821 enabled Calhoun to extend the system to more of the staff officers. In 1822 Monroe observed:

his *Memoirs*, 4:323–24. Parton's views are set forth with vigor in his *Life of Jackson*, 2:371–82.

[49] *American State Papers: Military Affairs*, 2:189–92; Jameson, *Correspondence of John Caldwell Calhoun*, pp. 133–34.

[50] The law was called an act to reduce the staff and was combined with the establishment of a commissariat. For a further account of its progress through Congress see Chapter VI.

There was some controversy as to who was the author of this law. Christopher Van Deventer, chief clerk of the War Department, suggested the establishment of a central staff. Jameson, *Correspondence of John Caldwell Calhoun*, pp. 791–92. General Brown assisted in drafting the bill. "The staff bill finally passed in the state which you left it, with the exception of the Judge Advocate General." Calhoun to Brown, April 25, 1818, Brown Letter Books. Certainly the credit for administering the law belongs to Calhoun.

[51] Upton's *Military Policy of the United States* fails to mention the law of 1818.

[52] *American State Papers: Military Affairs*, 2:345.

With the organization of the staff there is equal cause to be satisfied. By the concentration of every branch with its chief in this city, in the presence of the Department, and with a grade in the chief military station to keep alive and cherish a military spirit, the greatest promptitude in the execution of orders, with the greatest economy and efficiency, are secured.[53]

The importance and utility of the staff were recognized and the resulting economy met with approval.[54]

The reduction of the army to six thousand by the act of March 2, 1821, produced problems similar to those of 1815, and they were solved in a similar way. A board of officers, consisting of Brown,[55] Scott, and Gaines, met in April and completed their report on May 14. The results of their deliberations were announced in the general orders of May 17. Brown was appointed commander-in-chief of the whole army with headquarters at Washington. The two divisions and nine departments were abolished and two departments,[56] an Eastern and a Western, were substituted. The departments were divided approximately by a line drawn from the southern point of Florida to the northwestern extremity of Lake Superior. All of Kentucky and Tennessee, however, were in the Western Department.[57] Gaines was assigned to the Western Department, with headquarters at Louisville, and Scott to the Eastern Department, with headquarters at New York.[58] Brown at once assumed command and issued a general order on June 1 in which he urged careful attention to discipline, the cultivation of harmony, and correct

[53] Richardson, *Messages and Papers of the Presidents*, 2:188.
[54] *Niles' Weekly Register*, 13:274; *National Intelligencer*, May 15, 1818.
[55] Brown had been asked on March 10 to serve on the board. Brown Letter Books. Jackson had been appointed governor of Florida and soon ceased to be an officer of the army.
[56] The correct meaning of the word "department" cannot be determined without the date. If the word applies to the period from 1815 to 1821, it indicates one of nine units. After 1821 it refers to one of two units.
[57] See the map on page 103.
[58] Thian, "Notes Illustrating the Military Geography of the United States," Officers' Record Division, Adjutant General's Office; Gordon, *Compilation of Registers of the Army, 1815–1837; Niles' Weekly Register*, 20:191–92; 22:386; Rodenbough and Haskin, *The Army of the United States*, p. 27; *American State Papers: Military Affairs*, 2:411; *National Intelligencer*, March 22, May 16, 19, 1821.

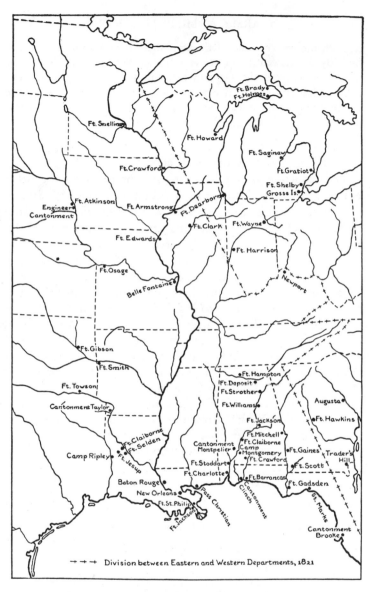

MILITARY POSTS IN THE UNITED STATES, 1815–25

social bearing on the part of officers in order to give the public a favorable impression of the army.[59]

The organization of the army appeared to be the most logical that it had ever had, but the commander-in-chief was unable to infuse much vigor into it. Brown's lack of energy was certainly due in part to sickness. After the reorganization in May he went to Brownsville, intending to return to Washington within a short time, but on October 17 he suffered a paralytic stroke and was unable to return to Washington until October, 1822. Even then there was considerable doubt about his fitness to perform the duties of commander-in-chief.[60] The paucity of his correspondence during this period indicates that he was not in active charge of the army, and it is doubtful if he ever again had complete control. The greater share of the work fell to Gaines and Scott, the department commanders.

The department commanders had large units to administer, and they had virtual autonomy because of the isolation of their posts. To secure closer coordination Gaines created a sub-department of the Missouri and upper Mississippi frontiers and placed Brigadier General Henry Atkinson in charge of the unit, which was variously called the Northwestern Frontier, the Western Wing, and the Right Wing.[61] From his headquarters at St. Louis, Atkinson supervised the posts on the Arkansas, Missouri, and upper Mississippi,[62] and Gaines assumed direct control of the southern part of his department. The department commanders not only issued orders and received reports but made tours of inspection and maintained close contact with the principal posts.[63]

[59] General Orders, 1818–21, p. 192, Old Records Division, Adjutant General's Office; *Niles' Weekly Register*, 20:235–36.

[60] Brown Letter Books, 2:208, 218.

[61] Order of July 14, 1821, Department Orders, Old Records Division, Adjutant General's Office.

[62] Order of July 26, 1823, *ibid.*

[63] At Gaines's request he and Scott exchanged departments in 1823. Scott secured a short leave of absence for a vacation, and Atkinson was for a time in command of the Western Department. In 1825 Gaines and Scott returned to their assignments of 1821. Letters Sent, 1821–24, pp. 364–65, 371–72, 417–18, Old Files Section, Adjutant General's Office; Department Orders, Old Records Division, Adjutant General's Office.

In the administration of the army perhaps no official was more important than the inspector. Unannounced he arrived at a post and observed its conditions and the conduct of officers and men. The typical inspection reports included observations on the following items: mess, sanitation, health, hospital, quarters, guardhouse, parade, arms, gun carriages, powder, instruction, discipline, records, and the utility of the post. The inspectors were not blind to defects, and the very nature of their position tended to make them critical. Hence the typical report gives a rather unfavorable impression of army life. Poorly cooked and unappetizingly served food seems to have been the rule. Sanitation was frequently neglected, and the care of the sick was far from satisfactory. Inspectors were inclined to lay it to the location if an undue proportion of the garrison was sick. Indifferent quarters, dirty guardhouses, worn or poorly kept arms, rotten gun carriages, and damp and spoiled powder were noted so frequently that one almost concludes that no camps were ever properly kept. Parades, instruction, and discipline were usually satisfactory, except among the artillery, who were often no better trained than the infantry. Record books were sometimes quite blank, even orders being omitted. The condition of the fort and the probable success or failure of the garrison to sustain an attack were reported. In many instances the inspector, finding the post to be poorly located and utterly useless in any scheme of defense, recommended its abandonment. Special comments on officers were frequently made, many of which were uncomplimentary. One was reported to be a "confirmed sot," another possessed "a great deal of vanity, duplicity, and intrigue," and a third was unable to cooperate with the officers under his charge.

Inspectors reported more than mere routine items. Their observations often reached the dignity of a consideration of national policies. In 1817 John M. Davis, assistant inspector general, visited Fort Gaines and observed: "We shall always be annoyed by Seminoles and their party until we get possession of East Florida, which time I hope is not far distant."[64] Inspector

<hr>

[64] Inspection Reports, Inspector General's Office, 1814–23, pp. 20–21.

General Samuel B. Archer pointed out the necessity of establishing a school for training the artillery. Infantry could learn their tasks during a war, but the artillery must study the firing of cannon and the range of guns before they could hope to succeed in battle.[65] The location and structure of forts, the methods of erecting army buildings, the storing of supplies, methods of transportation, and the shifting of frontier lines and garrisons were discussed by various inspectors. Blunt frankness characterized their reports, and many of their remarks would seem to reflect upon the secretary of war and the commanding generals.

The policy of maintaining post gardens and herds of livestock was inaugurated by Calhoun and doubtless helped to reduce expenses, yet Inspector General George Croghan denounced it most vehemently. After visiting Fort Atkinson [66] he observed that it was the weakest fort he had ever seen and the garrison about the most helpless and untrained. His explanation for such conditions was the policy of making farmers out of soldiers. The military had lost character among the Indians. No officer seemed to know his place in case of an alarm. Order a shell to be thrown and the time necessary for firing three or more would be taken up in finding one small enough for the bore. The men said there was no danger—well, then, as well argue that there should be no army, and he would as soon argue there be none. The present system was destroying military spirit and making officers the base overseers of a troop of awkward plowmen. Let the soldier be one. Let him no longer boast of his skill as a tiller of the soil, but as a soldier. They could raise gardens, but let them not boast of proficiency as farmers, of the advantages of the broadcast over the drill, or of the five bushels of corn per acre more raised by Company C than by Company B from relying more upon the plough than upon the hoe. What had been gained by this anti-military course? Nothing except the saving of a few dollars. "Look at Ft. Atkinson and you will see Barn yards that would

[65] *Ibid.*, pp. 196–97, 219–20, 245–49.
[66] In October, 1826.

not disgrace a Pennsylvania farmer, herds of cattle that would do credit to a Potomac grazier, yet where is the gain in this, either to the soldier or to the Government? Why all the corn and hay? To feed to cattle? Why the cattle? To eat the corn and hay." [67]

The inspection reports furnished the material from which the commander-in-chief formulated his plans and policies. On March 21, 1823, Brown advised Calhoun that the frontier line of posts should consist of Forts Brady, Howard, Crawford, Snelling, and Atkinson.[68] Posts within that line were useless and not worth garrisoning; the proposed line would hold the Indians in check. Discipline and training were difficult when the army was scattered in small units. The training of West Point graduates was likely to go for naught when they came into contact with small, careless, and indifferent groups of poorly trained men who had lost the military spirit.[69] Brown reported on May 12, 1823, that the army was in good condition, but that much of the equipment was poor. Guns were worn out by improper and too frequent cleaning; gun carriages were rotten and in most cases beyond repair; arsenals were dilapidated and poorly kept, even the inventories being inaccurate and incomplete. Many locations were unhealthful, namely, Pensacola, Baton Rouge, St. Marks, St. Augustine, Bellona Arsenal at Richmond, and Fort Johnson, North Carolina. He recommended the abandonment of Forts Edwards, Armstrong, Saginaw, Dearborn, and Detroit and St. Marks. Fort Crawford was worth temporary retention and Forts Brady and Atkinson should be permanently fortified.[70] Brown believed in shifting troops because some posts were agreeable "while a residence at others can be compared only to a state of continued penance," and troops who remained too long in one place obtained a proprietary sense and lost the military spirit.[71] They tended to become civilians instead of soldiers.

[67] Inspection Reports, Inspector General's Office, 1825–28, pp. 96–98.
[68] For the location of posts see the map on page 112.
[69] Brown Letter Books, 2:224–26.
[70] Ibid., pp. 227–38.
[71] Ibid., p. 265.

There is no clear and definite line between army administration on a national scale and its application to a specific post, but regulations and rules for the whole army had a local application. The policies and plans of the major general or the commander-in-chief were carried out by the post commanders. A view of the various frontiers will throw additional light on army administration.

CHAPTER VIII

THE NORTHERN FRONTIER

THE WISDOM of the military policy and the efficiency of army administration were tested on the frontiers. Pride in the vast extent of the country as well as a consideration of the exposed frontiers caused some congressmen to support the establishment of 1815. The proximity of the British and Spaniards and their Indian policies affected both the formation of the policy and its administration. The location, number, and disposition of the Indians had a more immediate effect upon army administration. Each frontier presented its particular difficulties and dangers. The northern frontier [1] received attention first.

The War of 1812 could not be terminated suddenly. News traveled slowly. The Battle of New Orleans is only one example of the regrettable results of slow communication. The feelings engendered by the war could not be quieted by official proclamation. The Indians were sullen and in no mood to accept peace even after the news was carried to them by their late allies. Indian attacks and outrages continued into the fall of 1815, for the British had spent time, money, and effort in enrolling the scattered tribes in their cause. The frontiersmen were uneasy and distrustful of both the Indians and the British. Many Americans recalled and commented on the fact that the British had made peace in 1783 but that they had held the frontier posts for years. Rumors that there were large armies in Canada and that re-enforcements were expected caused some concern. Whether such fears were groundless or not, whether they were shared

---

[1] The northern frontier is synonymous with the Fifth Department. Forts Armstrong, Crawford, and Snelling were in the Fifth Department from 1818 to 1821, but they were otherwise administered before and after that period and so are considered elsewhere. See the map on page 103.

by officials or not, the fact remained that official recognition of the fears was necessary. It was logically and naturally felt that the northern frontier should receive immediate attention. No one wanted to take the risk of a recurrence of the events following 1783.

The fear that the British would attempt to hold the posts was groundless, although some sensitive patriots complained of what they regarded as unnecessary delays. Forts Bowyer at Mobile and Castine in Maine were surrendered before May 17,[2] and Fort Niagara was given up on May 22.[3] The Americans surrendered Fort Malden on July 1, and troops were dispatched from Detroit on July 5 to occupy Mackinac, which was surrendered on July 18.[4] The British traders tried to import their goods for the fall trade before the transfer, and succeeded to some extent.[5]

As early as February 22, 1815, Monroe suggested the establishment of forts along the northern border [6] and on March 11 instructed the commissioners who were to negotiate treaties with the Indians to inform them that a chain of posts would be erected.[7] By May 22 a general program had been adopted, and Dallas informed Jackson of the plan "to establish posts along the course of the British traders, from Michilimackinac by Green Bay, the Fox River, and the Ouisconsin river, to Prairie du Chien, and thence up the Mississippi to St. Anthony's Falls." He asked Jackson's views in regard to the establishment of posts on the Chicago–Illinois River route.[8] Definite plans for the post at Green Bay were approved by Madison on June 20.[9] On the

[2] Brown Letter Books, 1:334–36.
[3] National Intelligencer, June 1, 1815.
[4] Niles' Weekly Register, 8:402; Missouri Gazette, September 2, 1815; Michigan Pioneer and Historical Collections, 16:177, 191, 200.
[5] Missouri Gazette, September 2, 1815; American State Papers: Indian Affairs, 2:83. A specific instance is recorded in Wisconsin Historical Collections, 19:397–98.
[6] Monroe, Writings, 5:325.
[7] American State Papers: Indian Affairs, 2:6, 13; Missouri Gazette, April 1, 1815.
[8] Bassett, Correspondence of Andrew Jackson, 2:206.
[9] Dallas' Report, Wisconsin Historical Collections, 19:380–81. Further proof that they had been long in preparation is found ibid., p. 383.

same day Governor Cass wrote to Dallas, giving his ideas as to the proper places to be garrisoned. He suggested the immediate occupation of three strategic points: Chicago in order to dominate the Chicago–Illinois River route; Green Bay and Prairie du Chien in order to control the Fox-Wisconsin route, which was the most important one; and a post near Grand Portage in order to hold the Lake Superior–Mississippi route, although he admitted that the third was less important than the others. He estimated that two-thirds of the British goods that were imported were smuggled into the country, and urged a display of force to impress the British traders and Indians.[10]

The plans soon resulted in the movement of troops to the northern frontier. It was obvious that the New York frontier, where many of them were stationed, was in no danger, for the natural barriers, the concentration of troops about Niagara, Sackett's Harbor, and Plattsburg, and the absence of hostile Indians eliminated any danger in that region. The frontier to the west of New York was regarded as the strategic area, and orders were given for the westward movement of regular troops to replace the volunteers whose services terminated with the end of the war.[11] The Navy Department assisted in transporting troops from Erie and Buffalo to Detroit.[12] On July 20, 1815, Brown left Sackett's Harbor and on August 9 reached Detroit, where he made arrangements for the distribution of troops.[13] Detroit was garrisoned by thirteen hundred men and became the headquarters for two regiments of infantry, the Third under Colonel John Miller and the Fifth under Lieutenant Colonel Joseph Lee Smith.[14] Mackinac was protected by four hundred men. Plans for the occupation of other posts were considered, but were postponed because of the advanced season and the

[10] *Ibid.*, pp. 376–79.
[11] Brown Letter Books, 1:342.
[12] *Ibid.*, pp. 350–51.
[13] *Ibid.*, pp. 308–09; *Niles' Weekly Register*, 8:402. Brown's tour was made in obedience to orders from the War Department of May 10, 1815. Military Books, Old Records Division, Adjutant General's Office.
[14] Rodenbough and Haskin, *Army of the United States*, pp. 433, 467.

shortage of supplies and transportation.[15] Brown returned to Buffalo on September 12, carrying enthusiastic reports of the garrisons, the strength of the forts, the favorable outlook for the fur trade, and the general prosperity of the region.[16] The allocation of garrisons was carried out in September, and the returns of the Fifth Department for October, 1815, show the following distribution of troops: Detroit, 683; Fort Shelby, 173; Fort Wayne, 88; Fort Knox, 54; Fort Harrison, 61; Fort Gratiot, 75; Grosse Isle, 77; Mackinac, 170; River Rouge, 67.[17]

The year 1816 witnessed the progress of the policy proposed by Monroe and developed by Dallas and Brown. Green Bay was fortified, Fort Dearborn reoccupied, and Fort Wayne, Fort Gratiot, and Detroit strengthened. On March 27 Brown ordered Macomb to prepare to send troops to Green Bay and Chicago. The force at Mackinac was to be reduced until the post at Green Bay was firmly established.[18] Two companies destined for Chicago and one destined for Mackinac left Detroit on June 9. The Chicago detachment, consisting of about a hundred men under Captain Hezekiah Bradley, reached that point on July 4 and erected a fortified camp.[19] The remainder of the detachment destined for Green Bay left Detroit on July 1 and went first to Mackinac.[20] Major Charles Gratiot of the Corps of Engineers was ordered to Green Bay to select the site for the fort.[21] Special precautions were taken because of the rumors that the Indians would oppose the movement, although Macomb himself regarded such reports as nonsense.[22] On July 26 about five hundred men under Colonel Miller left Mackinac in the schooners *Washington, Wayne,* and *Mink* and the sloop *Amelia,* and arrived at the head of Green Bay on August 8. Miller and Gratiot de-

[15] Brown Letter Books, 1:308–09; *Missouri Gazette*, October 21, 1815.
[16] Brown Letter Books, 1:375; *Missouri Gazette*, October 28, 1815; *Niles' Weekly Register*, 9:75.
[17] Department Returns, Officers' Record Division, Adjutant General's Office.
[18] Brown Letter Books, 2:4, 13.
[19] *Ibid.*, pp. 23, 35, 41; Quaife, *Chicago and the Old Northwest*, pp. 265–68.
[20] Brown Letter Books, 2:23, 35, 39.
[21] *Ibid.*, pp. 26–27.
[22] *Ibid.*, p. 39.

cided to build the new fort on the left bank of the Fox River near its mouth, on the site of the old French fort. The threatened attack did not materialize, and about two hundred men returned to Mackinac and left Lieutenant Colonel Talbot Chambers with about three hundred men to erect and garrison Fort Howard, as the new post was called.[23]

By the close of 1816 Fort Howard was firmly established, Fort Dearborn was re-established, and the old posts were well garrisoned. The total number of troops in the Fifth Department was no larger than it had been in the previous year, but they were more advantageously distributed. The total in the Fifth Department on January 1, 1817, was 1,297, and in the First Department 1,299.[24] Remarkably healthy conditions prevailed, no deaths having occurred at Fort Howard for over a year.[25] The troops were engaged in building forts, cutting roads, and performing garrison duties, but there was no fighting.

The bitterness of the Americans toward the British and the eagerness with which the northern frontier was occupied have been mentioned. By one of those rare and fortunate events that sometimes occur in international history, the fear and hostility that had inspired such precautions soon lost much of their intensity, and official confidence resulted. This change was the outcome of the agreement between Great Britain and the United States in regard to armaments on the Great Lakes. This agreement, proclaimed on April 28, 1817, limited the naval force of each nation to one vessel of one hundred tons and one eighteen-pound cannon for each of the four lakes on the border; all other armed vessels were to be dismantled. Either nation might abrogate the convention by giving six months notice.[26] The arrangement by no means eliminated local suspicion or commercial

[23] *Ibid.*, p. 45; Miller to Parker, August 22, 1816, *Mississippi Valley Historical Review*, 13:550–53; Wisconsin Historical Collections, 13:441–44; 19:437; Neville and Martin, *Historic Green Bay*, pp. 150–55.
[24] *American State Papers: Military Affairs*, 1:662.
[25] *Niles' Weekly Register*, 13:96; *Detroit Gazette*, July 25, November 28, 1817.
[26] Malloy, *Treaties, Conventions, and Agreements*, 1:628–30. For a discussion see Callahan, "The Neutrality of the American Lakes and Anglo-American Relations," Johns Hopkins Studies in Historical and Political Science, 16:84–86.

hostility, for the Indians and the fur trade occasioned intense rivalry, but official distrust was lessened, and the secretary of war felt safe in decreasing the strength of a garrison or abandoning a post altogether. Henceforth the control of the Indians rather than protection against the British became the motivating factor in the defense of the northern frontier.

Coincident with the increase in the size of the garrisons and the erection of new posts was the recession of the defense line. The abandonment of a useless fort was as necessary as the establishment of a new one, and the former step was sometimes necessary before the latter could be taken. In writing to Calhoun on February 5, 1818, Brown observed that some posts that had formerly been on the frontier were then far behind it. Forts were good or bad as their location was good or bad. If they were centers for idlers and begging Indians they were worse than useless. Settlements should be formed *behind* forts, not *around* them. He thought that the line of defense that ran from Detroit to St. Louis by way of Fort Defiance, Fort Wayne, and Fort Harrison should be abandoned altogether. The new line, according to Brown, should extend from Fort Gratiot to Sault Ste. Marie, and southward to the southern end of Lake Michigan and on to the headwaters of the Illinois River. All posts south or east of such a line should be abandoned. He recommended the rebuilding of Fort Gratiot, the occupation of Sault Ste. Marie, the strengthening of Fort Howard, the retention of Fort Dearborn, and the complete abandonment of Mackinac, Fort Harrison, and Fort Wayne.[27]

As early as December, 1815, Macomb contemplated the abandonment of Fort Harrison,[28] but an attack upon surveyors near Vincennes [29] caused the temporary continuance of the fort. Early in 1817 Benjamin Parke, Indian agent at Vincennes, advocated the removal of his agency, which served the tribes around Fort Harrison,[30] and on February 3, 1818, General Brown gave or-

[27] Brown Letter Books, 2:90–94.
[28] Morgan to Secretary of War, January 28, 1816, Old Records Division, Adjutant General's Office.
[29] Letters Received, 9:197, 295, Old Records Division, Adjutant General's Office.
[30] *Ibid.*, 10:270.

ders for the abandonment of the fort.[31] A similar course was followed with Fort Wayne. Damaged and neglected, it served no useful function in the defense plan, and Brown was unwilling to spend much for repairs.[32] The machinations of the Prophet and his party during the early part of 1817 [33] seemed to indicate the advisability of maintaining the fort, but Macomb reported that the establishment of new posts had caused the Indians to assume a more respectful attitude.[34] On April 19, 1819, the garrison of about one hundred left Fort Wayne to join the troops that were being sent to the upper Mississippi.[35] Fort Shelby at Detroit was not in first-class order, and Major Gratiot advised that Spring Wells was a better location.[36] The inspector reported, early in 1817, that Fort Gratiot was fast falling into decay,[37] but naturally Detroit was too important a center to be abandoned.

The supervision of the scattered posts was strenuous work. How it was performed in the summer of 1819 by General Brown is told by Captain Roger Jones, a member of the staff. The party left Sackett's Harbor on May 31 and reached Fort Niagara on June 2. Concerning this fort Jones observed, "The fort hitherto has been considered as a very important point; from its situation however 'tis no longer so regarded." [38] On June 12 they embarked at Buffalo on the *Walk-in-the-Water,* the first steamboat to be operated west of Lake Ontario, and reached Erie the next day. After making a visit to Put-in-Bay, they reached Detroit on June 15, where they were received by Macomb and Governor Cass. After inspecting the troops the party left for

[31] Brown Letter Books, 2:112, 119.
[32] Griswold, *History of Fort Wayne,* p. 229.
[33] Letters Received, 10:351, 388, Old Records Division, Adjutant General's Office.
[34] *Ibid.,* p. 204.
[35] Griswold, *History of Fort Wayne,* pp. 238–40; *Detroit Gazette,* May 14, 1819.
[36] Reports of the Corps of Engineers, 1812–23, pp. 41–42.
[37] Inspection Reports, Inspector General's Office, 1814–23, p. 37.
[38] Jones, "Gen. Brown's Inspection Tour up the Lakes in 1819," Publications of the Buffalo Historical Society, 14:301. The garrison at Fort Niagara had been reduced shortly before Jones's visit. Jones to Adjutant General, April 19, 1819, Letters Received, Old Files Section, Adjutant General's Office.

Fort Gratiot on the following day and reached Mackinac on June 19. The troops paraded and drilled for inspection, received official approval, and won commendation for Lieutenant Colonel William Lawrence, who had recently taken charge, and for Captain Benjamin Kendrick Pierce, who was credited with having drilled them thoroughly. The garrison inspection on the following day showed that the quarters were tastefully and comfortably arranged and that the utensils were brilliantly clean.

On June 21 the party left for Sault Ste. Marie, where they inspected the "talked-of fortifications," and returned to Mackinac. On June 29 they left for Green Bay on board the schooner *Tiger,* but were delayed by a storm and did not arrive until July 5. Jones observed that "Ft. Howard is miserably situated 3 miles from the mouth of the river, on a low sandy soil. A mile and a half above on the opposite shore would have afforded a lofty, eligible position." After the usual inspection, they embarked on the eighth and reached Detroit on the twelfth.

A holiday at Hog Island, three miles up the river, afforded relaxation for the party. Tents and bowers were prepared, and dances and cotillions were performed to the music of the military band. At sunset they embarked in three boats and glided down the river. Waving banners, martial music, and sunset glows were duly noted by Jones.[39] The party left Detroit on the *Walk-in-the-Water* on July 15 and reached Buffalo two days later, having performed a journey of 2,543 miles in little more than a month and a half.[40]

Brown was not satisfied with conditions on the northern frontier. He suspected the British of maintaining unduly large garrisons in Canada.[41] The Indians made frequent visits to Malden and to Drummond's Island,[42] where they received val-

---

[39] Jones's wife, who accompanied him as far as Mackinac, had returned to Detroit, where she awaited his return.

[40] Jones, in Publications of the Buffalo Historical Society, 14:296–321.

[41] In November, 1819, Brown estimated the troops in Canada at 8,950, 100 being stationed at Malden. Brown Letter Books, 2:173.

[42] The post at Drummond's Island was built in 1815 after the evacuation of Mackinac. In 1822 the boundary commissioners decided that the new post was

uable presents and liberal supplies. Such a policy on the part of the British appeared ominous. If there was no diplomatic or military motive, there was at least the commercial object of securing the fur trade of the Indians.[43] Writing to Calhoun on September 27, 1819, Brown advocated the occupation of Sault Ste. Marie and the erection of permanent quarters. He also emphasized the importance of Fort Howard and proposed that stone barracks be erected on a new and more healthful site.[44] Brown's plans were furthered by Governor Cass's tour of the lakes in 1820.

On November 19, 1819, Governor Cass, in writing to Calhoun, proposed a trip for the purpose of (1) securing information about the Indians, (2) procuring cessions of land at Green Bay, Prairie du Chien, and Sault Ste. Marie, (3) examining the copper deposits on Lake Superior, (4) treating with the Indians near Chicago in regard to the removal to that vicinity of the Six Nations, and (5) ascertaining the extent and nature of the British fur trade. Calhoun answered on January 14, 1820, approving Cass's plans and suggesting that he discover a route from Lake Superior to the Mississippi. Later Calhoun informed Cass that Schoolcraft would accompany him and that a tract of land at Sault St. Marie only was to be bought. He enclosed a map and asked that Cass obtain an area ten miles square on which to erect a fort.[45]

On May 24, 1820, the party, consisting of Cass, Schoolcraft, Captain David B. Douglas of West Point, James Doty, and soldiers, Indians, and *voyageurs,* numbering all told about thirty-four men, set out from Detroit in three canoes. A large

within the United States, although it was not until six years later that the British withdrew. *Detroit Gazette,* June 7, August 2, 1822; *Missouri Gazette,* August 2, 1822; *Niles' Weekly Register,* vol. 9, sup. 80; Wisconsin Historical Collections, 19:146.

[43] The evidence of the Indian visits is abundant. See *Niles' Weekly Register,* 9: 429; 10:64; Wisconsin Historical Collections, 19:377, 419, 421, 423, 426, 430, 472, 473; *Missouri Gazette,* March 9, 1816, August 16, 1817; *Detroit Gazette, passim.*

[44] Brown Letter Books, 2:156–58.

[45] *American State Papers: Indian Affairs,* 2:318–20; Smith, *Life and Times of Lewis Cass,* pp. 118–24.

American flag flew from each canoe, and the boatmen chanted
their songs as they pulled away from the shore.[46] The *Detroit
Gazette* praised Calhoun for approving the tour and declared
it to be more important than the Yellowstone Expedition.[47]
Maps were to be made, eligible sites for forts selected, the land
purchased, and the source of the Mississippi ascertained.[48]

The party arrived at Fort Gratiot on May 27, where they were
entertained by Major Alexander Cummings. They reached
Mackinac on June 6. Accompanied by Captain Pierce and
twenty-two soldiers, the party pushed on to Sault Ste. Marie,
which they reached on June 14. The British very properly regarded the Straits as the key to the upper country, and the
American government, entertaining a similar view, had decided
to build a post there. Doty mistakenly prophesied that it would
be established "next season." Cass's bravery in snatching down
a British flag raised by an Indian won the admiration of both
whites and Indians. A council confirmed the land cession, and
the party moved on westward.[49]

Skirting the southern shore of Lake Superior, they touched at
various points and examined the copper deposits on the Ontono-
gon River. On July 5 they reached the western end of Lake
Superior and began the ascent of the St. Louis River. Doty
pointed out that a practicable route was by way of the Bois
Brulé–St. Croix. On the thirteenth the party reached Sandy Lake,
where they found a fur trading post of Astor's. Cass ascended
the Mississippi to Red Cedar Lake, erroneously estimated by
Doty to be three hundred and fifty miles above Sandy Lake.
On July 25 they left Sandy Lake and reached Camp Coldwater,
or St. Peter's, on the thirty-first. They left St. Peter's on August 2.
At Chicago the party divided, Schoolcraft and most of the party
returning by the Lakes, and Cass by way of Chicago.[50] The

[46] Doty, "Official Journal, 1820," Wisconsin Historical Collections, 13:164–65;
Detroit Gazette, May 26, 1820.
[47] March 3, 1820.
[48] Wisconsin Historical Collections, 13:163.
[49] *Ibid.*, pp. 167, 176–80.
[50] Doty, in Wisconsin Historical Collections, 13:190, 192, 193, 194, 202, 203,
204, 210, 212, 215, 216, 219.

Detroit Gazette [51] hailed Cass's return and praised him for having secured the fort site at Sault Ste. Marie, for securing much information about the Indians, and for making good maps of the regions visited.

The long-deferred post at Sault Ste. Marie was established in 1822. It had been planned as early as 1797, when General James Wilkinson visited the site.[52] In 1815 a party of forty-five soldiers had made a reconnoitering expedition around the eastern end of Lake Superior. In August, 1818, Macomb had inspected the grounds,[53] and in 1819 Brown had recommended the establishment of the post. Cass completed the arrangements with the Indians and indorsed the plan. To establish the fort an expedition was sent in 1822. In June two hundred and fifty men under Colonel Hugh Brady left Sackett's Harbor in the steamboat *Superior* and reached Detroit early in July. The steamboat was unable to reach Sault Ste. Marie on account of the uncharted waters, but the troops arrived there on July 6. A council with the Indians was held, and the troops began the erection of winter quarters. Six large houses sixty-two by twenty feet and officers' quarters were completed by the middle of October.[54]

Fort Saginaw was also erected in 1822. In September, 1819, Cass had secured a large cession of land bordering Saginaw Bay and projecting far to the southwest.[55] The settlers on the new cession complained of Indian outrages, and a fort was planned for their protection. Early in July, 1822, Major Daniel Baker left Fort Howard with about a hundred men and reached Detroit on July 21. They proceeded at once to the Saginaw River, where a site was chosen on the west bank twenty-five miles from its mouth and near the principal Indian village. A stockaded

---

[51] September 15, 1820.

[52] Michigan Pioneer and Historical Collections, 12:270–71.

[53] Johnston, "Reminiscences," Michigan Pioneer and Historical Collections, 12: 605–06, 607–08; 16:631. Johnston's memory was unreliable as to names and years. His statements must be checked.

[54] *Detroit Gazette*, July 5, 26, September 12, 20, 1822; *Niles' Weekly Register*, 22:240, 387.

[55] Kappler, *Indian Affairs, Laws, and Treaties*, 2:185–87. A fuller account of the treaty may be found in Dustin, *The Saginaw Treaty of 1819*.

fort and quarters were ready for occupation early in October.[56] In the same month the troops began the cutting of a road to Detroit. The task was completed by January, half of it having been performed by the troops in twenty-one days.[57]

The post at Saginaw was short-lived. Throughout the summer and fall the health of the troops was good,[58] but during the winter sickness was common. Within little more than a year nine of the garrison of less than a hundred men died,[59] among them being a fifteen-year-old son of Major Baker. The post surgeon became ill; a doctor from Detroit who came to the relief of the garrison was also afflicted; and a third doctor was employed.[60] Rumors that the post would be abandoned aroused the protests of thirty-nine residents of Detroit, who filed a vigorous protest with Governor Cass. Cass added his own protest, asserting that the fort was necessary to guarantee the safety of the settlers, who were moving into the new cession in great numbers. The Indians had previously been troublesome, but the fort had produced a marked improvement in their conduct.[61] Cass followed his protest with another six days later.[62] Calhoun denied any intention of removing the troops.[63] Sickness continued, and in October Captain John Garland ordered members of the garrison who were able to march to go to Detroit, where they arrived on the twenty-ninth.[64] A small detachment under Lieutenant Henry Bainbridge remained at Saginaw, but the post

[56] *Detroit Gazette*, July 7, 26, August 2, 16, September 12, 1822.

[57] Baker to the Adjutant General, January 8, 1823, Letters Received, Old Files Section, Adjutant General's Office.

[58] *Detroit Gazette*, October 11, December 6, 1822.

[59] Reservation File: Saginaw, Old Files Section, Adjutant General's Office. The garrison numbered 93 in 1822 and 94 in 1823. *American State Papers: Military Affairs*, 2:455–56, 558.

[60] Letters Received, Old Files Section, Adjutant General's Office. The Indians warned the troops against erecting the fort on the burial ground of the chiefs.

[61] Cass *et al.* to Calhoun, June 5, 1823, Old Files Section, Adjutant General's Office.

[62] Cass Letter Books, 4:162–68, Indian Office.

[63] *Detroit Gazette*, July 25, 1823.

[64] Letters Received, Old Files Section, Adjutant General's Office; *Detroit Gazette*, October 8, 17, 31, 1823. The severity of conditions is indicated by the fact that four men deserted during the short occupation of Fort Saginaw. *American State Papers: Military Affairs*, 3:194–95.

was never fully garrisoned again, and in July, 1824, the guard was withdrawn.[65]

Garrison life on the northern frontier was alternately monotonous and exciting, enervating and strenuous. The performance of garrison duties, the preparation of winter quarters, and the cutting of wood were tasks that occupied all the troops. The erection of forts and the construction of roads were under the direction of the engineers, who had charge of the troops during working hours.[66] Occasional outrages were committed by the Indians. In 1821 they killed an army surgeon as he was journeying from Fort Howard to Chicago.[67] In 1824 two soldiers deserted from Fort Howard, carrying four guns. They were pursued by Indians, who were generally employed to catch and restore deserters. The two men resisted capture and killed four Indians before they themselves were killed.[68] The suffering in winter must have been considerable. Late in December, 1817, a Mr. Collins left Detroit with a load of shoes on pack horses and set out to supply the garrisons at Chicago and Green Bay. He returned in the following March, having lost several horses in the snow. He reported that the temperature at Fort Howard was thirty-five degrees below zero.[69]

Uniformity and high standards of discipline and camp life were insured by regular inspection. Brown's tour of inspection in 1819 has been mentioned. Samuel B. Archer, inspector general, visited Detroit on September 1, 1822,[70] and in the following year Colonel John E. Wool, assistant inspector general, made a tour of the forts on the northern frontier.[71] On September 22, 1824, Gaines, acting as inspector, arrived at Fort Howard. He found the food supply ample and the meals well cooked, but thirty-four men were in the hospital, a situation for which he accounted by observing that the location was unhealthful. He inspected Mack-

[65] *Saginaw Courier-Herald*, March 13, 1910.
[66] Brown Letter Books, 2:9–10.
[67] Jameson, *Correspondence of John Caldwell Calhoun*, p. 189.
[68] *Niles' Weekly Register*, 27:16.
[69] *Detroit Gazette*, December 26, 1817, April 3, 1818.
[70] Inspection Reports, Inspector General's Office, 1814–23, pp. 233–34.
[71] *Detroit Gazette*, June 6, 1823.

inac on October 3 and observed that the Indians did not frequent the place as they had formerly because they secured supplies at Green Bay. He found the fort poorly constructed. Four days later he inspected Fort Brady, which he thought could withstand an Indian attack but was useless against artillery. He was enthusiastic about the location of the fort and urged that it be made strong and permanent. He also recommended a large garrison for Fort Gratiot. Traveling by Detroit, Gaines reached Fort Niagara, a post that was nearly beyond repair, on October 25.[72] In 1825 the tour of inspection was again performed by Wool.[73]

The plans for the northwestern frontier and the strengthening of Forts Brady and Howard necessitated the removal of garrisons. The abandonment of Forts Harrison and Wayne in 1818 and 1819, respectively, has been mentioned. The contemplated abandonment of Detroit and the actual reduction of the force at that point provoked some criticism.[74] Referring to Fort Gratiot, Doty observed in 1820, "I should think government must be ill advised to abandon it." [75] In that year, however, the garrison was transferred to Fort Howard.[76] The establishment of the artillery school in 1823 forced the withdrawal of the artillery from the upper Great Lakes and the abandonment of Chicago. The petition of the Detroit citizens and the protests of Cass were unavailing.[77] In writing to Solomon Sibley, Calhoun pointed out that the line of protection from the Lakes to the Missouri rendered some garrisons useless. Since Chicago was south of the new line, it had been abandoned.[78] The garrison at Fort Shelby, Detroit, numbered less than a hundred from 1820 to 1825 and was abandoned altogether in 1826. During the same period

[72] Inspection Reports, Inspector General's Office, 1823–24, pp. 339–424.
[73] Detroit Gazette, July 12, 1825.
[74] Ibid., May 26, 1819. The secretary of Michigan Territory filed a vigorous protest against weakening the forces at Detroit and Fort Gratiot. Annals of Congress, 16th Congress, 1st Session, pp. 2480–82.
[75] Wisconsin Historical Collections, 13:168.
[76] Detroit Gazette, May 26, 1820.
[77] Jameson, Correspondence of John Caldwell Calhoun, pp. 207–09; Letters Received, 1823, Old Files Section, Adjutant General's Office; Cass Letter Books, 4:162–68.
[78] Detroit Gazette, July 25, 1823.

Mackinac had a garrison of less than two companies and was supplanted in importance by Fort Brady, where a garrison of nearly three hundred was maintained.[79] Green Bay on the route to the West was equally well protected.[80]

The policy of reducing the number of troops on the northern frontier was not popular with the editor of the *Detroit Gazette,* who asked why the company of artillery was to be placed on the Atlantic coast and the Straits left unprotected. He asked why troops should be stationed at Sackett's Harbor and Fort Niagara, where they were useless. He argued that they were needed to overawe the Indians and prevent British communications with them. In 1825 he pointed to the two or three thousand Indians who visited Malden and the three hundred thousand dollars that were being spent annually by the British for presents for the Indians at Drummond's Island.[81] In spite of local protests, the northern frontier slowly and surely lost its strategic position, and because of the remarkably rapid settlement, the decreasing importance of the Indians, and the good understanding with Great Britain, it soon ceased to be a military frontier.

[79] Stephen H. Long thought Mackinac should be strongly fortified to eliminate the need for posts at Green Bay and Chicago. Keating, *Long's Expedition,* 2:242–43.

[80] Returns for 1822, 1823, 1824, and 1825, *American State Papers: Military Affairs,* 2:455–56, 557, 706; 3:115.

[81] *Detroit Gazette,* June 20, 27, July 4, 1823, August 2, 16, 1825.

CHAPTER IX
THE MISSISSIPPI–MISSOURI FRONTIER

THE WAR OF 1812 came to an end with reasonable promptness on the northern frontier, where the British predominated, but the situation was quite different on the Mississippi-Missouri frontier,[1] where the Indians had been the chief combatants against the Americans. The news of peace spread slowly, and when it did arrive the Indians received it with sullen acquiescence or open hostility. On March 22 Governor William Clark of Missouri Territory wrote a note to the British officer on the Mississippi enclosing a copy of the *National Intelligencer* containing the news of peace. Three days later Colonel William Russell, commandant at Belle Fontaine, wrote a note to the commander at Prairie du Chien notifying him of the peace and asking him to inform the Indians.[2] On the twenty-ninth Major Taylor Berry set out from Belle Fontaine on board the gunboat *Governor Clark* and reached Rock River early in April. He dispatched a note to Captain Duncan Graham, British Indian agent at Rock River, telling him of the peace and asking for the surrender of two American prisoners. Graham refused to surrender the prisoners and warned Berry to be cautious until the Indians were convinced of the truth of the reported peace. He agreed to forward Russell's note to Prairie du Chien,[3] where it arrived on April 16, just in time to prevent the departure of an expedition of considerable proportions against the St. Louis area.[4]

[1] The term Mississippi-Missouri frontier is here used to designate the region from central Missouri to Prairie du Chien, including Fort Clark at Peoria and Fort Osage on the Missouri.
[2] "The Bulger Papers," Wisconsin Historical Collections, 13:126–27, 130.
[3] *Missouri Gazette*, April 29, 1815.
[4] Bulger, "Last Days of the British at Prairie du Chien," Wisconsin Historical Collections, 13:156–57.

Governor Ninian Edwards of Illinois Territory also notified the Indians of the peace treaty, but outrages continued. The Sauk of Rock River were particularly hostile. Scarcely a week passed without one or more murders, and skirmishes were of frequent occurrence. Two of them, the attack on Cotes sans Dessein and the Sink Hole fight, might almost be called battles.[5] Horses were stolen, women and children tomahawked, and men ambushed, and on one occasion a ranger was killed almost within a fort. The outrages continued with undiminished frequency until late summer. The peace parleys at Portage des Sioux at last convinced the Indians that peace had really been declared.[6]

The grand conclave at Portage des Sioux, which assembled on July 6, was poorly attended at first, and the Indians seemed sullen and indifferent about making peace.[7] The news reached Jackson that a renewal of the Indian war seemed inevitable,[8] and he directed Governor Clark to hold the militia in readiness. Adjutant General David Delaunay of the militia accordingly issued a proclamation on July 19 calling on members to be ready to proceed against the Indians if a treaty was not effected.[9] No active steps were necessary, however, for most of the tribes made peace by early September,[10] and the frontier entered upon an era of greater security than it had known since the preaching of the Prophet had stirred the Indians to activity in the years before the war.

[5] Cotes sans Dessein was on the Missouri opposite the mouth of the Osage, and the Sink Hole was near Fort Howard, in what is now Lincoln County, Missouri. For accounts of these battles see the *Missouri Gazette*, April 8, 29, May 27, June 3, 17, 1815. A shortened version of the Sink Hole fight appears in *Niles' Weekly Register*, 8:311–12, 361–62.

[6] The news of peace was announced in the *Missouri Gazette*, March 11, 1815. Nearly every issue from that date until August contains accounts of murders and attacks by the Indians.

[7] *Missouri Gazette*, July 15, 1815. For a fuller account of the treaties, see Fisher, "The Treaties of Portage des Sioux," *Mississippi Valley Historical Review*, 19:495–508.

[8] *Niles' Weekly Register*, 8:436.

[9] Military Books, 8:291–92, Old Records Division, Adjutant General's Office; *Missouri Gazette*, July 22, 1815.

[10] Kappler, *Indian Affairs, Laws, and Treaties*, 2:110–17, 119–23; *American State Papers: Indian Affairs*, 2:1–25.

The Sauk, Foxes, Kickapoo, and Winnebago of Rock River refused to attend the peace meeting at Portage des Sioux. Their refusal emphasized the necessity of providing for the defense of the western frontier. Early in March, 1815, five hundred men under Colonel James Miller had been ordered to St. Louis to insure the good conduct of the Indians, and an additional five hundred were to follow as soon as possible.[11] The troops were distributed among the posts already established, Belle Fontaine, Fort Osage, and Fort Clark. New forts were to be established near the mouth of the Des Moines, at Rock River, and at Prairie du Chien.[12]

In the autumn of 1815 a contingent under Colonel Robert Carter Nichols ascended the Mississippi and erected temporary quarters, known as Cantonment Davis, a half mile below the site of the future Fort Edwards.[13] The troops spent a pleasant winter and enjoyed excellent health. In the spring a delay in the delivery of supplies by the contractors was offset by a supply of fish, which were caught in great numbers.[14] In June the troops began the erection of Fort Edwards, named in honor of Governor Edwards, and completed the task the following year.[15] For several years the fort was occupied by a garrison, which was strategically situated to control the tribes on both sides of the Mississippi.

Shortly after the troops arrived at Cantonment Davis they heard that British traders had erected houses among the disaffected tribes at Rock River and were instrumental in keeping their disaffection alive.[16] Such facts tended to hasten the occu-

[11] Secretary of War to Clark, March 10, 1815, Territorial Papers, State Department; *Missouri Gazette*, April 8, 1815; *National Intelligencer*, May 16, 1815.

[12] *Missouri Gazette*, September 30, October 28, 1815; *Niles' Weekly Register*, 9:172; 10:57. Niles gives the strength and distribution of the army on March 7, 1816, in a report which is not in *American State Papers: Military Affairs*.

[13] The camp was on the site of Fort Johnson, which was built in September, 1814, and evacuated and destroyed in the following month. See Wesley, "James Callaway in the War of 1812," Missouri Historical Collections, 5:69–72. For the location of forts see the map on page 112.

[14] *Missouri Gazette*, December 23, 1815, May 18, 1816; *Niles' Weekly Register*, 10:352; Flagler, *History of Rock Island Arsenal*, pp. 14–15.

[15] Mahan, *Old Fort Crawford and the Frontier*, p. 302.

[16] *Missouri Gazette*, December 23, 1815.

pation of the Rock River country. In April, 1816, Brigadier
General Thomas A. Smith with a considerable force ascended
the Mississippi to Cantonment Davis, where he assumed command. Leaving a garrison at the cantonment, Smith and several
hundred men proceeded to Rock Island, which was reached on
May 10. Choosing a site on the lower end of the island, the
troops began the erection of Fort Armstrong, in spite of the
objections of the Indians, who professed to fear that the erection
of a fort would incite the young braves to deeds of violence.[17]
Smith treated the Indians civilly and proceeded with the work of
erecting the fort.[18] It was of the usual type, with a square court
enclosed by palisades and blockhouses, but the lower part of the
walls was made of stone.[19]

Two new forts had been established with reasonable promptness. A third was to follow fast upon the second. Posts on the
upper Mississippi had been suggested by Monroe, planned by
Dallas, and sanctioned by Jackson.[20] In the summer of 1815
Jackson ordered Colonel William S. Hamilton to proceed with
his regiment to Prairie du Chien by way of the Ohio and
Mississippi. Additional troops were to be added at Newport,
Kentucky, and at Smithland, at the mouth of the Cumberland,[21]
but the slow movement of the troops forced a postponement
until the following year.[22] In the spring of 1816 Hamilton left
Belle Fontaine with about three hundred riflemen and proceeded to Fort Armstrong, where Smith took command. The
troops ascended the Mississippi to Prairie du Chien, where they
arrived on June 20. Richard Graham, Indian agent,[23] accompanied the expedition. John W. Johnson, factor, had already
reached Prairie du Chien and had opened trade with the In-

[17] On May 13, 1816, the Sauk of Rock River signed a treaty of peace at St.
Louis. They were doubtless aware of the plans and movements of the army.
Kappler, *Indian Affairs, Laws, and Treaties*, 2:126–28.

[18] *Missouri Gazette*, June 15, 1816.

[19] Flagler, *History of Rock Island Arsenal*, pp. 16–17.

[20] See Chapter VIII.

[21] *Missouri Gazette*, September 2, 1815.

[22] Wisconsin Historical Collections, 19:383; Bassett, *Correspondence of Andrew
Jackson*, 2:206.

[23] For a further account of Graham's activities see Chapter III.

dians.[24] Thus the new post illustrates the threefold policy of force, diplomacy, and trade.

Smith assumed control of the town. Private property was appropriated for public use without formality or delay; traders were subjected to rigid inspection; and the citizens, many of whom had aided the British, were treated with severity and contempt. The necessity of establishing American control doubtless justified some of Smith's severe measures. The erection of the fort was unusually burdensome. Neither wood nor stone was to be found near the site, and the troops had to secure the materials at a considerable distance and transport them in boats.[25] In spite of difficulties the post was firmly established and well garrisoned by the close of 1816.

The War Department and the division commander had acted with commendable promptness. Within little more than a year all the posts that would be needed on the Mississippi-Missouri frontier for a decade had been erected and occupied. In March, 1816, about 850 soldiers were at Belle Fontaine, which was the distributing center for the western area.[26] The returns of February, 1817,[27] show a total of 767 men, distributed as follows: Belle Fontaine, 170; Fort Osage, 83; Fort Clark, 86; Fort Edwards, 84; Fort Armstrong, 79; Fort Crawford, 265. The returns for December, 1817,[28] show slight variations in all the garrisons, and the total number on the frontier was by no means constant.

A view of the three forts on the Mississippi is afforded by Long's account of 1817.[29] With fifteen men and two boats he set out from Belle Fontaine on June 1 and inspected the sites around the Falls of St. Anthony and returned to Prairie du Chien on July 21. He regarded the location of Fort Crawford as unsuitable for several reasons. It was too low; it did not command the

[24] Wisconsin Historical Collections, 19:424–25.
[25] Mahan, Old Fort Crawford and the Frontier, pp. 71–73.
[26] Niles' Weekly Register, 10:57.
[27] Southern Division Returns, Officers' Record Division, Adjutant General's Office.
[28] American State Papers: Military Affairs, 1:671–72.
[29] Long, "Voyage in a Six-Oared Skiff to the Falls of Saint Anthony in 1817," Minnesota Historical Collections, 2:9–88.

river; and stagnant water endangered the health of the garrison. Its location had been determined by general geographic facts rather than by specific local considerations, and Long was forced to admit, after careful examination, that no site in the vicinity was more desirable. The fort was a square stockaded court, measuring 340 feet on each side, and enclosed mostly by buildings, the stockade occupying only about one-fourth of the sides. Two-storied blockhouses occupied the northeastern and northwestern corners. He found the troops busy cutting shingles and completing their quarters, which were capable of accommodating five companies.[30]

On July 27 Long set out for Fort Armstrong and en route met Hugh Glenn, the contractor who supplied the troops and who had already left supplies at Forts Edwards and Armstrong. He found Fort Armstrong well located, with ample command of the river and prairies, and surrounded by abundant supplies of timber and stone. Three miles distant was a Sauk village of some two thousand Indians, and on the mainland opposite the fort was a Fox village of thirty cabins. These tribes had caused much trouble during the war, and the fort was strategically located to quell future uprisings. The stockade was 288 by 277 feet and contained three blockhouses.[31]

On August 2 Long left for Fort Edwards, where he arrived two days later. He noted that Cantonment Davis, where the troops had been quartered before and during the erection of the fort, was deserted. He regarded Fort Edwards as useless because it did not command the river, because a ravine enabled an enemy to approach within range unobserved, and because a height to the northeast made its defense difficult or impossible.[32]

The development of defense plans made possible a renewal of the advance of the frontier. During the war the frontiersmen

[30] Minnesota Historical Collections, 2:9, 10, 41, 51, 52, 56–59. The post was under the command of Lieutenant Colonel Talbot Chambers, who arrived with two companies on April 22, 1817. Johnson to Sibley, April 28, 1817, Sibley Letter Books, Missouri Historical Society.
[31] Minnesota Historical Collections, 2:64, 65, 67, 68–74.
[32] Ibid., pp. 74–80.

had frequently been forced to live in stockaded forts, and the growth of Missouri and Illinois territories was slight. With the return of peace and the assurance of protection, settlers came in greater numbers. A road to the Osage River was cleared in the winter of 1815–16. Immigrants were assured that no stumps higher than eight inches would be found in the new road and that the route was blazed to Cole's Fort on the Missouri. A hundred families moved into Howard County, Missouri, in 1816.[33] The *Missouri Gazette*[34] remarked that it seemed as though Virginia, Kentucky, Tennessee, and the Carolinas planned to gain statehood for Missouri and Illinois as soon as possible. Roads and ferries were crowded, and the hospitable editor welcomed everyone, saying that there were ample food supplies and millions of acres of land.

The line of defense that facilitated the influx of settlers was rendered useless by their arrival. When an area that had required the protection of garrisons became well populated, it needed them no longer. The study of frontier defense is thus twofold, including consideration of the advancing line of defense and of the abandonment of posts that had served their purpose.

In 1815 Fort Clark at Peoria was considered an important post. It had been erected during the War of 1812,[35] and in 1816 Major Stephen H. Long was sent to survey the grounds for a new structure. In September he reported that a new site, two hundred yards below the old fort, had been chosen.[36] Before the plans could be carried out, the population of Illinois Territory had grown so rapidly that the fort was no longer regarded as necessary. In December, 1817, the garrison numbered only thirty.[37] Early in 1818 Long again inspected the fort and on

[33] *Missouri Gazette*, March 23, 1816; *Missouri Intelligencer*, April 1, 1820; Sibley to Mask, March 29, 1817, in Darby, *Emigrant's Guide*, pp. 301–05. Sibley says that many settlers moved into the Boon's Lick country during the war.
[34] *Missouri Gazette*, October 26, 1816.
[35] For an account of the building of Fort Clark in 1813 see Wesley, "James Callaway in the War of 1812," Missouri Historical Collections, 5:45–47, 57–59.
[36] Letters Sent, Old Files Section, Adjutant General's Office; Reports of the Corps of Engineers, 1812–23, p. 138; *Missouri Gazette*, May 24, 1817.
[37] *American State Papers: Military Affairs*, 1:672.

May 12 reported that it was fast falling into decay and that the erection of a new building was imperative if the post was to be continued. He observed that the number of Indians in the vicinity was so small that the fort was no longer necessary.[38] In accordance with his recommendation it was immediately abandoned.[39] About November 20 it was partially destroyed by fire during a riot of Indians.[40] In 1815 Fort Clark had been regarded as an important post; in 1818 the situation was so altered that it was not worth rebuilding.

In the same way Fort Osage on the Missouri diminished in importance. In January, 1816, it was garrisoned by more than two hundred men, but in June, 1818, there were only forty-six.[41] In 1818 Colonel Arthur P. Hayne, inspector for the Southern Division, recommended its abandonment.[42] When the Missouri Expedition ascended the river in 1819, the garrison, consisting of twenty-two men, was attached to the main force, leaving a guard of seven men to protect the factory.[43] The editor of the *Missouri Intelligencer* [44] looked upon the evacuation with complacency, because, as he observed, the line of settlement extended almost to the fort. In obedience to Calhoun's orders the fort was reoccupied in the following year,[45] but the garrison continued to be small. In 1822 Jacob Fowler stopped at Fort Osage and observed that "the garreson at this time Was Commanded by one officer of the united States armey—Haveing two men under His Command Both of them Haveing disarted a few days ago and Carryed off all His amenetion—" [46]

[38] Reports of the Corps of Engineers, 1812–23, pp. 282, 285.
[39] The returns of June, 1818, show no garrison at Fort Clark. Southern Division Returns, Officers' Record Division, Adjutant General's Office.
[40] Hubbard, *Autobiography*, p. 49; *History of Peoria County*, pp. 278–79.
[41] Southern Division Returns, Officers' Record Division, Adjutant General's Office.
[42] Reservation File: Fort Osage, Old Files Section, Adjutant General's Office.
[43] Order of August 29, 1819, Department Orders, Old Records Division, Adjutant General's Office.
[44] September 3, 1819. For a description of Fort Osage in 1819 see James, *Long's Expedition*, in Thwaites, *Early Western Travels*, 14:168.
[45] Atkinson to Calhoun, October 18, 1820, in *Missouri Intelligencer*, February 5, 1821.
[46] Coues, *Journal of Jacob Fowler*, p. 173.

The importance of Fort Edwards fluctuated, but it was never considered one of the major posts. The force that ascended the Mississippi in 1815 for the purpose of founding it numbered one hundred and forty-six, but the regular garrison consisted of about sixty men.[47] In May, 1818, Long recommended its abandonment,[48] and about April, 1819, the garrison was removed. On June 16 of that year Thomas Forsyth stopped at Fort Edwards and found the barracks occupied by some families who were awaiting an allotment of land for services in the War of 1812. He observed that "a few troops would be well stationed at this place."[49] On July 30 Atkinson gave orders that the factor, Robert B. Belt, have sole authority to occupy the fort buildings.[50] On May 1, 1820, Belt wrote an urgent letter to James Kennerly, factory agent at St. Louis, saying that the Winnebago were about to attack the factory and requesting that a boat in which to forward the furs and goods be sent at once.[51] On May 16 Atkinson dispatched a lieutenant and twenty men to protect the factory.[52] In 1823 Gaines recommended that Fort Edwards be abandoned and dismantled. He considered that the posts on the western frontier had been entirely successful, but Missouri and Illinois were so thickly settled that there was no longer any danger from the Indians.[53] A small garrison continued to occupy the fort until June 11, 1824, when the force, with the exception of a guard of seven men left to care for the crops and public property, was transferred to Fort Armstrong.[54]

The advance of the frontier and the abandonment of posts did not signify that there was no longer need for defense. Indian

[47] Southern Division Returns, Officers' Record Division, Adjutant General's Office.
[48] Reports of the Corps of Engineers, 1812–23, p. 282.
[49] Forsyth, "Narrative," Minnesota Historical Collections, 3:141, 167.
[50] Department Orders, Old Records Division, Adjutant General's Office.
[51] Kennerly Collection, Missouri Historical Society; Niles' Weekly Register, 18: 257.
[52] Department Orders, Old Records Division, Adjutant General's Office; Porter, "Journal of Stephen Watts Kearny," Missouri Historical Collections, 3:127.
[53] Inspection Reports, Inspector General's Office, 1823–24, pp. 190–92.
[54] Western Department, Order No. 36, in Gregg, History of Hancock County, Illinois, pp. 379–80; Order of July 22, 1824, Department Orders, Old Records Division, Adjutant General's Office.

outrages and intertribal wars continued to make vigilance necessary. The Sauk, Osage, and Winnebago were inclined to be hostile; they stole horses and slaves and committed murders.[55] In March, 1820, the Winnebago killed two soldiers near Fort Armstrong. When the chiefs were called to account, they left hostages to insure the delivery of the murderers.[56] In September of that year another murder was committed near Fort Armstrong,[57] and in 1824 two deserters and four travelers from Fort Snelling were killed, supposedly by Chippewa.[58] The Iowa and Sauk and the Foxes and Sioux carried on intertribal wars that endangered the lives of traders.[59] Outrages and intertribal wars were not prevented by the garrisons, but their presence tended to lessen and restrict such activities.

The soldier's work on the Mississippi-Missouri frontier was strenuous, his amusements few, and his punishments severe. Erecting forts, cutting roads, making punitive expeditions against the Indians, assisting factors, guarding the lead mines,[60] cutting wood, raising crops, and fishing and hunting to offset the delays of contractors[61] were some of the principal tasks. His amusements were drinking, gambling, reading, shooting contests, and horse racing. Most posts maintained a band[62] and a reading room, where a few books and newspapers were available. Imprisonment in the guard house, fines, and hard labor were

[55] *Missouri Gazette*, June 8, 13, 1816, January 18, 25, February 22, March 15, 1817; *Missouri Intelligencer*, July 29, August 26, 1820.

[56] *St. Louis Enquirer*, April 19, 1820; *Missouri Gazette*, June 28, 1820; *Niles' Weekly Register*, 18:224, 257.

[57] *St. Louis Enquirer*, October 21, 28, 1820.

[58] *Niles' Weekly Register*, 27:144.

[59] Forsyth to Clark, July 2, September 11, 18, 30, 1818, Forsyth Collection, Missouri Historical Society.

[60] Meeker, "Early History of the Lead Region of Wisconsin," Wisconsin Historical Collections, 6:271; *Detroit Gazette*, September 12, 1822; *St. Louis Enquirer*, June 24, 1822.

[61] One example of the delay of contractors has been mentioned. Another was reported on December 14, 1816, by Colonel William Lawrence, who said that Forts Edwards and Osage were unsupplied. Letters Received, Old Records Division, Adjutant General's Office.

[62] The commander at Belle Fontaine made a request for musical instruments. Smith to the Secretary of War, June 3, 1817, Letters Received, Old Records Division, Adjutant General's Office.

punishments frequently imposed by courts-martial. In 1824 Scott conducted a court-martial at Fort Edwards and condemned two soldiers to wear nine-pound collars with two projecting points nine inches long.[63]

The Mississippi-Missouri frontier was important in the decade after the war. Its fertility and accessibility made the area highly desirable in the eyes of settlers. The War Department recognized its value and the necessity for its defense. The rapid growth of the population and the development of plans for the fortification of the upper Missouri and the Mississippi above Prairie du Chien centered government attention on a more advanced frontier. These plans were cited by Long as justification for recommending the abandonment of Forts Clark and Edwards.[64] The necessity for defense on the Mississippi-Missouri frontier was by no means removed by 1825, but the crisis was over, and local wars were recognized as such. Military officials no longer had to consider foreign influence and unknown combinations of Indians.

[63] Department Orders, Old Records Division, Adjutant General's Office.
[64] Reports of the Corps of Engineers, 1812–23, pp. 282–85.

CHAPTER X

THE NORTHWESTERN FRONTIER[1]

THE RAPID settlement of the northern and western frontiers facilitated the military occupation of more remote regions. The United States government endeavored to protect the fur traders wherever they went and to counteract foreign influence over the Indians by substituting American control. The fur traders operated far beyond the settled areas and traded with remote tribes. The carrying out of the government policy thus necessitated the establishment of a military frontier in advance of settlement. Such a frontier was established by the erection of posts at the mouth of the Minnesota and at Council Bluffs on the Missouri.

James Monroe, secretary of war, in writing to the Senate Committee on Military Affairs on February 22, 1815, proposed the erection of posts on the upper Mississippi and near the boundary in order to secure the friendship, allegiance, and "exclusive commerce" of the Indians.[2] He did not refer to the upper Missouri,[3] but he did plan for a post as far north as the Falls of St. Anthony.[4] In 1816 Governor Clark recommended the establishment of a post on the Platte,[5] but nothing was accomplished toward the extension of the military frontier in the Northwest until two years later.

[1] The term "northwestern frontier" is here used to designate the Missouri above Fort Osage, the Missisippi above Prairie du Chien, and the region between the rivers.
[2] Monroe, *Writings*, 5:325.
[3] The editor of the *St. Louis Enquirer* (January 13, 1824) said that in 1815 Monroe had advocated "extending our military posts far up the Missouri." In view of Monroe's explicit statement to the Indian peace commissioners on March 11, 1815, it seems improbable that he referred to the Missouri. *American State Papers: Indian Affairs*, 2:6, 13.
[4] Bassett, *Correspondence of Andrew Jackson*, 2:206.
[5] Clark to the Secretary of War, May 28, 1816, Letters Received, Old Records Division, Adjutant General's Office.

On March 16, 1818, Calhoun informed Colonel Thomas A. Smith at Belle Fontaine that a post was to be erected at the mouth of the Yellowstone in order "to extend and protect our trade with the Indians."[6] On August 22, in writing to Jackson, Calhoun said:

From information since received [i. e., since sending instructions to Smith], I am inclined to think the principal post ought to be at the Mandane village.[7] It is the point on the Missouri nearest to the British post on the Red River, and the best calculated to counteract their hostilities against us, or influence with the Indians. It appears to be very important, that a strong post should be taken at the mouth of the St. Peter's on the Mississippi.[8]

Calhoun's ideas were further developed by October. In a letter to General Brown on the seventeenth he advised that the post at the mouth of the Minnesota be made unusually strong because of its "proximity" to Selkirk's colony and because it would be near the powerful Sioux. He also announced plans for a fort at the head of navigation on the Minnesota, which would form a communication with the proposed fort at the Mandan village. Still another post at the head of navigation on the St. Croix was planned to complete the cordon of forts that would restrain "foreign traders."[9] In his report to the House on December 11 Calhoun announced the plans for the occupation of the mouths of the Minnesota and the Yellowstone.[10] By March 6, 1819, he had definitely decided that the principal post would be at the Mandan village and that no attempt would be made to occupy a higher position until that one was firmly established; he doubted whether the troops would reach even the Mandan village during the year. If the officers found the circumstances unfavorable for so extended an advance, they were to erect an

---

[6] Jameson, *Correspondence of John Caldwell Calhoun*, pp. 134–36.

[7] This statement plainly shows that the so-called Yellowstone Expedition ceased to be the *Yellowstone* expedition before it ever started.

[8] Jameson, *Correspondence of John Caldwell Calhoun*, p. 138. The St. Peter's is now called the Minnesota River.

[9] *Ibid.*, pp. 147–48.

[10] *American State Papers: Military Affairs*, 1:779–82.

intermediate post either at Council Bluffs or at the Great Bend.[11]

The supposed unity of the Northwest and the resulting unity of plans are further shown by Calhoun's letter to Brown, in which he said, "The same principle will govern both of the expeditions which have the same objects, the complete security of our frontier and the extension of our trade with the Indians." [12] In writing to Colonel Henry Atkinson, who was to command the Missouri Expedition, he said: "In the event of hostilities the Commandant of the 5th Regiment on the Upper Mississippi is ordered to receive your orders. The distance between the Mississippi and Missouri is not too great for cooperation and the country is said to be very open and may easily be past over." [13] Calhoun's report of December 29, 1819, contains, perhaps, the most explicit statement of the comprehensiveness of his plans. "The expedition ordered to the mouth of the Yellow Stone, or rather to the Mandan village, (for the military occupation of the former, depending on circumstances, is not yet finally determined on,) is a part of a system of measures, which has for its objects, the protection of our northwestern frontier, and the greater extension of our fur trade." [14] Further proof of the unity of the northwestern expeditions is found in another part of the same report. The entire document is entitled "Expedition to the Mouth of the Yellow Stone River," but its subdivisions deal with the Missouri and Mississippi expeditions.[15] Thus it is evident that the term Yellowstone Expedition was used in a broad, loose sense to include the whole military expansion into the Northwest.

[11] Jameson, *Correspondence of John Caldwell Calhoun*, p. 153. The Great Bend is about forty miles above the mouth of White River in south-central South Dakota.

[12] *Ibid.*, p. 155.

[13] *Ibid.*, pp. 159–60.

[14] *American State Papers: Military Affairs*, 2:33.

[15] *Ibid.*, pp. 31–32. William Wirt, attorney general, in reviewing the contest over the Johnson contracts for the transportation of troops and supplies, called attention to the unified plans, which were, as he saw it, interrupted by Johnson's failure. House Document No. 110, House Documents, 16th Congress, 2d Session, 8:258.

The Missouri Expedition,[16] the first of the military movements into the Northwest, attracted widespread attention. It received the enthusiastic indorsement of frontiersmen and western editors. In fact, it suffered at the hands of its friends and was made to appear as an event heralding a new day. One writer said that it would add to the security of the West; keep the Indians in check; tend to destroy British influence over the Indians; throw additional light on the geography of the West; encourage western immigration; protect and encourage the fur trade; and help to open communication with the Pacific. These were "a few" of the benefits that were to result from the expedition.[17] Another wrote, "It is a large step toward actual possession of the whole American Territory."[18]

[16] The term "Missouri Expedition" is here used to designate the movement of troops which resulted in the founding of Fort Atkinson at Council Bluffs. It is synonymous with the usual term "Yellowstone Expedition," which is obviously, in view of the facts given above, inappropriate and misleading. Failure to appreciate the breadth and inclusiveness of the plans for the Northwest has resulted in the confusion with which writers have regarded the expedition. Chittenden (*American Fur Trade*, 2:562) says it "was everywhere popularly known in its day as the Yellowstone Expedition, but is now always spoken of as Long's Expedition." Neither statement is correct. The terms "Missouri," "Mandan," and "Northwestern" were frequently used, and it is a confusion of fact to regard Long's explorations as the Yellowstone Expedition. It was a separate affair, which merely coincided in part with the Missouri Expedition.

Long's expedition of 1820 is not considered in this study because it had little or no relation to the development of frontier defense. Long recommended no posts as a result of the expedition, and no defense plans were furthered by his report. Indeed, the only justification there would be for considering Long's expedition is the fact that it had a deterrent effect. His gloomy report tended to limit and restrict defense plans rather than forward them. The positive effect of the expedition on frontier defense was approximately zero.

[17] *Missouri Gazette*, April 21, 1819.

[18] *Ibid.*, September 22, 1819. There are many examples of similar prophecies. See the *National Intelligencer*, June 30, 1819; *Niles' Weekly Register*, 15:117, 182; 16:320; *St. Louis Enquirer*, September 4, 1818; *Edwardsville Spectator*, June 5, 1819; *Argus of Western America* (Frankfort, Kentucky), April 2, 1819.

Chittenden (*American Fur Trade*, vol. 2, chap. 2) considered the Missouri Expedition as an isolated and misguided effort, devoid of sensible objectives and barren of results. He went astray on three important points and so naturally misjudged the expedition, which appeared to him as a mere episode. In the first place, he did not appreciate the larger plans of which it was only a part. In the second place, he did not understand Calhoun's reasonable and practicable plans for the expedition itself. In the third place, he set up the expectations and chimerical prophecies of western expansionists and exploiting editors as the standard by which the expedition should be judged. In spite of these errors Chittenden has

The official beginning of the Missouri Expedition is found in Calhoun's orders of March 16, 1818, to Colonel Smith, who was directed to prepare for the establishment of a post at the mouth of the Yellowstone which would serve "to extend and protect our trade with the Indians." The strength of the detachment, the means of transportation, and the supplying of the troops were left to Smith's discretion. He was advised to consult with Governor William Clark and arrange for Indian presents to the value of three thousand dollars. Two hundred recruits from Pennsylvania and Ohio were to be transferred to the rifle regiment, and the ordnance department was to furnish four pieces of light artillery. Since the season would be advanced before the troops could reach their destination, they were to occupy an intermediate point.[19] The *Washington City Gazette* announced the plans and said that two intermediate posts were to be built, probably at the Great Bend and at Mandan.[20] Early in the summer Colonel James Johnson of Kentucky contracted to furnish supplies and offered to employ steamboats, which he calculated would be able to make the journey in sixty days.[21] The well-known fur trader Manuel Lisa was sent up the river to prepare the Indians for the coming of the troops.[22]

The advance contingent of the Missouri Expedition, consisting of about three hundred and fifty men [23] under the command of Lieutenant Colonel Talbot Chambers, left Belle Fontaine on

been regarded as the authority on the subject, and his account, retold by numerous writers, has been generally accepted for more than a quarter of a century. These facts constitute the apology for giving additional details of supposedly well-known events and drawing therefrom an interpretation different from that given by Chittenden.

See Goodwin, "A Larger View of the Yellowstone Expedition," *Mississippi Valley Historical Review*, 4:199–313, for a more just evaluation of the Missouri Expedition.

[19] Jameson, *Correspondence of John Caldwell Calhoun*, pp. 134–36.

[20] Quoted in the *Missouri Gazette*, June 12, 1818; *Niles' Weekly Register*, 14: 192.

[21] *Niles' Weekly Register*, 14:344.

[22] *Ibid.*, 15:117.

[23] On November 2 the troops numbered 347. *Detroit Gazette*, January 8, 1819. The *Gazette* quotes a St. Louis newspaper. Since the item is not in the *Missouri Gazette*, it must have been in the *St. Louis Enquirer*, of which no file for the year 1818 exists.

August 30, 1818. Their equipment, which was extensive, was transported in six keelboats and a tender. They reached Isle au Vache or Cow Island [24] in October and prepared winter quarters. Chambers returned to Belle Fontaine, leaving Captain Wyly Martin in command. In his honor the camp was named Cantonment Martin. In the spring Lieutenant Colonel Willoughby Morgan was in charge of the troops, which in May numbered 272. The delayed arrival of supplies endangered their health, but they were able to supplement their scanty fare by hunting until the arrival of Long's party in August relieved their shortage.[25]

During the fall and winter further plans for the expedition were made. The addition of a scientific corps under Major Long was decided upon about October 1.[26] No commander for the main expedition had been selected by the first of the year, and Calhoun, who attached great importance to it, asked Jackson to select the ablest and most experienced officer, leaving him to determine the fitness of Captain Martin, who was then in charge.[27] Calhoun himself made the selection, however, and on March 6, 1819, he informed Jackson that Colonel Henry Atkinson had been selected to command the expedition, that Major Benjamin O'Fallon, Indian agent for the Missouri, would accompany or precede the troops, and that Long would ascend the river about the same time.[28]

The most important steps in the preparation of the expedition were, in view of the results, the three contracts made with James Johnson of Kentucky. The first contract was for transporting clothing, ordnance, and medical stores from Pittsburg to St. Louis; the second for furnishing supplies; and the third for supplying transportation such as might not be per-

[24] Cow Island is a few miles above Leavenworth, Kansas.
[25] Niles' Weekly Register, 15:117, 160, 182; Detroit Gazette, January 8, 1819 (three of these items originated with the St. Louis Enquirer); James, Long's Expedition, in Thwaites, Early Western Travels, 14:175; House Document No. 110, House Documents, 16th Congress, 2d Session, 8:19, 220.
[26] Niles' Weekly Register, 15:111. Curiously enough, Thwaites's edition of Long's Expedition gives no clue as to the origin of the expedition.
[27] Jameson, Correspondence of John Caldwell Calhoun, pp. 150–51.
[28] Ibid., pp. 152–54.

formed by the troops. The third contract, which was made on December 2, 1818, obligated Johnson to furnish steamboats for transporting the troops and supplies.[29] Four steamboats, the *Expedition, Johnson, Calhoun,* and *Jefferson,* were accordingly built or bought. The navigation of the Missouri was uncertain, and Calhoun was severely criticized for obligating the War Department to depend upon an untried method, although a few hopeful and enthusiastic Westerners proclaimed the method to be entirely feasible. In May and June the light steamer *Independence* made a successful trip to Franklin and Chariton,[30] but the voyage by no means demonstrated the practicability of navigation on a large scale. In addition to this proof Calhoun received the emphatic and repeated assurances of Atkinson that "I have not the least doubt of the practicability of navigating the Missouri with steam power, notwithstanding the almost universal opinion to the contrary." [31]

The concentration of a thousand men for the Missouri Expedition was a mobilization of considerable proportions for that day. Troops were moved from Plattsburg, Philadelphia, and Prairie du Chien and were concentrated at Belle Fontaine.[32] Some of the troops reached St. Louis on board Johnson's steamboats, which arrived on May 12, 17, and 19.[33] The Sixth Regiment left Plattsburg on March 11 and reached Pittsburg on May 2, where it was delayed six days because the contractor failed to have transports ready.[34] It reached St. Louis on June 6.[35] Atkinson had preceded his regiment, having arrived on June 1 aboard the steamboat *St. Louis.*[36] Atkinson congratulated the

[29] The contracts are summarized in House Document No. 110, House Documents, 16th Congress, 2d Session, 8:258, and the third one is given in full on pages 6–7. See also *American State Papers: Military Affairs,* 2:68, 324.

[30] *Missouri Intelligencer,* May 28, June 4, 11, 1819, July 20.

[31] House Document No. 110, House Documents, 16th Congress, 2d Session, 8:159, 160, 161, 163–65.

[32] *American State Papers: Military Affairs,* 2:31.

[33] *St. Louis Enquirer,* May 19, 1819; *Missouri Gazette,* May 26, 1819.

[34] Atkinson to the Adjutant General, March 11, April 8, 18, May 2, 22, 1819, Letters Received, Old Files Section, Adjutant General's Office; *Niles' Weekly Register,* 16:143.

[35] *Missouri Gazette,* June 9, 1819; *St. Louis Enquirer,* June 9, 1819.

[36] *Missouri Gazette,* June 2, 1819; *Atkinson to Calhoun,* June 7, 1819, in House Document No. 110, House Documents, 16th Congress, 2d Session, 8:159.

regiment on its good conduct during the long journey from Plattsburg and pointed out that the journey was still incomplete. He asked that every man be ready to move on short notice and informed them that they were to be transported in steamboats to Council Bluffs, "where permanent arrangements" would be made for their accommodation. "The Council Bluffs are situated in the finest climate, & district of the country, in America, & may be, justly esteemed, the most desirable post, on the Continent—" [37]

The brief stop that Atkinson contemplated grew into weeks before the main body of troops began their ascent of the Missouri. The delay was caused by the necessity of unpacking the supplies for inspection, by the necessity of repairing the steamboat, and by Johnson's legal battles with the Bank of Missouri. Johnson objected to unpacking the supplies for inspection on the ground that they were already government property, but the quartermaster refused to accept them without careful inspection. Since they were Johnson's property until they were accepted by inspectors, he had to submit, but he dared not unload them at St. Louis nor at Belle Fontaine lest they be seized under a writ of attachment, issued for the benefit of the Bank of Missouri, to which Johnson was indebted. An agreement was finally made by which the goods were unloaded, inspected, and repacked on the Illinois side near the mouth of the Missouri. Johnson blamed the quartermaster and inspectors for the delay and they blamed him. Certainly much time would have been saved if the goods could have been inspected at Belle Fontaine.[38]

The movement of troops up the Missouri did not depend

[37] Order of June 8, 1819, Department Orders, Old Records Division, Adjutant General's Office.

[38] It is difficult to arrive at the true explanation of the delay. Johnson arrived at Belle Fontaine with the supplies far behind the contracted time. For a convincing summary of the case against him, see William Wirt's decision, House Document No. 110, House Documents, 16th Congress, 2d Session, 8:258–73. The report of the House committee may be found in *American State Papers: Military Affairs*, 2:324. Johnson had received large sums in advance and so was in an advantageous position.

entirely upon Johnson's steamboats. On June 14 Colonel Talbot Chambers with about two hundred and sixty men of the rifle regiment set out from Belle Fontaine in five keelboats. The troops reached Franklin on July 2 and Fort Osage on July 20. There they awaited the arrival of the main force. In the meantime the main contingent, traveling in keelboats and on the three steamboats that ascended the Missouri, left Belle Fontaine on July 4 and 5.[39] Their ascent was irregular and uncertain. The steamboats ran onto snags and sandbars, blew out pistons, and sprang leaks. They made no attempt to keep together.

The steamboat *Expedition* was fairly well constructed for the navigation of the Missouri and would probably have reached Council Bluffs had it not been for low water. It arrived at Franklin on July 22, at Chariton on August 5, and at Fort Osage on August 16. It left Fort Osage on the twenty-fourth and reached Cantonment Martin three days later, but was unable to proceed because of low water. The cargo was transferred to keelboats, which arrived at Council Bluffs on September 29.[40] The *Johnson,* running less successfully than the *Expedition,* reached Franklin on August 3 and Fort Osage about September 7. About ten miles below the mouth of the Kansas River its machinery gave out, and its load was transferred to keelboats.[41] The *Jefferson* failed to reach Franklin, and its supplies were also transferred to keelboats.[42]

[39] *Missouri Gazette,* June 23, July 14, 21, August 18, September 8, 1819; *Missouri Intelligencer,* July 2, 9, 23, August 20, 1819; *St. Louis Enquirer,* June 16, 1819; Atkinson to Calhoun, June 7, 1819, House Document No. 110, House Documents, 16th Congress, 2d Session, 8:159, 163.

[40] *Missouri Intelligencer,* July 23, August 13, 27, September 3, 17, November 5, 1819; House Document No. 110, House Documents, 16th Congress, 2d Session, 8:163, 167–68; *St. Louis Enquirer,* October 30, November 27, 1819; *Missouri Gazette,* September 15, 22, 29, November 3, 1819.

[41] *Missouri Intelligencer,* August 6, September 17, November 5, 1819; *Missouri Gazette,* November 3, 1819; *St. Louis Enquirer,* November 27, 1819; Atkinson to Calhoun, October 19, 1819; House Document No. 110, House Documents, 16th Congress, 2d Session, 8:169–71. Scattered and not entirely reliable notes about the expedition may be found in *Niles' Weekly Register,* 16:320, 368; 17:44, 96, 143, 160, 288.

[42] *Missouri Intelligencer,* August 13, 18, 19; Atkinson to Calhoun, August 13, 1819, House Document No. 110, House Documents, 16th Congress, 2d Session, 8:163–65. Johnson's favorable reports of his progress and success are recorded in

During the summer and fall, while the troops were making their slow ascent of the Missouri, the public attitude toward the expedition was materially altered. Johnson's delay in delivering the supplies, the deficiency of his steamboats, and his legal troubles with the Bank of Missouri placed the whole expedition in an unfavorable light. When the plans had been announced, they had been greeted with universal approval by western editors, and only the cautious had expressed a doubt as to the wisdom of using steamboats on the untried waters of the Missouri. But when the contractor failed to meet his engagements promptly, when he became embroiled in a quarrel with a bank, he forfeited the confidence of many persons, and the expedition itself became the object of unmerited ridicule.

The chief spokesman of this changed attitude was the owner of the *St. Louis Enquirer,* Thomas Hart Benton, who was also interested in the Bank of Missouri. He soon made his influence felt against the whole expedition. There is no denying that the contracts for transportation were unwise [43] and that the provisions were hopelessly inadequate, but the *Enquirer* included the expedition itself in its criticisms instead of confining them to the real point at issue. The criticisms were severe and not entirely unmerited, but to some extent they were based on mistakes of fact.[44] The *Enquirer* was rebuked by more than one editor for its attitude.[45] But its criticisms furnished a weapon for Calhoun's enemies, for those who opposed a large army, and incidentally for those who posed as defenders of the treasury. The unwise contracts and the unwise criticisms finally brought about a rigid curtailment of the expedition.

The changed attitude toward the expedition is clearly shown

the *Argus of Western America,* April 2, 9, May 14, 28, June 4, 11, July 9, August 13, 20, September 3, October 29, 1819.

[43] It is very certain that all the blame for liberality in dealing with Johnson cannot be placed upon Calhoun. On July 5, 1819, Monroe ordered Calhoun to advance $50,000 to Johnson and $57,500 additional upon the delivery of the four steamboats. *American State Papers: Military Affairs,* 2:69.

[44] *St. Louis Enquirer,* July 14, 21, 28, August 11, September 4, October 9, 30, November 27, 1819.

[45] *Edwardsville Spectator,* September 11, 1819; *Niles' Weekly Register,* 17:288; *Missouri Gazette,* September 22, 1819; *Missouri Intelligencer,* July 30, 1819; *Argus of Western America,* August 13, 20, September 3, 1819.

by Atkinson's letters, but he, naturally, did not confuse the method of transportation with the expedition itself. His approval of the use of steamboats was hearty and enthusiastic, and not until the boats demonstrated their poor mechanism did he voice any complaint. His letter addressed to Calhoun from St. Charles on July 11 was the first to express any anxiety, and then it was merely a lament that transportation had been placed in the hands of others than the quartermaster. As late as August 13 he had no fear of the failure of the *Expedition* and *Johnson,* but on the following day he repeated that the management of transportation should not have been taken from the quartermaster general. He declared that keelboats, although slower, were much surer. He also expanded upon the advantages of buying supplies in the Boon's Lick country, thereby saving time, cost, and transportation.[46]

As noted before, Atkinson, the rifle regiment, and five and a half companies of the Sixth Regiment arrived at Council Bluffs on September 29. Atkinson selected a rich bottom tract one mile above the bluffs as the site for the fort and put the men to work. Other contingents arrived and joined in the work of erecting barracks. By October 19 they were ready for the roofing. The whole fort was 520 feet square and the barrack rooms were 20 by 20. Because of the deficiency in supplies Atkinson contracted for two hundred beef cattle, which were delivered about the middle of October. In order to facilitate communication, he ordered the survey and cutting of a road from Council Bluffs to Chariton, and the latter town became the postoffice for the troops.[47]

In the meantime Long's party had arrived and established themselves five miles below Camp Missouri, the name temporarily given to the encampment at Council Bluffs. The *Western Engineer,* built at Pittsburg and launched on March 26,

[46] House Document No. 110, House Documents, 16th Congress, 2d Session, 8:159, 160, 161, 162, 163–65, 166.
[47] *Ibid.,* pp. 168–71; *Missouri Intelligencer,* November 5, 1819; *Missouri Gazette,* November 3, December 15, 1819. Chariton, a few miles above Franklin, contained thirty families in 1819. Peck, *Memoir,* p. 143.

1819, had made the voyage successfully.[48] Its strange appearance, resembling that of a huge serpent, was well calculated to inspire awe and did not seem to interfere with its mechanical construction.[49] It left St. Louis on June 21, reached Franklin on July 13, and arrived at Fort Osage on August 1. At Cow Island the scientific corps was assigned a guard of fifteen men in a keelboat. The entire expedition reached Fort Lisa, just below Council Bluffs, on September 17 and immediately began the erection of quarters, which were known as Engineer Cantonment.[50]

The troops were scarcely settled at Council Bluffs before a legislative battle began that was to result in the frustration of Calhoun's plans for an advance up the Missouri. On December 21 the House requested that it be informed of the objects and expense of the expedition. When the information was furnished, additional inquiries were made, and the Johnson contracts were demanded.[51] As a result of the agitation over the contracts, the House insisted upon cutting the appropriations of the quartermaster's department in order to stop the progress of the expedition and confine it to Council Bluffs. It was denounced as useless, expensive, and dangerous—useless because it was not directed against the Great Lakes region, the real source of British influence, expensive because of the vast distances, dangerous because it would create a string of settlements impossible to defend. In spite of Calhoun's warning that little, if anything, would be saved by curtailing the expedition and in spite of the stubborn resistance of the Senate, the House finally had its way, and the appropriations were cut down so that the expedition could not proceed.[52]

[48] *Missouri Gazette*, April 28, 1819.

[49] Full descriptions may be found in the *National Intelligencer*, July 17, 1819; *St. Louis Enquirer*, June 19, 1819; *Missouri Intelligencer*, May 21, June 25, 1819; *Niles' Weekly Register*, 16:368; James, *Long's Expedition*, in Thwaites, *Early Western Travels*, 14:178.

[50] James, *Long's Expedition*, pp. 121, 148, 161, 221, 222.

[51] *Annals of Congress*, 16th Congress, 1st Session, pp. 750, 848, 936, 1047; House Document No. 110, House Documents, 16th Congress, 2d Session, 8:6–7, 258; *American State Papers: Military Affairs*, 2:31–34, 68–69; *Niles' Weekly Register*, 17:329.

[52] *Annals of Congress*, 16th Congress, 1st Session, pp. 545, 549–50, 555, 598–99, 1634, 1783–90, 1807, 1821, 2142.

The Missouri Expedition had reached its destination. It was not the mouth of the Yellowstone, or the Mandan villages, or even the Great Bend, but Council Bluffs. A series of events had brought ridicule upon it. Contemporary critics confused the contracts for transportation, the unwise advances of money, Johnson's legal battles with the Bank of Missouri, the failure of the steamboats, and Benton's attacks with the expedition itself, and so it is not surprising that subsequent writers have fallen into the same errors. The plan for occupying the Yellowstone or the Mandan villages may or may not have been a wise one. Calhoun intended no such occupation until intermediate posts had been established. Congress saw fit to stop the expedition when it had occupied the first intermediate post, but it is certain that the plans themselves were not the cause of the action of Congress. Thus Calhoun's original plans cannot be judged in the light of accomplishment, since they were never carried out. The nearest one can come to applying a fair test is to consider the wisdom of the establishment of Fort Atkinson. A new post several hundred miles beyond the frontier was established. The military frontier line was extended at one stroke to include areas that would by the process of settlement have required decades to occupy. Forts far behind the new line could be and were abandoned.[53] The Indians on the Great Plains realized for the first time the strength and greatness of the United States. Judged by a pragmatic standard, the Missouri Expedition was no failure.

While the expedition was proceeding on its way, the movement on the Mississippi was also in progress. Plans for the post at the mouth of the Minnesota had been made in conjunction with those for the Missouri post.[54] Long's voyage of 1817 had been made for the purpose of selecting sites for forts, and he had examined and approved the position near the mouth of the Minnesota.[55] The fact that the post was to be built was public

[53] See Chapter IX.
[54] See *supra*, pp. 144–47.
[55] Long, "Voyage in a Six-Oared Skiff to the Falls of Saint Anthony in 1817," Minnesota Historical Collections, 2:41.

knowledge as early as September, 1818.[56] Calhoun instructed General Brown to order the movement of troops to the Mississippi.[57] Brown's order of February 10, 1819, directed the concentration of the Fifth Regiment at Detroit preparatory to the westward movement. Two detachments left Detroit about May 10; on May 14 Colonel Henry Leavenworth left with about ninety men and reached Prairie du Chien on June 30.[58] A delay of more than a month ensued because of Johnson's tardiness in sending supplies and in transporting a detachment of the Fifth from Belle Fontaine. Ninety men from the Fifth were sent to Belle Fontaine to join the rifle regiment of the Missouri Expedition and twenty-seven men were sent to Fort Armstrong.[59]

The arrival of supplies on August 2 enabled the expedition to proceed, and Leavenworth decided not to wait for the additional troops.[60] On August 8 they set out, accompanied by Thomas Forsyth,[61] the Indian agent, who was sent to make treaties and assure the Indians of the kindly intentions of the United States. They arrived at the mouth of the Minnesota on August 24 and set to work preparing winter quarters. On September 1, 120 recruits arrived, bringing the total to 235.[62] In spite of delays the Mississippi Expedition was successful, and the troops were well established before winter.[63]

[56] *Missouri Gazette,* October 2, 1818.

[57] Calhoun to Brown, October 17, 1818, in Jameson, *Correspondence of John Caldwell Calhoun,* p. 147.

[58] *Detroit Gazette,* May 14, 1819, February 18, 1820; *Missouri Gazette,* March 1, 1820; Forsyth, "Narrative," Minnesota Historical Collections, 3:145. A detailed account of the march from Green Bay to Fort Crawford was made by Captain Henry Whiting. Reports of the Corps of Engineers, 1812–23, pp. 397–411.

[59] *Missouri Gazette,* June 23, September 22, 1819, March 1, 1820; Minnesota Historical Collections, 3:148; *Niles' Weekly Register,* 16:440.

[60] The *Detroit Gazette* (October 1, 22, 1819) shows a natural sectional pride by calling attention to the superiority and economy of the lake route over the Mississippi route.

[61] Forsyth received his order to accompany the expedition on March 15, 1819. Tesson Collection, Missouri Historical Society.

[62] Fifth Regiment Returns, December, 1819, Officers' Record Division, Adjutant General's Office; Minnesota Historical Collections, 3:149–54, 156. For fuller accounts see Folwell, *A History of Minnesota,* vol. 1, chap. 6; Hansen, *Old Fort Snelling, 1819–1858,* chap. 2.

[63] Calhoun congratulated Brown upon the facility with which the Fifth had moved over to Prairie du Chien. Jameson, *Correspondence of John Caldwell Calhoun,* p. 163; *Missouri Gazette,* January 5, 1820.

Affairs at the new forts were none too cheerful. At both places the troops suffered dreadfully from scurvy. Forty men died at the post on the Minnesota,[64] and at Camp Missouri half the garrison was sick and nearly one hundred died.[65] At both forts the quarters were badly located, and removals to better sites were made in the spring. At Camp Missouri there was a scarcity of wood, and much sickness and suffering resulted. Spring brought relief, and sickness gradually decreased. Only one man died between April 15 and October 1. New barracks, covered with shingles and equipped with good brick chimneys, were erected at Camp Missouri, and immense crops of corn, turnips, and potatoes were raised.[66]

Calhoun reported to the House on January 3, 1820, that five objects were contemplated for the season of 1820: (1) to move the rifle regiment on up the Missouri to the Mandan villages and erect barracks for five hundred men; (2) to remove obstructions in the Missouri; (3) to open a road from Chariton to Council Bluffs and on to the Mandan villages; (4) to open a road from Council Bluffs to the mouth of the Minnesota; and (5) to connect the Fox and Wisconsin rivers by a canal or road.[67]

The first object was defeated by the reduced appropriation. The second involved great expense and so was not undertaken. The road from Chariton to Council Bluffs was surveyed by Atkinson's order,[68] and Calhoun approved the project.[69] The road was made within the year by a group of men under Lieutenant Fields.[70] On April 20 Calhoun ordered Atkinson to send an

---

[64] Doty, "Official Journal, 1820," Wisconsin Historical Collections, 13:214.

[65] Inspection Reports, Inspector General's Office, January-February, 1820; Missouri Intelligencer, May 14, 1820. An early report said that the soldiers were recovering. Missouri Gazette, February 23, 1820.

[66] Atkinson to Calhoun, October 18, 1820, in Missouri Intelligencer, February 5, 1821; St. Louis Enquirer, July 15, 1820.

[67] American State Papers: Military Affairs, 2:32.

[68] Atkinson to Calhoun, October 19, 1819, House Document No. 110, House Documents, 16th Congress, 2d Session, 8:171.

[69] Calhoun to Atkinson, February 7, 1820, in Jameson, Correspondence of John Caldwell Calhoun, pp. 168–71.

[70] Missouri Intelligencer, November 26, 1819; Atkinson to Calhoun, October 18, 1820, ibid., February 5, 1821.

exploring party to mark a route to the mouth of the St. Peter's.[71] Stephen Watts Kearny, acting adjutant at Council Bluffs, issued the order directing Captain Matthew J. Magee to take fifteen men and mark the route.[72] The party set out on July 2 and crossed what is now Iowa in a northeasterly direction. They reached the Mississippi several miles below the fort and ascended the river, arriving at the mouth of the Minnesota after a journey of twenty-three days. They reported that the scarcity of wood and water and the rugged character of the hills rendered the route impracticable except for small parties.[73]

Those who had claimed that steamboats could navigate the Missouri saw the fulfillment of their prophecies in 1820. Early in April the two stranded steamboats, the *Expedition* and the *Johnson,* descended the river.[74] The former left St. Louis for Council Bluffs on May 19 and arrived at its destination on July 23. It was claimed that the voyage could be made in thirty days. The *Western Engineer* made the trip from Council Bluffs to Franklin in four running days.[75] In 1821, when the *Washington* traveled from St. Louis to Franklin in six days, the editor of the Franklin paper observed, "The practicability of navigating the Missouri with safety and facility may be considered as established beyond the possibility of doubt."[76]

Major Benjamin O'Fallon, Indian agent for the Missouri, was active in promoting good relations with the Indians, and the troops assisted by impressive parades. The wonders of a moving steamboat were shown to the collected natives by putting the *Expedition* in motion.[77] O'Fallon's efforts to promote peace with the Indians were not entirely successful. In the spring of 1820 Bernard Pratte, Jr., a fur trader, was attacked several miles above Camp Missouri and lost all his furs. Early in August two

[71] Brown Letter Books, 2:180–81.
[72] Department Orders, Old Records Division, Adjutant General's Office.
[73] Porter, "Journal of Stephen Watts Kearny," Missouri Historical Collections, 3:8–29, 99–131. An excellent map is furnished by the editor.
[74] *Missouri Intelligencer,* April 8, 1820.
[75] *Ibid.,* May 27, June 24, August 5, 1820.
[76] *Ibid.,* April 30, 1821.
[77] *Ibid.,* February 5, 1821.

Frenchmen belonging to Manuel Lisa's post were killed. The
St. Louis Enquirer, which reported these incidents, declared that
the Mandan villages had to be occupied if Congress did not want
the Northwest Company to obtain the fur trade.[78] This paper,
notwithstanding its temporary criticisms of the expedition,
consistently urged the advance of the troops.

In 1820 Fort Atkinson[79] made great progress toward self-
support. A large sawmill was erected to supply the lumber
necessary for new buildings. Fifteen thousand bushels of corn
and great herds of cattle and hogs were raised.[80] In 1821 General Atkinson was placed in charge of the Western Department,
and Leavenworth took command of the Sixth Regiment at Fort
Atkinson.[81] The number of troops varied, but at all times it was
considerably larger than at any other frontier post. They numbered in 1820, 851;[82] in 1821, 548; in 1822, 490; in 1823, 379; in
1824, 423; in 1825, 694; in 1826, 472; and in April, 1827, 490.[83]

The long-deferred advance up the Missouri was finally made
in 1823, but in a manner totally unforeseen and with temporary
and perhaps unimportant results. In that year William H. Ashley, owner and leader of the Rocky Mountain Fur Company,
ascended the Missouri on his way to the mountains. As Ashley's
outfit passed the Arikara villages on June 2, they were attacked;
fourteen men were killed and eleven wounded, and some property was taken. Ashley notified Benjamin O'Fallon, Indian agent,
of the disaster. The letter was shown to Leavenworth, who decided that the occasion required action and that his instructions
gave him authority to proceed against the Indians.[84]

[78] June 7, September 23, 1820.
[79] Camp Missouri became Fort Atkinson by the explicit order of Calhoun.
Calhoun to Atkinson, January 5, 1821, Military Books, Old Records Division,
Adjutant General's Office.
[80] *St. Louis Enquirer,* October 13, 1821, April 27, 1822.
[81] Heitman, *Register of the United States Army,* 1:174, 622. He was transferred
on October 1 and left Washington for Council Bluffs on October 3. *National Intelligencer,* October 6, 1821.
[82] *Annals of Congress,* 16th Congress, 2d Session, p. 879. The *American State
Papers: Military Affairs,* 2:37, give the number as 1,120, which included those
at Belle Fontaine and Fort Osage.
[83] Post Returns, Officers' Record Division, Adjutant General's Office; *American
State Papers: Military Affairs,* 2:456, 558, 706; 3:115.
[84] News of the war caused a general movement of troops toward the Missouri.
Six companies from Baton Rouge were ordered to the scene of trouble, but they

On June 22 the troops, numbering two hundred and twenty, with some small artillery began the ascent of the river in four keelboats. One of the boats ran onto a snag and sank, causing the death of seven men, the only fatalities among the whites during the war. Joshua Pilcher, president of the Missouri Fur Company and a sub-agent under O'Fallon, decided to accompany the punitive expedition and added about forty men to the regulars. He also persuaded some four or five hundred Sioux to become allies. Ashley's force of about eighty men brought the total expedition to about eight hundred when it was assembled before the Arikara villages.

The expedition reached and attacked the villages on August 9. Two Sioux and thirteen Arikara were killed, but the attack was not very spirited nor very determined. On the next day the attack was renewed, but the artillery fire was ineffectual and did no great damage, although it terrorized the Arikara. The eleventh was spent in peace negotiations, for the Indians were willing to make terms. Pilcher, disgusted with Leavenworth's pusillanimity, as he regarded it, refused to draw up the treaty and consented to it only under protest. Leavenworth considered that the objects of the expedition had been attained and drew up the treaty, which provided for the return of Ashley's stolen goods, for good conduct toward the traders in the future, and for peace with the United States. The Indians restored part of the goods, and Leavenworth accepted the partial fulfillment of the agreement. During the night they deserted their villages and on August 15, after a vain search for them, the troops began their return. Just as the troops withdrew, the villages were set on fire, much to the regret of Leavenworth, who charged Pilcher and his *engagés* with the act. Pilcher denied the charge, although he justified the destruction of the villages. The troops returned to Fort Atkinson.[85]

were halted at Belle Fontaine. Department Orders, Old Records Division, Adjutant General's Office; *Detroit Gazette,* September 19, 1823; *Niles' Weekly Register,* 15:32.
[86] Information about the Arikara War is fairly full. The official correspondence may be found in South Dakota Historical Collections, 1:181–256. This is the most

The expedition was successful in its immediate object of rescuing Ashley's men and securing at least a part of their stolen property, but it was unsuccessful in impressing the Indians. Pilcher, angered by Leavenworth's order refusing the further help of the Missouri Fur Company and displeased with the conduct of the campaign, wrote a most violent and abusive letter to the general, who seems to have ignored it.[86]

A further result of the war was to open the whole question of the moral right of the whites to hunt furs on Indian lands. On December 30 Charles Rich of Vermont introduced a resolution in the House of Representatives asking that laws be framed to restrain citizens from trespassing on Indian lands. He said that the Arikara War was caused by intruding fur traders and cited Atkinson and Ashley as authorities for his statement. The resolution was adopted.[87] Niles thought that the Indians owned the fur-bearing animals just as whites owned livestock and that the whites had no right to hunt on unceded land.[88] O'Fallon said that Americans did not hunt on Indian lands and that no beaver nor bears were to be found in the Mandan or Arikara country.[89] The *St. Louis Enquirer* objected most vehemently to Rich's resolution, declaring that Americans had as much right to the furs on the east side of the Rockies as the Russians had to those on the west side, and that fur traders deserved protection as much as Cape Cod fishermen, Nantucket whalers, and New York and Boston China merchants. It bitterly assailed the idea of refusing protection because the fur trade produced no direct revenue.[90]

important source and formed the basis of Chittenden's account (*American Fur Trade*, vol. 2, chap. 3), which is partial to Pilcher and consequently uncomplimentary to Leavenworth. Further information may be found in *American State Papers*, 2:454. Dale's account (*Ashley-Smith Explorations*, pp. 71–85) contains some errors, resulting from his use of scattered newspaper reprints of the official letters instead of the collected and correct version cited above.

[86] *St. Louis Enquirer*, October 13, 25, December 20, 1823.
[87] *Annals of Congress*, 18th Congress, 1st Session, pp. 896–97.
[88] *Niles' Weekly Register*, 24:393.
[89] *St. Louis Enquirer*, February 9, 1824; *American State Papers: Indian Affairs*, 2:454.
[90] February 9, 16, 1824.

While these events were taking place on the Missouri, the fort at the mouth of the Minnesota was being built. In the spring of 1820 Colonel Leavenworth chose the permanent site, and the barracks were erected under the supervision of Colonel Josiah Snelling, who succeeded Leavenworth in August. The post soon became known as Fort St. Anthony because of its proximity to the falls of that name; the name Fort Snelling was adopted upon the recommendation of General Scott, who inspected it in the spring of 1824. The presence of the troops impressed the Indians, and the few who remained at Selkirk's colony on the Red River wished to be under the protection of the United States.[91]

Various expeditions visited the fort during the first few years. On July 25, 1820, Captain Magee's party arrived from Council Bluffs, having tried to find a practicable route for a road between the posts. They were well received by the officers, "who were a little astonished at the sight of us, we having been the First Whites that ever crossed at such a distance from the Missouri to the Mississippi river." [92] Only five days later Cass arrived from the upper Mississippi. He stayed at the post for three days and held a council with the Indians. The official secretary of Cass's party noted that preparations for the new fort were under way.[93]

Long's expedition of 1823 arrived at the fort on July 3 and remained six days. When it left, twenty-one soldiers from the garrison and Joseph Snelling, son of the colonel, accompanied the expedition. Long ascended the Minnesota River and descended the Red to Pembina. There his astronomer ascertained that the forty-ninth parallel of latitude ran just north of the town. Long found that it was impracticable to follow the route directly eastward to Lake Superior and so returned in canoes by way of Lake Winnipeg, Lake of the Woods, and the Great

[91] *Niles' Weekly Register*, 21:224; *Detroit Gazette*, May 24, 1822, May 28, 1824; Hansen, *Old Fort Snelling*, pp. 29–30.
[92] Porter, "Journal of Stephen Watts Kearny," *Missouri Historical Collections*, 3:105–06.
[93] Schoolcraft, *Narrative Journal*, pp. 292–315; Doty, "Official Journal, 1820," *Wisconsin Historical Collections*, 13:212–16.

Lakes. He reported that no military force could attack the United States west of Lake Superior because the region was "a sterile dreary waste" three or four hundred miles wide and fourteen hundred miles long. Nature had thus protected the nation, and no forts were needed.[94]

Comprehensive and far-flung as was Calhoun's plan for the northwestern frontier, it failed to include enough territory to satisfy many western expansionists. Agitation for the occupation of Oregon was renewed soon after the end of the War of 1812. Commodore D. Porter, in writing to Madison on October 31, 1815, suggested a voyage to the Pacific,[95] and the *Missouri Gazette* gave a detailed scheme for the erection and location of a string of thirteen posts from the mouth of the Kansas to the mouth of the Columbia.[96] It estimated the average distance between the posts at two hundred and sixty miles and proposed a force of two thousand men for garrison duty. The fur traders were much interested in the scheme. The *Detroit Gazette* argued that the Missouri Expedition was sent out not to repel Indians, in which case the posts would be established near the settlements, but to counteract British influence and to secure the route to Oregon. It urged attention to that region.[97]

Beyond the reoccupation of Astoria in 1817[98] and the partial recognition accorded by the Convention of 1818 with England, no further efforts were made toward the occupation of Oregon until Congress assembled in December, 1820. John Floyd, at the suggestion of Benton, introduced a resolution inquiring into the expediency of occupying the Columbia River.[99] He declared that

[94] Keating, *Long's Expedition*, 1: map; 312, 314; 2:46–47, 242–43. Long's recommendation is noted later; see *infra*, p. 165. The details of his expedition are accessible and are summarized here merely to show the basis of his recommendation.

[95] *National Intelligencer*, January 29, 1816, republished January 25, 1821; *Niles' Weekly Register*, 20:21–25. Captain Thomas Biddle's letter of December 6, 1817, proposing a similar scheme may be found in Letters Received, Old Records Division, Adjutant General's Office.

[96] November 9, 1816.

[97] October 15, 1819.

[98] Greenhow, *Oregon and California*, p. 304.

[99] Benton, *Thirty Years' View*, 1:13.

the Northwest Company had establishments within the United States. He advised that a few troops be placed on the upper Missouri and a small force at the mouth of the Columbia. The resolution was adopted, and the report gave a summary of the fur trade, but no action was taken.[1] Further agitation occurred within the decade,[2] but no military steps were taken. Niles remarked in 1825 that the project of establishing a chain of posts to the Pacific was being agitated again, and he hoped that it would be postponed "yet a little while." [3]

In 1825 there were on the northwestern frontier just two forts, Atkinson and Snelling. The cessation of the advance on the Missouri was due, according to Chittenden, to the scandal growing out of the Johnson contracts of 1819. There is no denying their importance as a political factor in cutting down the appropriations, but other factors entered in to postpone indefinitely the program on which Calhoun had expended so much feeling and thought.[4] The fur traders, who were eager for an advance up the river, overreached themselves and awakened the hostility of the East and the North. The Arikara War was, perhaps, as important in solidifying opposition as any other single event. Humanitarianism, economy, indifference, and sectional interests combined to frustrate all attempts to extend the posts. Another factor was the report Long made after his trip of 1823. He saw no reason for fortifying the northern frontier west of Lake Superior.[5] Finally the Atkinson Expedition of 1825—sometimes, and very properly, called the Yellowstone Expedition—put an authoritative end to the old rumor of British instigation of the Indian disturbances.[6]

[1] *Annals of Congress*, 16th Congress, 2d Session, pp. 946–59.
[2] *Ibid.*, 18th Congress, 1st Session, pp. 890, 1203, 1622–23; 2d Session, pp. 13–28, 36–42, 44, 59, 684, 687–95, 698–713.
[3] *Niles' Weekly Register*, 24:151.
[4] His feeling of disappointment and hostility is revealed in a letter to Benton, February 23, 1824. *American State Papers: Indian Affairs*, 2:448–49.
[5] Keating, *Long's Expedition*, 2:242–43.
[6] Atkinson Journal, 1825, MS. in the Missouri Historical Society; House Document No. 118, House Documents, 19th Congress, 1st Session, 6:118; *American State Papers: Indian Affairs*, 2:605–08.

CHAPTER XI

THE FLORIDA FRONTIER

BECAUSE OF Indian disturbances and international complications the Florida frontier required special attention in the period after the War of 1812. The dissatisfied Creeks who had fled across the border and the Seminole of Florida presented a problem that was made more difficult by the fact that they were the subjects of a foreign power. The conflicting claims of Spain and the United States to West Florida influenced the allocation of troops.[1] The running of the Creek line in accordance with the Treaty of Fort Jackson[2] required the presence of troops, and the removal of Indians and the restraint of intruders required constant vigilance.

One of the first tasks confronting Jackson when he assumed command of the Southern Division in 1815 was the protection of the commissioners who ran the Creek boundary line. The activity of Lieutenant Colonel Edward Nicholls, commander of the British forces in Florida during the War of 1812, had led the Creeks to expect a restoration of the lands lost by the Treaty of Fort Jackson. Nicholls took the unique position that the Indians were a party to the Treaty of Ghent and encouraged them to believe that England would protect their interests. In a letter to Colonel Benjamin Hawkins he complained that settlers were not moving off the Creek lands, "according to the ninth article of the treaty of peace"[3] and protested against the running of the line.[4] General Gaines received information concerning the expectations of the Indians and learned that Nicholls had

[1] Bassett, *Correspondence of Andrew Jackson*, 2:206.
[2] For the terms of the Treaty of Fort Jackson see *supra*, p. 15.
[3] *American State Papers: Foreign Relations*, 4:548–49.
[4] Bassett, *Correspondence of Andrew Jackson*, 2:211.

delivered a fort on the Apalachicola, equipped with cannon and powder, into the hands of the Indians. Outrages by the Creeks lent color to the story of their expectations and probable opposition to running the line.[5]

As soon as Jackson learned of the probable opposition of the Creeks, he ordered troops toward their lands. A company of rangers was ordered to Fort Strother[6] to protect the commissioners until the arrival of the regulars. A detachment was moved from Mobile to Fort Jackson, and recruits from Knoxville were ordered to Fort Deposit.[7] Gaines called on the governor of Georgia to be ready to furnish two thousand militia in the event that the Indians interfered with the marking of the boundary in southern Georgia.[8] Eight hundred regulars were assembled near the junction of the Flint and the Chattahoochee, where they erected temporary quarters, afterwards known as Fort Scott. These precautions overawed the Indians, and the commissioners were enabled to complete their task in safety.[9]

The marking of the Creek line having been practically completed, Jackson planned the erection of a line of forts to exclude foreign influence and afford protection to settlers on the new cession. In the interior troops were already stationed at Forts Hawkins, Hampton, Jackson, and Montgomery, and General Jackson proposed three sites for new posts, one each on the Escambia, the Choctawhatchee, and the Apalachicola near the points where they crossed the Florida line.[10] Early in March, 1816, Jackson ordered Gaines to erect the posts on the Escambia[11] and the Choctawhatchee.[12] Early in April Gaines began the construction of Fort Gaines on the east bank of the Chatta-

[5] *American State Papers: Foreign Relations,* 4:551–52.
[6] For the location of forts see the map on page 112.
[7] Bassett, *Correspondence of Andrew Jackson,* 2:210–11.
[8] *National Intelligencer,* October 24, 30, 1815.
[9] Bassett, *Correspondence of Andrew Jackson,* 2:222; *Niles' Weekly Register,* 9:42–43, 151, 187–88, 202, 215.
[10] Bassett, *Correspondence of Andrew Jackson,* 2:222.
[11] The Escambia above the Florida line was called the Conecuh.
[12] Jackson to Crawford, March 15, 1816, Old Records Division, Adjutant General's Office.

hoochee one mile below the Creek line.[13] Fort Crawford, three miles west of the Conecuh, was established at about the same time. The proposed post on the Choctawhatchee were never erected. In addition to the border posts, Cantonment Montpelier, nine miles northwest of Fort Montgomery, was established the same year. The site was chosen for a large encampment because of its high elevation and healthful surroundings.

The new posts and the large number of troops on the Florida frontier did not insure complete safety for all the settlers. The Indians continued to steal negroes, horses, and cattle, and to commit occasional murders. The marauding Indians found a refuge in the fort on the Apalachicola, which was situated fifteen miles from the mouth of the river and several miles below the boundary of Georgia. It had been erected during the war by the British, who had left a few cannon and a large supply of powder in the hands of the Indians. The fort soon fell into the hands of a motley collection of negroes and a few Seminole and Choctaw. In March, 1816, Crawford ordered Jackson to call the fort to the attention of the Spanish authorities and to recommend its destruction. If they did nothing, the president would decide whether its reduction could be accomplished without the approval of Congress.[14] Jackson ordered Gaines to make inquiries about the fort and expressed the opinion "that it ought to be blown up regardless of the ground it stands on." [15] On April 23 Jackson sent Captain Ferdinand Amelung to carry a letter to the Spanish commandant of Pensacola, in which he demanded that some action be taken to control the band that occupied the negro fort.[16] The commandant, Mauricio de Zuniga, answered that the fort had been erected illegally and that its occupants were outlaws. He assured Jackson that he had reported the matter to the captain general and expressed the hope that the United States would take no steps "prejudicial to the sov-

[13] Gaines to Crawford, April 6, 1816, Old Records Division, Adjutant General's Office.
[14] Bassett, *Correspondence of Andrew Jackson*, 2:236–37.
[15] *Ibid.*, p. 239.
[16] *Ibid.*, pp. 241–42.

ereignty of the King" until he had heard from his government.[17] Amelung gave a favorable report of the intentions of the commandant.[18] Jackson seized upon the point that the Spanish commandant had officially acknowledged that the fort was held by outlaws. He urged Crawford to issue an order for its destruction, since such action would not endanger relations with Spain.[19]

The development of events made an explicit order from Crawford unnecessary. Gaines had ordered Colonel D. L. Clinch to establish a fort near the Florida line below Fort Gaines. As Colonel Clinch moved down the Chattahoochee he encountered some difficulties. The Indians stole thirty cattle, captured two privates who were guarding them, and escaped into Florida. The transportation of supplies to troops below Fort Gaines was a difficult problem, and Gaines determined to have supplies sent up the Apalachicola. He accordingly requested Commodore Daniel T. Patterson at New Orleans to send a gunboat to protect the two transports that conveyed the supplies. Patterson sent Jarius Loomis in command of *Gunboat No. 149* and James Bassett in charge of *Gunboat No. 154* to accompany the transports. The vessels arrived at the mouth of the Apalachicola on July 10.

During the voyage a band of Creeks, friendly to the United States, besieged the negro fort but were unable to capture it. Colonel Clinch with a detachment of regulars joined in the attack, but they also failed to effect its capture. The gunboats ascended the river and reached the fort on July 28. After firing eight shots and learning the correct range, Loomis gave orders for heating a shot. The first hot shot penetrated the magazine. A terrible explosion followed. The fort was blown to pieces and about two hundred and seventy persons — negroes, Indians,

[17] *American State Papers: Foreign Relations*, 4:556–57. Jackson's letter and the commandant's answer are also printed on pages 499–500, where the answer is incorrectly dated March 26 instead of May 26.

[18] Bassett, *Correspondence of Andrew Jackson*, 2:242–43.

[19] Jackson to Crawford, June 15, 1816, *American State Papers: Foreign Relations*, 4:557.

women, and children—were killed.[20] The destruction of the
negro fort was followed by the establishment of Fort Scott on
the right bank of the Flint seven miles above its mouth, but the
fort was maintained for only a short time when the troops were
removed. The buildings and stores were entrusted to a settler.
The Florida Creek band, known as the Red Sticks, drove him
off and plundered the buildings.[21]

The inspection report of John M. Davis, who made a tour of
the southern posts in the spring of 1817, affords a view of conditions on that frontier.[22] Fort Hawkins, one mile east of the
Oakmulgee on the site of what is now East Macon, consisted
of a stockade and two blockhouses. It was large enough for
two companies, but at the time of Davis' visit only a small
detachment was there for the purpose of protecting the factory. Fort Scott was on a high bank above the river and had
well-constructed barracks. It was unoccupied by troops, but a
company had been ordered to put it in readiness. Fort Gaines,
on the east bank of the Chattahoochee, was large enough for the
accommodation of only one company. It consisted of a stockade
and two blockhouses. Supplies had to be transported by wagons
for one hundred miles. Since Fort Scott was not garrisoned, Fort
Gaines was the post nearest and most accessible to the Red
Sticks and the Seminole. Fort Crawford was large enough for
four companies, but the buildings were unfinished and at the
time of Davis' inspection were occupied by only two companies.
It was regarded as a healthful place. Supplies were transported
in wagons from Camp Montgomery, although Gaines planned
to have supplies sent past Pensacola and up the Escambia and
Conecuh. Camp Montgomery, formerly called a fort, was located
ten or twelve miles above the junction of the Alabama and Tombigbee and three miles east of the former. The old fort had

---

[20] The official reports are given in *American State Papers: Foreign Relations*,
4:558–61. Some items are given in the *National Intelligencer*, August 27, September 2, October 9, 1816; *Niles' Weekly Register*, 11:14–15, 37–38.

[21] *American State Papers: Military Affairs*, 2:681.

[22] For a careful description of Alabama at this time, see Abernethy, *The Formation Period in Alabama*.

fallen into ruins, but fairly extensive barracks of round logs had been built for the accommodation of a large force.[23] It was the headquarters for the Seventh Regiment. A hospital was maintained. The buildings at Cantonment Montpelier were almost completed and were occupied by a considerable force.[24] In September, 1817, the forts were garrisoned as follows: Fort Hawkins, 34; Fort Scott, 117; Fort Gaines, 25; Fort Crawford, 95; Camp Montgomery, 368; and Cantonment Montpelier, 368.[25]

The troops were soon to see active service. The Creek War of 1813–14 and the Treaty of Fort Jackson caused many of the Creeks to flee across the Florida border into Spanish territory, and from there they made a series of raids on the frontier. The destruction of the negro fort added fuel to their hatred and furnished them with some new allies from among the Seminole. The dissatisfied Creeks who lived in southern Georgia and northern Florida continually threatened the settlers and tried to prevent the settlement of the Creek cession. Their outrages and threatening attitude caused Gaines to order the reoccupation of Fort Scott. By September, 1817, more than a hundred men were on duty there, and the force was greatly increased after the attack on Lieutenant R. W. Scott, which occurred on November 30. The Seminole War followed. Jackson swept through Florida, captured St. Marks[26] and Fort Barrancas, executed two English subjects, and returned to Tennessee, leaving Florida in the hands of American troops.[27]

In November, 1817, Calhoun ordered Gaines to seize Amelia Island and eject the filibusters. Later orders advised him to return to Fort Scott unless he had already reached Amelia Island, in

[23] It numbered nearly eight hundred in February, 1817.
[24] Inspection Reports, Inspector General's Office, 1814–23, pp. 17–23.
[25] Southern Division Returns, September, 1817, Officers' Record Division, Adjutant General's Office.
[26] For the location of forts see the map on page 112.
[27] The causes, engagements, and diplomatic aspects of the Seminole War do not fall within the scope of this study, but the changes that the war brought about in the military situation will receive attention. Information on the war may be found in *American State Papers: Military Affairs*, 1:680–769; *American State Papers: Indian Affairs*, 2:154–62; Bassett, *Correspondence of Andrew Jackson*, vols. 2 and 3, *passim;* Bassett, *Life of Jackson*, 1:233–93.

which event he was to return through Florida and assist in the attack on the Indians. Gaines did not go to Amelia Island, and on December 23 it was occupied without opposition by Major James Bankhead with a detachment from Charleston. The two movements against Florida occurred at about the same time and rendered American occupation more complete.[28]

Jackson's invasion of Florida necessitated a new allocation of troops and an extension of defense plans. In June, 1818, the forces in Florida were distributed as follows: at Fort Gadsden, which Jackson had erected on the site of the old negro fort, 338; at St. Marks, 243; at Pensacola, 418; and at Amelia Island, 239.[29] In addition to the fortifications in Florida, a post was established at Trader's Hill on the north side of the St. Mary's River, a few miles above its mouth. Calhoun advised that it be guarded with special care,[30] and about one hundred men were stationed there. Two companies of rangers patrolled the country between Mobile and the Apalachicola. The removal of the artificial boundary of the thirty-first parallel simplified the problem of defense, for the attempt to secure the frontier by a chain of posts as long as Florida was open to every enemy was, according to Jackson, "visionary in the extreme."[31] In August, 1818, he advised Gaines to capture St. Augustine and imprison or deport the garrison.[32] He ordered Captain James Gadsden of the Corps of Engineers to draw up a plan for the defense of the coast, including Florida, which Jackson hoped would be permanently retained.[33]

Jackson's invasion of Florida interrupted the negotiations for its transfer to the United States. While the invasion strengthened the probability of the eventual cession of Florida, it undoubtedly

---

[28] Bassett, *Correspondence of Andrew Jackson*, 2:342; *Niles' Weekly Register*, 13:190, 348. For an account of the preceding phase of the history of Amelia Island, see Davis, "MacGregor's Invasion of Florida, 1817," in the *Florida Historical Society Quarterly*, 7:3–71.

[29] Southern Division Returns, June, 1818, Officers' Record Division, Adjutant General's Office.

[30] Jameson, *Correspondence of John Caldwell Calhoun*, p. 146.

[31] In spite of the fact that Florida had not been ceded, Jackson expected its permanent retention.

[32] Bassett, *Correspondence of Andrew Jackson*, 2:380, 384.

[33] *Ibid.*, p. 386.

weakened the diplomatic position of the United States with respect to its claim to Texas. Compensation for the loss of Texas was found in the relinquishment by Spain of its claims to the Oregon country.[34] The signing of the treaty on February 22, 1819, brought about an unusual situation. Spain had demanded the withdrawal of American troops from Florida, and the condition had not been met when the treaty was signed. In March, 1819, American troops were stationed at Amelia Island, St. Marks, Pensacola, Barrancas, and Fort Gadsden, but they were to be withdrawn from territory that had, according to Adams,[35] already become American soil. By June, 1819, the American troops had been withdrawn from all the Florida posts except Fort Gadsden, which was garrisoned by 192 men.[36] American troops continued to occupy it until the final ratifications of the Treaty of 1819.

The delay in the ratification of the treaty by Spain aroused Monroe's anger. On November 22, 1819, he ordered Christopher Van Deventer, chief clerk of the War Department,[37] to inform Jackson that a rapid military movement into Florida might be ordered shortly after the assembling of Congress. Gaines was ordered to withdraw the troops from Trader's Hill and Jackson was to assemble his forces on the Alabama. Troops from the Northern Division were to move south and reduce eastern Florida. Final orders depended upon news from the American minister at Madrid.[38] On December 7 Monroe asked Congress to decide upon the wisdom of carrying out the treaty "in the same manner as if it had been ratified by Spain."[39] He was willing, however, to suspend the operation of a law authorizing the seizure of Florida and to await the arrival of a new Spanish

[34] Marshall, *Western Boundary of the Louisiana Purchase*, pp. 46–70.
[35] *American State Papers: Foreign Relations*, 4:657–58.
[36] Southern Division Returns, March, 1819, Returns of Eastern Section, Southern Division, June, 1819, Officers' Record Division, Adjutant General's Office. Amelia Island was also held, but it scarcely belongs in the same category as the other Florida posts.
[37] Calhoun was in South Carolina and was unable to return on account of sickness.
[38] Brown Letter Books, 2:168.
[39] Richardson, *Messages and Papers of the Presidents*, 2:57.

envoy, who was said to be on his way. Jackson was in his normal frame of mind and promised, "with the smiles of heaven I will endeavour to place once more the american Eagle upon the ramparts" of the Florida posts.[40] In spite of a strong report by the Committee on Foreign Relations favoring the occupation of Florida, no action was taken by Congress. In fact, Monroe requested on March 27, 1820, that Congress take no action. He gave as the reasons for his request the revolution in Spain and the friendly intercession of other powers.[41] Calhoun was glad to avoid the expense of a campaign, for he feared that it would endanger the appropriations for his department.[42]

The movement into Florida, the temporary occupation, the withdrawal of some troops, and the contemplated reoccupation naturally produced many changes in the location of troops. After the construction of Fort Scott and the barracks at Trader's Hill, both of which were on the Florida border, the continued occupation of Forts Gaines and Hawkins was unnecessary. Early in 1820 Jackson rearranged his forces with a view to the early seizure of Florida.[43] By June they were located as follows: Fort Scott, 595; Cantonment Montpelier, 368; Encampment Blakely, 110; Fort Gadsden, 194. Mere guards were stationed at other posts.[44] Jackson insisted upon maintaining the garrison at Fort Gadsden, and Major A. C. W. Fanning, who was in charge of the fort, strengthened it by erecting a row of pickets, digging a ditch, and resetting the cannon. In spite of the unhealthful location the maintenance of the post was regarded as necessary because of the proximity of the Spanish garrison at St. Marks.[45]

The patience of Monroe was finally rewarded, and in October, 1820, the Spanish government ratified the cession of Florida.

[40] Bassett, *Correspondence of Andrew Jackson*, 2:446, 447, 448; Jameson, *Correspondence of John Caldwell Calhoun*, pp. 165, 167–68.

[41] Richardson, *Messages and Papers of the Presidents*, 2:70.

[42] Jameson, *Correspondence of John Caldwell Calhoun*, p. 171.

[43] His plans were outlined in detail on January 10. Bassett, *Correspondence of Andrew Jackson*, 3:2–6.

[44] Eastern Section, Southern Division Returns, June, 1820, Officers' Record Division, Adjutant General's Office. Blakely was on the Gulf, southeast of Mobile. It was a place for the storage of rations.

[45] Inspection Reports, Inspector General's Office, 1814–23, pp. 128–29.

Because of the lapse of the time limit appended to the treaty, a second ratification by the Senate was necessary. This was voted on February 21, 1821, and formal ratifications were exchanged on the following day.[46] The Florida border ceased to be of international importance, and the American occupation was attended with no opposition. St. Marks, Pensacola, and St. Augustine were occupied by American troops. Fort Gadsden was abandoned, and new encampments were established near Pensacola. The coast fortifications were strengthened, and Cantonment Brooke was established on Tampa Bay.[47]

With the final occupation of Florida the southern frontier ceased to be of importance from a military standpoint. The Seminole and Creeks required some restraint, and the control and removal of other tribes necessitated the performance of routine duties by the army, but no further major operations were necessary within the decade from 1815 to 1825.

[46] Marshall, *Western Boundary of the Louisiana Purchase*, p. 70.

[47] Western Department Returns, Officers' Record Division, Adjutant General's Office.

CHAPTER XII

THE SOUTHWESTERN FRONTIER

THE DEFENSE of the southwestern frontier had two phases: the control of the Indians and the maintenance of order along the Louisiana-Texas border. Both phases continued throughout the decade, though the supervision of the border was not adequately performed until 1819 and the troops required for the control of the Indians were not sent in any considerable numbers until the termination of the Florida troubles. From 1815 until 1819 such forces as were in the Southwest were occupied with the control of the domestic tribes. After that, troops that had been stationed on the Florida frontier were available, and the adequate policing of the border, as well as the control of the Indians, was possible.

At the close of the War of 1812 Fort Claiborne at Natchitoches was the only post on the southwestern frontier. In the summer of 1815 Jackson ordered two companies of the rifle regiment to proceed from Smithland, at the mouth of the Cumberland, to Natchitoches.[1] About a year later two more companies were sent to Fort Claiborne; in February, 1817, the garrison numbered 154.[2] In 1816 Baton Rouge was selected as the distributing point for the western part of the Eighth Department, and the building of extensive barracks was begun. In February, 1817, the troops at that point numbered 308, which number was increased or decreased from time to time as the needs of the department required.[3] For two or three years the troops found little to do aside from routine duties, but in the meantime the Indian situation slowly changed.

[1] *Missouri Gazette,* September 2, 1815; *Niles' Weekly Register,* 10:57.
[2] Southern Division Returns, Officers' Record Division, Adjutant General's Office; *Missouri Gazette,* November 9, 1816; *Niles' Weekly Register,* 11:259.
[3] Southern Division Returns, Officers' Record Division, Adjutant General's Office.

The native tribes on the southwestern frontier had been peaceably disposed toward the United States, but the influx of Indians from the east side of the Mississippi altered the situation. By 1820 bands from nearly every tribe south of the Ohio and from many tribes north of that river had crossed the Mississippi. Their arrival naturally decreased the hunting and farming lands of the native tribes and resulted in constant friction. The Indian agents tried to provide for the immigrant bands and at the same time to do justice to the native tribes.

The situation was aggravated by the arrival of white settlers and traders, who came in considerable numbers and occupied the choice locations. One group of squatters and outlaw traders settled at Pecan Point [4] on the Red River. These settlers sold whiskey and incited the Indians against factors and agents; according to one writer, they were "a band of the most abandoned wretches." [5] The remoteness of the settlement placed the inhabitants practically beyond the control of the law. John Jamison, Indian agent at Natchitoches, in his several reports to the secretary of war on the activities of the outlaws at Pecan Point, presented an alarming pictures of the conditions there: native Indians, crowded and restricted; immigrant tribes, dissatisfied and restless; squatters, intent upon seizing the best lands; and lawless traders, who ignored laws and regulations, sold whiskey, and stirred up the Indians. [6] Intertribal wars resulted, outrages against whites were frequent, and the outlaw traders were beyond the reach of ordinary legal processes. Such a situation called for the presence of troops. [7]

Amid the confusion of outrages and intertribal wars one struggle stands out because it involved strong tribes and was closely associated with the establishment of posts. This was the

[4] Pecan Point was in the southeastern part of what is now McCurtain County, Oklahoma.

[5] *Missouri Gazette*, October 25, 1817; Nuttall, *Journal*, in Thwaites, *Early Western Travels*, 13:221–22.

[64] For further details of the situation along the Red River see pages 28–30.

[7] Nuttall, who visited various points on the southwestern frontier in 1819, did not think that the "expensive forts, now established and still extending," were successful in controlling the Indians. *Journal*, in *Early Western Travels*, 13:222.

Cherokee-Osage War. From time to time the Cherokee enrolled allies from nearly all the tribes south of the Arkansas, and the Clermont band of Osage, who were the chief antagonists, at various times secured the aid of other Osage, the Kickapoo, Delawares, Sauk, and Foxes. The Clermont Osage had their village on the Verdigris, several miles above the Arkansas, but they hunted south of the river and came into conflict with the immigrant Cherokee. As early as 1814 William L. Lovely, Cherokee agent, asked Clark, superintendent of Indian Affairs, to send troops to the Arkansas. In July, 1816, Lovely succeeded in bringing the chiefs of the two principal combatants together for a peace conference at the mouth of the Verdigris, but the settlement proved to be only temporary, and on October 8 he again wrote to Clark requesting that troops be sent.[8] In the early summer of 1817 a coalition of Cherokee, representatives of tribes south of the Arkansas, and eleven white men, numbering all told about six hundred, marched against Clermont's town. Clermont and most of the warriors were absent on a hunting expedition, and the allies had no difficulty in defeating those who remained at the village. They killed fourteen Osage warriors and sixty-nine women and children, captured over a hundred, burned the village, and destroyed the crops. The Cherokee lost several warriors and the Delawares one.[9]

The establishment of a post on the Arkansas was ordered before news of the battle reached Nashville or St. Louis, but the outrages resulting from the war undoubtedly caused the order.[10] In 1816 Clark had reported Indian outrages and recommended a post on the Arkansas.[11] Late in September, 1817, Majors Wil-

[8] House Executive Document No. 263, House Documents, 20th Congress, 1st Session; Forsyth Collection, Missouri Historical Society; National Intelligencer, March 10, 1816; Foreman, Pioneer Days in the Early Southwest, p. 29.

[9] This battle was noted by many newspapers and writers. Perhaps the most reliable account is found in Clark's letter to Sibley, November 11, 1817, Sibley Collection, Missouri Historical Society. Other accounts are those in Missouri Gazette, August 23, 1817; Niles' Weekly Register, 13:80, 312, 378; Nuttall, Journal, in Early Western Travels, 13:192, and James, Long's Expedition, in Early Western Travels, vol. 20.

[10] Missouri Gazette, August 16, 1817. The issue of August 23 contains the first news of the battle.

[11] Clark to the Secretary of War, May 28, 1816, Letters Received, Old Records Division, Adjutant General's Office.

liam Bradford and Stephen H. Long, accompanied by about seventy men of the rifle regiment, left St. Louis to establish a post on the Arkansas near the Osage boundary line.[12] The site selected for the new post was at the junction of the Poteau and the Arkansas, and the name Fort Smith, honoring Brigadier General Thomas A. Smith, soon supplanted the original name Belle Point.

The establishment of Fort Smith did little toward stopping intertribal wars. In April, 1818, four hundred Pawnee met forty-eight Osage and killed all but one.[13] In the following year the Cherokee stole forty horses from the Osage and killed four warriors. The tribes north of the Arkansas planned to help the Osage, but Major Bradford persuaded the Cherokee to return the stolen horses. He visited Clermont's village to effect peace between the Pawnee and Osage and to dissuade the latter from again attacking the Cherokee.[14] The Osage soon killed a number of Cherokee hunters, and in April, 1820, Governor James Miller of Arkansas Territory visited the tribes and induced them to hold a council at Fort Smith in October, but practically nothing was accomplished. Hostilities continued throughout 1821 and during the first few months of 1822, resulting in the loss of several warriors, the death of a few settlers, and a demonstration by the Osage against Fort Smith.[15] Matthew Lyon, factor at Spadra Bluffs, feared an attack upon the factory, and Calhoun ordered Bradford to see that it was protected.[16]

These occurrences led to the re-enforcement of the garrison and the the establishment of Fort Gibson. In the summer of 1821

[12] *Niles' Weekly Register,* 13:176; *Southern Division Returns,* June, 1818, Officers' Record Division, Adjutant General's Office. For descriptions of Fort Smith see Nuttall, *Journal,* in *Early Western Travels,* 13:201–02; James, *Long's Expedition,* in *Early Western Travels,* 16:187–88; Morse, *Report to the Secretary of War on Indian Affairs,* p. 254.

[13] *Missouri Gazette,* June 19, 1818.

[14] James, *Three Years among the Indians and Mexicans; Niles' Weekly Register,* 16:287; 17:376.

[15] *Missouri Intelligencer,* February 19, 1821; *St. Louis Enquirer,* February 24, 1821; *National Intelligencer,* October 10, 1821, April 6, May 15, 1822; *Niles' Weekly Register,* 21:112, 381; Foreman, *Pioneer Days in the Early Southwest,* pp. 57–59.

[16] War Department Letter Book E, in Indian Office, p. 133.

the Seventh Regiment was ordered from the Florida frontier to the southwestern frontier. Four companies under Colonel Matthew Arbuckle ascended the Mississippi on board the steamboat *Tennessee* and arrived at the mouth of the Arkansas late in November.[17] From here they continued in keelboats and arrived at Fort Smith on February 26, 1822. Arbuckle assumed command and Bradford was transferred to Natchitoches.[18] The augmented garrison numbered 239,[19] a force large enough to command more respect from the Indians. On August 9 Governor Miller and Arbuckle succeeded in effecting a treaty at Fort Smith which put an end to the long-continued intertribal war,[20] although it did not prevent later outrages against whites.[21]

Fort Smith was too far down the river to control the Osage effectively, and it was thought that a post higher up the Arkansas would help to protect the Santa Fé trade.[22] As early as May, 1818, Long had recommended a post above Fort Smith.[23] In December, 1823, Gaines recommended that the Seventh Regiment be stationed above the Verdigris to restrain the Indians.[24] In January, 1824, Henry W. Conway, delegate in Congress from Arkansas Territory, urged Calhoun to establish a post at the mouth of the Verdigris. Brown accordingly suggested to Scott that such a movement might be advisable,[25] but Calhoun acted directly without waiting to hear from Scott. On March 6 the adjutant general ordered Arbuckle to move the troops to the Verdigris.[26] The removal was effected in April, and the new post, Fort Gibson, was established on the east bank of the Grand River, three

[17] *Louisiana Herald* (Alexandria), November 17, 1821.
[18] *National Intelligencer*, May 18, 1822, quoting the *Arkansas Gazette* of April 2, 1822.
[19] *American State Papers: Military Affairs*, 2:456.
[20] Foreman, *Pioneer Days in the Early Southwest*, p. 62; *Detroit Gazette*, August 22, 1822, quoting *Arkansas Gazette*, June 4, 1822.
[21] Arbuckle to Secretary of War, September 3, October 27, November 2, 1823, Old Records Division, Adjutant General's Office, *St. Louis Enquirer*, January 13, 1824.
[22] *American State Papers: Indian Affairs*, 2:456.
[23] Reports of the Corps of Engineers, 1812–23, p. 285.
[24] Inspection Reports, Inspector General's Office, 1823–24, p. 188.
[25] *St. Louis Enquirer*, April 26, 1824, quoting *Arkansas Gazette*.
[26] General Orders, Old Records Division, Adjutant General's Office.

miles from the Arkansas.[27] At the time of the removal the garrison numbered 226, and a hundred additional men were expected, but the returns show that only 261 were present in the summer of 1825.[28]

Conditions similar to those along the Arkansas existed on the Red River. The principal Caddo villages were located near the mouth of Sulphur Fork, just above the Louisiana-Arkansas line. To offset the corrupting influence of lawless traders, a factory had been located at the mouth of Sulphur Fork in 1818. In 1820 the Caddo ceded a tract of land north of the Red River for the use of the Choctaw,[29] but the Caddo repented of their action and opposed the carrying out of the terms. In June, 1821, a guard of ten men was sent to protect the factory, and in the following year Gaines ordered a whole company to Sulphur Fork. The troops constructed a post known as Cantonment Taylor and continued to occupy the position until May, 1824.[30]

The disturbing activities of traders, adventurers, and squatters at Pecan Point and at the mouth of the Kiamichi made a further advance up the Red River advisable. The need for troops above the settlements had been pointed out in 1816 by John Jamison, and two years later Long had recommended the establishment of such a post.[31] In January, 1824, Henry W. Conway, delegate from Arkansas Territory, called the attention of Calhoun to outrages at the mouth of the Kiamichi. In the following month Brown suggested to Scott that the company stationed at Cantonment Taylor might be moved to the Kiamichi.[32] In May, 1824, a detachment from Fort Selden and the garrison at Cantonment Taylor, numbering all told about one hundred men, ascended the Red River and established Fort Towson near the mouth of

[27] *Natchitoches Courier*, May 10, 1825, quoting the *Arkansas Gazette;* Foreman, *Pioneer Days in the Early Southwest*, pp. 63–64.
[28] *American State Papers: Military Affairs*, 2:706; 3:115.
[29] Kappler, *Indian Affairs, Laws, and Treaties*, 2:192.
[30] Cantonment Taylor, Post Returns, Officers' Record Division, Adjutant General's Office; Inspection Reports, Inspector General's Office, 1823–24, pp. 159–60; *American State Papers: Military Affairs*, 2:456, 558, 706.
[31] Reports of the Corps of Engineers, 1812–23, p. 285.
[32] *St. Louis Enquirer*, April 26, 1824, quoting *Arkansas Gazette*.

the Kiamichi.[33] Although the fort was designed primarily to control traders, squatters, and domestic tribes, its location on the boundary enabled the garrison to exercise some influence over the Texas tribes who frequently crossed the Red River to trade. The fort thus illustrates a combination of the two phases of frontier defense, the control of the Indians and the policing of the border.

The second phase of defense on the southwestern frontier consisted of attempts to maintain order along the Louisiana-Texas border. The control of the domestic tribes engaged the attention of the soldiers, but the factors and Indian agents were keenly aware of the situation in Texas and of its effects upon the border tribes. The claim of the United States to Texas had tended to produce uncertainty, and the impracticable arrangement of a neutral zone [34] had promoted, rather than allayed, friction. The Napoleonic wars had interrupted all attempts to adjust the boundary, and the Mexican revolution aggravated the situation. As a result of these factors Texas became the scene of Indian outbreaks,[35] revolutions, piracy, filibustering, and confusion. From 1815 to 1818 Perry, Herrera, Aury, Mina, Lafitte,[36] and Lallemand [37] tried to accomplish their various purposes, all of which tended toward the continued disruption of Texas. The stern objection of the Spanish minister and the fear of postponing the settlement of the Florida question prevented the United States from suppressing the pirates along the coast and the revolutionists and filibusters in the interior.

The signing of the Treaty of 1819 with Spain altered the situation. The claim to Texas was surrendered, and the Sabine became an international frontier. Caution had prevented the United States from pursuing an aggressive policy along the border for fear of interrupting the negotiations for Florida. The

[33] Monthly Post Returns; Cantonment Taylor, Officers' Record Division, Adjutant General's Office; American State Papers: Military Affairs, 3:115.
[34] Marshall, Western Boundary of the Louisana Purchase, p. 30.
[35] For a contemporary account of the Indian situation in Texas see Padilla, "Texas in 1820," Southwestern Historical Quarterly, 23:47–68.
[36] For a brief account of each see Bancroft, North Mexican States and Texas, 2:33–52.
[37] For an account of Lallemand, see Reeves, "The Napoleonic Exiles in America," Johns Hopkins Studies in Historical and Political Science, 23:531-656.

signing of the treaty removed the necessity for such caution. The treaty also produced an event which had an immediate effect upon the defense of the frontier.

The surrender of the American claim to Texas angered many persons in the Southwest who had wished to see that province definitely added to the United States. Disappointment over the treaty and sympathy for the Texan patriots resulted in an expedition into Texas. The citizens of Natchez held a mass meeting to protest against the surrender of Texas and to enlist support for the patriot cause. Dr. James Long was selected as the leader, and in June, 1819, he started for Nacogdoches with seventy-five men. By the time he reached that place his force had grown to three hundred. A provisional government was established and independence declared. Long sent out a call for volunteers to whom he promised liberal grants of land. A newspaper, the *Texas Republican,* was started and paper money was issued. Some volunteers passed through Natchitoches and a small force from Pecan Point joined the new republic, but its forces never reached more than a few hundred. Long was unsuccessful in enlisting sufficient help, his assistants proved incapable, and the royalists easily defeated and scattered his divided forces.[38]

Long's expedition was the occasion, if not the cause, of an advance to the Sabine by the United States soldiers. As early as 1817 General Ripley, writing from headquarters at New Orleans to the secretary of war, had advocated the placing of a considerable force on the border,[39] but the status of the Florida negotiations made such an advance at that time inadvisable.[40] On December 12, 1818, three companies had embarked from Baton Rouge for Fort Claiborne at Natchitoches. In June, 1819, the troops occupied Fort Selden[41] and Fort Claiborne was abandoned.[42]

[38] *Missouri Gazette,* September 1, October 6, November 10, 1819; *St. Louis Enquirer,* September 18, October 9; *Missouri Intelligencer,* October 1, December 3, 1819; Yoakum, *History of Texas,* 1:199–202; Bancroft, *North Mexican States and Texas,* 2:47–52.
[39] Letters Received, 10:309, Old Records Division, Adjutant General's Office.
[40] Jameson, *Correspondence of John Caldwell Calhoun,* pp. 147, 150.
[41] Fort Selden at Natchitoches was established in 1817.
[42] Fort Claiborne was said to be a healthful site, whereas Fort Selden was unhealthful. A dispute over the ownership of the land on which Fort Claiborne was located caused its abandonment. Inspection Reports, Inspector General's Office,

Four companies were ordered to move to Crow's Ferry on the Sabine where they established Camp Ripley in September.[43] In the following year the force numbered 105.[44] The situation along the border became less acute, and in 1822 the troops moved back from the Sabine and established quarters on more healthful grounds. The new post, known as Fort Jesup, was located about midway between Natchitoches and the Sabine. It was established in May, 1822, by four companies of the Seventh Regiment under the command of Lieutenant Colonel Zachary Taylor. In June, 1823, the garrison numbered 252.[45] Fort Jesup continued to be an important post, especially during the troubled period of the Texan republic, and did not lose its military importance until after the close of the Mexican War.

Garrison life on the southwestern frontier did not differ materially from that on other frontiers. In accordance with widespread practice the troops erected their own quarters and helped to support themselves by hunting and farming. Perhaps the most spacious and best constructed quarters were those at Fort Gibson. Cabins about twenty feet square, built of squared white oak logs of substantial dimensions, faced a court ninety-eight by eighty-eight yards. Each room was provided with a door and a window on the side toward the court.[46] The soldiers at all the posts supplemented their rations with frequent supplies of buffalo, deer, and bear meat. The gardens were large and were industriously cultivated. In 1819 the corn crop at Fort Smith amounted to four thousand bushels.[47] Herds of cattle and hogs were raised. In 1822 the garrison at Fort Smith owned one hundred

1814–23, p. 75; Military Books, 9:105, Old Records Division, Adjutant General's Office.

[43] The movements of the troops are recorded in Captain Ferdinand L. Amelung's Orderly Book, Company H, First Infantry, Old Records Division, Adjutant General's Office.

[44] *American State Papers: Military Affairs*, 2:37.

[45] Monthly Post Returns, Fort Jesup, Officers' Record Division, Adjutant General's Office.

[46] Inspection Reports, Inspector General's Office, 1825–28, pp. 19–22. Samuel B. Archer, inspector, recommended that windows be cut in the rear walls of the cabins in order to improve ventilation.

[47] *St. Louis Enquirer*, December 8, 1819; *Niles' Weekly Register*, 17:376.

cattle and four hundred hogs. The inspector who visited Fort Towson in May, 1825, reported that the food was good, the quarters excellent, and the gardens ample and well cultivated.[48] The health of the troops was unusually good. The mild climate and the variety of food reduced disease to the minimum. A few cases of dysentery, however, did occur at Fort Smith during the winter of 1822.[49]

Not all of the time of the soldiers was consumed in building quarters and cultivating gardens. They frequently performed duties of a military character, such as guarding factories, attending councils with the Indians, making incursions into disturbed regions, protecting a trader, guarding the border, and ejecting squatters. The fertile lands along the many tributaries of the Arkansas and Red rivers tempted settlers to occupy unceded lands. In spite of warnings and orders the number of such squatters was large. In 1819 Jackson ordered that no one be allowed to settle west of a line connecting the sources of the Kiamichi and Poteau. In June of that year Major Bradford with six soldiers rode through the tract west of the line and warned settlers that they would have to move. He found about two hundred families, some of whom had planted crops and erected cabins. He allowed those who had growing crops to remain until October. A similar task had to be performed repeatedly.[50]

In 1815 there was only one post, Fort Claiborne, on the southwestern frontier. By 1825 Fort Smith, a post at Baton Rouge, Fort Selden, Fort Gibson, Cantonment Taylor, Fort Towson, Camp Ripley, and Fort Jesup had been established, and Fort Claiborne, Fort Smith, Cantonment Taylor, and Camp Ripley had been abandoned, leaving five posts in operation in that year. They were sufficient for the control of the Indians, and no greater danger seemed imminent. The Mexican revolution had de-

[48] Inspection Reports, Inspector General's Office, 1825–28, pp. 17–18.

[49] *National Intelligencer,* May 18, 1822, quoting *Arkansas Gazette,* April 2, 1822; *Niles' Weekly Register,* 22:196.

[50] Calhoun to Jackson, December 15, 1818, *Niles' Weekly Register,* 45:159; *American State Papers: Indian Affairs,* 2:557; *National Intelligencer,* February 6, April 10, 1821.

stroyed the feeble control which Spain had exercised over Texas and substituted one which was but little stronger. The maintenance of peace along the border became more difficult since the burden fell almost wholly upon the United States. The continued immigration of Indians, the unsurveyed boundary line, the influx of Americans into Texas, and the subsequent revolution in that province made the southwestern frontier a strategic area until after the Mexican War.

APPENDIXES, BIBLIOGRAPHY,
AND INDEX

APPENDIXES

A. List of Indian Agents and Sub-Agents, 1815–25 [1]

AGENTS

AGENT   TRIBE OR LOCATION

Biddle, John.....................................Green Bay
Boilvin, Nicholas..............................Prairie du Chien
Bowyer, John....................................Green Bay
Boyd, George....................................Mackinac
Brearly, David.....................Cherokee Indians in Arkansas
Brevoort, Henry B..............................Green Bay
Chouteau, Peter................................Osage Indians
Cocke, William...............................Chickasaw Indians
Crowell, John...................................Creek Indians
Duval, Edward W...................Cherokee Indians in Arkansas
Forsyth, Thomas...............................Fort Armstrong
Graham, Richard........................Illinois, then Missouri
Gray, George...................................Natchitoches
Hawkins, Benjamin.............................Creek Indians
Hayes, John.....................................Fort Wayne
Humphrey, Gad...............................Seminole Indians
Jamison, John..................................Natchitoches
Johnston, John.....................................Piqua
Jouett, Charles.....................................Chicago
Kennerly, George H...................Upper Missouri River
Lovely, William L................................Arkansas
McKee, John...................................Choctaw Indians
McMinn, Joseph...................Cherokee Indians in Tennessee
McNair, Alexander.................................Missouri
Meigs, Return J....................Cherokee Indians in Tennessee
Mitchell, David Brydie..........................Creek Indians
Nicholas, R. C................................Chickasaw Indians

---

[1] *American State Papers: Indian Affairs,* 2:31–33, 76, 163, 289, 365, 403–04, 450; Kappler, *Indian Affairs, Laws, and Treaties,* 2:110–264; Letters Received, Old Records Division, Adjutant General's Office; War Department Letter Books, *passim.*

O'Fallon, Benjamin..............................Council Bluffs
Posey, Thomas ....Vincennes
Prince, William ....Vincennes
Puthuff, William H................................Mackinac
Schoolcraft, Henry R.........................Sault Ste. Marie
Sherburne, Henry...........................Chickasaw Indians
Smith, Benjamin F..........................Chickasaw Indians
Stickney, Benjamin F.............................Fort Wayne
Taliaferro, Lawrence..............................St. Peter's
Tipton, John.....................................Fort Wayne
Ward, William..............................Choctaw Indians
Wolcott, Alexander..........................Chicago, Detroit

SUB-AGENTS

SUB-AGENT	TRIBE OR LOCATION
Alexander, W. B.	Missouri
Barber, D.	Osage Indians
Bell, Robert	Choctaw Indians
Blondeaux, Maurice	Peoria
Bullett, Judge	Arkansas
Campbell, John	Missouri
Chouteau, Auguste P.	St. Louis
Chouteau, Pierre L.	Osage Indians
Cook, David Godfrey	Chickasaw Indians
Crowell, H.	Creek Indians
Dougherty, John	Council Bluffs
Forsyth, Robert A.	Detroit
Godfroy, Gabriel	St. Joseph, Michigan
Gooding, George	St. Peter's
Hawkins, Philemon	Unknown
Houston, Samuel	Cherokee Indians
Johnson, John W.	Fort Madison, Prairie du Chien
Kenzie, John	Chicago
Kercheval, Benjamin	Fort Wayne
Knaggs, Whitmore	Ottawa Indians, Chippewa Indians
Latham, James	Peoria
Lisa, Manuel	Upper Missouri
McPherson, James	Wapakoneta
Malbone, R.	Chickasaw Indians
Menard, Pierre	Kaskaskia
Miller, Jacob	Quapaw Indians
Montgomery, James	Sandusky River

Parke, Benjamin.....................................Vincennes
Parrish, Jasper.....................................New York
Philbrook, Nathaniel..................Osage Indians on Arkansas
Pilcher, Joshua...........................Upper Missouri River
Ruland, John.......................................St. Louis
Schoolcraft, Henry Rowe........................Sault Ste. Marie
Shaw, John.....................................Upper Sandusky
Sherburne, Thomas J.........................Chickasaw Indians
Sibley, George C...................................Fort Osage
Stephenson, Benjamin.......................Edwardsville, Illinois
Trowbridge, C. C....................................Michigan
Williams, J. G.....................Cherokee Indians in Tennessee
Wilson, P..............................Upper Missouri River

B. List of Factors, 1795–1822 [2]

FACTOR	FACTORY
Ballio, Paul	Marais des Cygnes, Missouri
Bayley, R. P.	Chickasaw Bluffs, Tennessee
Belknap, Eben	Chicago, Illinois
Belt, Robert B.	Fort Edwards, Illinois / Fort Armstrong, Illinois
Byers, Nicholas	Tellico, Tennessee / Hiawassee, Tennessee
Chambers, Joseph	Fort St. Stephens, Alabama
Fowler, John	Natchitoches, Louisiana / Sulphur Fork, Arkansas
Gaines, George S.	Fort St. Stephen, Alabama
Halstead, Jonathan	Fort Hawkins, Georgia
Hersey, John	Fort Confederation, Alabama
Hogg, David	Chickasaw Bluffs, Tennessee
Hooker, John W.	Tellico, Tennessee
Hughes, Daniel	Fort Hawkins, Georgia
Irwin, Matthew	Chicago, Illinois / Green Bay, Wisconsin
Johnson, John W.	Fort Madison, Iowa / Prairie du Chien, Wisconsin
Johnston, John	Fort Wayne, Indiana
Jordan, James	Coleraine, Georgia
Linnard, Thomas M.	Natchitoches, Louisiana
Lyon, Matthew	Spadra Bluffs (Bayou), Arkansas
McClellan, William	Sulphur Fork, Arkansas
Munro, Robert	Detroit, Michigan
Owens, Barak	Spadra Bluffs, Arkansas
Peterkin, Thomas	Chickasaw Bluffs, Tennessee
Rawlings, Isaac	Chickasaw Bluffs, Tennessee
Tillier, Rudolph	Belle Fontaine, Missouri
Sibley, George C.	Fort Osage, Missouri
Treat, John B.	Arkansas, Arkansas / Chickasaw Bluffs, Tennessee
Tupper, Samuel	Sandusky, Ohio
Varnum, Jacob B.	Mackinac, Michigan / Chicago, Illinois
Wright, Edward	Fort Wilkinson, Georgia

[2] *American State Papers: Indian Affairs*, 1:653, 769; 2:36, 57, 371, 421, 532–34, 537; Factory Account Books.

C. Indian Peace Commissioners, 1815–25 [3]

Adams, David
Atkinson, Henry
Calhoun, John C.
Cass, Lewis
Chouteau, Auguste
Clark, William
Coffee, John
Crittenden, Robert
Duval, William P.
Edwards, Ninian
Forney, Daniel M.
Forsyth, Thomas
Franklin, Jesse
Gadsden, James
Graham, George
Graham, John
Graham, Richard
Harrison, William Henry
Hinds, Thomas
Jackson, Andrew

Jennings, Jonathan
McArthur, Duncan
McIntosh, John
McIntosh, William
McKee, John
McMinn, Joseph
Mather, Thomas
Meriwether, David
Mitchell, David Brydie
Newman, Daniel
O'Fallon, Benjamin
Parke, Benjamin
Reeves, Benjamin H.
Rhea, John
Segui, Bernard
Shelby, Isaac
Sibley, George C.
Sibley, Solomon
Stephenson, Benjamin

[3] Kappler, *Indian Affairs, Laws, and Treaties*, 2:110–264.

D. Secretaries of War, 1815–25

James Monroe..................August 30, 1814–March 2, 1815 [4]
A. J. Dallas, *ad interim*............March 14, 1815–August 8, 1815 [5]
George Graham, chief clerk.......August 8, 1815–December 1, 1815 [6]
William H. Crawford..........December 1, 1815–October 22, 1816 [7]
George Graham, chief clerk......October 22, 1816–December 8, 1817
John C. Calhoun................December 8, 1817–March 3, 1825

E. Strength of the Army, 1815–25 [8]

1815	9,413	1821	6,183
1816	10,024	1822	5,211
1817	8,221	1823	5,949
1818	7,676	1824	5,779
1819	8,688	1825	5,719
1820	10,281		

[4] Monroe, *Writings*, 5:335. He was officially appointed on September 26 and confirmed on September 27, 1814.

[5] Bassett, *Correspondence of Andrew Jackson*, 2:190.

[6] Military Books, vol. 8, *passim*.

[7] *Ibid.*, p. 396. His appointment was confirmed by the Senate on March 3 preceding and his commission is dated August 1. Bassett in *Correspondence of Andrew Jackson*, 2:221.

[8] *American State Papers: Military Affairs*, 1:662; 2:38, 195, 454, 557, 705; 3:114.

BIBLIOGRAPHY

I. PRIMARY MATERIALS

RECORDS FILED IN THE INDIAN OFFICE, DEPARTMENT OF THE INTERIOR

Lewis Cass Letter Books, 1814–31. 27 vols. The first four are copied into ledgers. The others are bound originals, marked "Letters Received, Gov. Cass, Indian Office."

Factory Account Book. This is a general account book for the whole system.

Factory Account Books. Many but not all the factories are represented.

Factory Files. These consist of data of various kinds from the factors.

Indian Trade Department Letter Books, 1807–22. The books are marked A, B, C, D, and F. Book E, covering the period from April, 1818, to July, 1820, is missing. The books contain copies of the letters to the factors from the superintendent of Indian Trade.

Indian Trade Department Letter Book No. 1, March 18, 1821–May 3, 1825. This volume and its successors contain copies of the letters received by the superintendent of Indian Trade from the factors. Before 1821 letters from the factors were not entered in any systematic way. Some of them were addressed to the secretary of war and are filed in the Old Records Division of the Adjutant General's Office.

War Department Letter Books, 1800–24. 6 vols. The volumes are lettered and consist of copies of letters sent from the secretary of war to Indian agents. Letters from agents to the secretary are filed in the Old Records Division, Adjutant General's Office.

RECORDS FILED IN THE DEPARTMENT OF STATE

Territorial Papers MS. This voluminous manuscript consists of copies of important documents relating to territories. It was compiled under the direction of Dr. Newton D. Mereness. Congress has appropriated the funds necessary for its publication, and it is now being edited by Dr. Clarence Carter.

RECORDS FILED IN THE WAR DEPARTMENT

ADJUTANT GENERAL'S OFFICE: OFFICERS' RECORD DIVISION

Department Returns, 1821–28. The varied use of the words "department" and "division" is explained in Chapter VII. In this bibliography the present labeling of the War Department is followed.

Department Returns. Various dates are included in any one bundle.

Division Returns, 1815–20.

Outline Index of Military Forts and Stations. 26 vols. The volumes are lettered from A to Z. This is probably the most complete and accurate list of forts that has been made, although some of the information was derived from secondary materials. Compiled by a clerk in the War Department.

Post Returns. Returns from some posts are fairly complete, while other posts are not represented at all. Some post returns are filed in the Old Records Division of the Adjutant General's Office.

Thian, Raphael P. Notes Illustrating the Military Geography of the United States. Some notes are printed, others are typed, and still others are in handwriting. The work was never completed.

ADJUTANT GENERAL'S OFFICE: OLD FILES SECTION

Letters Received, 1814–25. 8 vols. The ledgers give the place, date, name of the writer, and a summary of the contents of letters received by the Adjutant General's office. In many instances the letter itself can be obtained from the files.

Letters Sent, 1814–27. 5 vols. The ledgers contain complete copies of the letters sent out by the adjutant general.

Reservation File. Data of various kinds concerning many posts are available, but much of it is based upon secondary materials.

ADJUTANT GENERAL'S OFFICE: OLD RECORDS DIVISION

Company Orderly Books. Nine books of various companies stationed at Camp Montgomery, Fort Scott, Fort Gadsden, Baton Rouge, New Orleans, Fort Claiborne, Fort Selden, Camp Ripley, Pass Christian, and Shieldsboro from 1815 to 1820 are represented.

Company Returns. Miscellaneous companies are represented.

Department Orders, 1819–25. This volume contains the orders issued by the commander of the Ninth Department from 1819 to 1821, and the orders of the commander of the Northwestern Frontier, the Western Wing of the Western Department, and the Western Department from 1821 to 1825.

Department Orders, Eighth Department. New Orleans, December, 1816–December, 1817.

Edmund Pendleton Gaines (Major General). Letter Book, November 20, 1817–March 26, 1819.

General Orders, 1815–27. 27 vols. Many of the orders are printed and bound with handwritten copies of other orders.

Letter Book, Eighth Department. New Orleans, May, 1817–May, 1821.

Letter Book, Southern Division, 1817–20. This volume contains Jackson's orders and many letters which have never been printed.

Letters Received. These volumes contain accurate digests of the letters relating to military affairs received by the secretary of war from the adjutant general. Numbers 8 to 19 inclusive cover the period from 1814 to 1825. The letters are filed and can be found readily. The ledgers are so full and so accurate that they compensate to some extent for the loss of occasional letters.

Military Books. These volumes contain copies of the letters sent out by the secretary of war. Numbers 8, 9, 10, 11, and 12 cover the period from 1814 to 1829.

Regimental Returns of the Sixth Infantry.

INSPECTOR GENERAL'S OFFICE

Inspection Reports, 1814–28. 3 vols. Original reports from the inspectors are bound into volumes with numbered pages.

ENGINEER'S OFFICE

Corps of Engineers, Reports, 1812–23. Copies of the reports are entered in large ledgers. Bernard, Swift, Long, and Macomb are some of the engineers represented. Nearly all the reports deal with coast fortifications, although two by Long are concerned with interior surveys.

MANUSCRIPTS IN THE LIBRARY OF CONGRESS

Jacob Brown Letter Book, 1814–27. 2 vols. These volumes contain copies of letters sent and received.
Factory System Accounts. These accounts supplement those in the Indian Office.
Gaines Papers. This scanty collection is of little value.

PERSONAL PAPERS IN THE MISSOURI HISTORICAL SOCIETY

William H. Ashley Letters
Gen. Henry Atkinson Journal
Thomas Biddle's Observations
Pierre Chouteau Papers
Chouteau–Maffit Papers
John Dougherty Papers
Andrew Drips Collection
Thomas Forsyth Collection
* Photostatic copies.

Richard Graham Collection
Charles Gratiot Collection
James and George Kennerly Collection
William Lewis Lovely Papers *
John O'Fallon Papers
George C. Sibley Letter Books
Tesson Collection, including a vast number of Forsyth papers.

PUBLISHED MATERIALS

PUBLICATIONS OF THE UNITED STATES GOVERNMENT

American State Papers: Foreign Relations. 6 vols. Washington, 1832–57.
American State Papers: Indian Affairs. 2 vols. Washington, 1832–34.
American State Papers: Military Affairs. 7 vols. Washington, 1832–61.
American State Papers: Miscellaneous. 2 vols. Washington, 1834.
Annals of Congress, 3d Congress, 2d Session; 4th Congress, 1st Session; 9th Congress, 2d Session; 13th Congress, 3d Session; 14th Congress, 1st and 2d Sessions; 15th Congress, 1st and 2d Sessions; 16th Congress, 1st and 2d Sessions; 17th Congress, 1st and 2d Sessions; 18th Congress, 1st Session.
Congressional Globe, 25th Congress, 2d Session; 30th Congress, 1st Session.
DE CAINDRY, WILLIAM A. *A History of the War Department* (Senate Document No. 555, 45th Congress, 3d Session). Also published in Thomas H. S. Hamersly, *Complete Regular Army Register of the United States for One Hundred Years, 1779–1879* (3d ed., Washington, 1881), pp. 215–379.
GORDON, WILLIAM A., editor, *A Compilation of Registers of the Army of the United States from 1815–1837.* Washington, 1837.
HEITMAN, FRANCIS B. *Historical Register and Dictionary of the United States Army, 1789–1903.* 2 vols. Washington, 1903.
Journals of the American Congress from 1774 to 1788. 4 vols. Washington, 1823.
Journals of the Continental Congress, 1774–1789 (edited by Gaillard Hunt and Worthington Chauncey Ford), vols. 1–25. Washington, 1904–22.
KAPPLER, CHARLES J., editor. *Indian Affairs, Laws, and Treaties.* 2 vols. Washington, 1904.
RICHARDSON, JAMES D., editor. *Compilation of the Messages and Papers of the Presidents, 1789–1897.* 10 vols. Washington, 1899.

THIAN, RAPHAEL P. *Legislative History of the General Staff* (Senate Document No. 229, 56th Congress, 2d Session).

United States Statutes at Large, 1789–1845 (edited by Richard Peters). 8 vols. Boston, 1856–61.

UPTON, EMORY. *The Military Policy of the United States.* Washington, 1917.

WILLIAM M. MALLOY, compiler. *Treaties, Conventions, International Acts, Protocols, and Agreements between the United States and Other Powers, 1776–1902.* 2 vols. Washington, 1910.

OTHER PRINTED SOURCE MATERIALS

ADAMS, JOHN QUINCY. *Memoirs* (edited by Charles Francis Adams). 12 vols. Philadelphia, 1874–77.

"Affairs at St. Stephens in 1810," *Gulf States Magazine,* 1:443–45.

"Arrival of American Troops at Green Bay in 1816," Wisconsin Historical Collections, 13:441–44.

BABCOCK, RUFUS, editor. *Memoir of John Mason Peck.* Philadelphia, 1864.

▸ BASSETT, JOHN SPENCER, editor. *Correspondence of Andrew Jackson,* vols. 1–4. Washington, 1926–28.

"Bulger Papers," Wisconsin Historical Collections, 13:10–153.

Copies of Papers on File in the Dominion Archives at Ottawa, Canada, Pertaining to the Relations of the British Government with the United States during and Subsequent to the Period of the War of 1812 (Michigan Pioneer and Historical Collections, vol. 16).

COUES, ELLIOTT, editor. *The History of the Expedition under the Command of Lewis and Clark.* 3 vols. New York, 1893.

———. *The Journal of Jacob Fowler.* New York, 1898.

DALE, HARRISON CLIFFORD. *The Ashley-Smith Explorations and the Discovery of a Central Route to the Pacific, 1822–1829.* Cleveland, 1918.

DOTY, JAMES DUANE. "Official Journal, 1820: Expedition with Cass and Schoolcraft," Wisconsin Historical Collections, 13:163–219.

EDWARDS, NINIAN WIRT. *History of Illinois from 1778–1833 and Life and Times of Ninian Edwards.* Springfield, 1870.

A FOREIGNER. *Letters from Washington on the Constitution and Laws with Sketches of some prominent public Characters of the United States, written during the Winter of 1817–1818.* Washington, 1818.

FORSYTH, THOMAS. "Narrative," Minnesota Historical Collections, 3:139–67.

FRANKLIN, BENJAMIN. *Writings of Benjamin Franklin* (edited by Albert Henry Smyth). 10 vols. New York, 1905–07.

GRISWOLD, BERT J. *Fort Wayne, Gateway of the West, 1802–1813: Garrison Orderly Books: Indian Agency Account Book* (Indiana Historical Collections, vol. 15). Indianapolis, 1927.

HUBBARD, GURDON SALTONSTALL. *Autobiography.* Chicago, 1911.

JAMES, EDWIN. *Account of an Expedition from Pittsburg to the Rocky Mountains, performed in the Years 1819, 1820 by Order the Hon. J. C. Calhoun, Secretary of War, under the Command of Maj. S. H. Long . . . in Reuben Gold Thwaites, editor, Early Western Travels, vols. 14–17. Cleveland, 1905.*

JAMES, THOMAS. *Three Years Among the Indians and Mexicans* (edited by Walter B. Douglas). St. Louis, 1916.

JAMESON, J. FRANKLIN, editor. *Correspondence of John Caldwell Calhoun* (Annual Report of the American Historical Association for 1899, vol. 2). Washington, 1900.

JOHNSTON, GEORGE. "Reminiscences of Sault Ste. Marie, 1815," Michigan Pioneer and Historical Collections, 12:605–11.

JONES, CAPTAIN ROGER. "Gen. Brown's Inspection Tour up the Lakes in 1819," Publications of the Buffalo Historical Society, 24:295–323.

KEATING, WILLIAM H. Narrative of an Expedition to the Source of St. Peter's River, Lake Winnepeek, Lake of the Woods, and performed in the Year 1823 . . . under the Command of Stephen H. Long . . . 2 vols. Philadelphia, 1824.

LONG, STEPHEN HARRIMAN. "Voyage in a Six-Oared Skiff to the Falls of Saint Anthony in 1817," Minnesota Historical Collections, 2:9–88.

MCAFEE, ROBERT B. A History of the late War in the Western Country. Lexington, 1816.

MARSHALL, THOMAS MAITLAND, editor. The Life and Papers of Frederick Bates. 2 vols. St. Louis, 1926.

————. "Remnants of the Letter Files of the Dearborn Family," Mississippi Valley Historical Review, 2:407–24.

"The Military Occupation of Green Bay," Mississippi Valley Historical Review, 13:550–53.

MONROE, JAMES. Writings of James Monroe (edited by Stanislaus Murray Hamilton). 7 vols. New York, 1898–1903.

MORSE, JEDIDIAH. A Report to the Secretary of War on Indian Affairs. New Haven, 1822.

NUTTALL, THOMAS. Journal, in Reuben Gold Thwaites, editor, Early Western Travels, vol. 13. Cleveland, 1905.

PADILLA, JUAN ANTONIO. "Texas in 1820" (Mattie Austin Hatcher, translator), Southwestern Historical Quarterly, 23:47–60.

PARTON, JAMES. Life of Andrew Jackson. 3 vols. New York, 1860.

PORTER, VALENTINE MOTT, editor. "Journal of Stephen Watts Kearny," Missouri Historical Collections, 3:8–29, 99–131.

ROBINSON, DOANE, editor. "Official Correspondence of the Leavenworth Expedition into South Dakota for the Conquest of the Ree Indians in 1823," Publications of the South Dakota State Historical Society, 1:181–256.

ROWLAND, DUNBAR, editor. Official Letter Books of W. C. C. Claiborne, 1800–1816. 6 vols. Jackson, 1917.

SCHOOLCRAFT, HENRY ROWE. Journal of a Tour into the Interior of Missouri and Arkansas. London, 1821.

————. Narrative Journal of Travels through the Northwestern Regions of the United States, extending from Detroit through the great Chain of American Lakes to the Sources of the Mississippi River. Performed as a Member of the Expedition under Governor Cass in the Year 1820. Albany, 1821.

SCOTT, WINFIELD. Memoirs of Lieut.-General Scott. 2 vols. New York, 1864.

SHAW, JOHN. "Narrative," Wisconsin Historical Collections, 2:197–232.

STONE, W. L. The Life of Joseph Brant. 2 vols. New York, 1838.

THOMAS, ALFRED B. "The Yellowstone River, James Long, and Spanish Reaction to American Intrusions into Spanish Territory, 1818–1819," West Texas Historical Yearbook, 1928, pp. 1–12.

WASHINGTON, GEORGE. Writings of George Washington (edited by Worthington Chauncey Ford). 14 vols. New York, 1889–93.

————. Writings of George Washington (edited by Jared Sparks). 10 vols. New York, 1837.

WESLEY, EDGAR BRUCE. "James Callaway in the War of 1812: Letters, Diary, and Rosters," Missouri Historical Collections, 5:38–81.

————. "A Letter from Colonel John Allen," *Ohio Archaeological and Historical Society Quarterly,* 36:332–39.
WESLEY, EDGAR BRUCE, editor. "Diary of James Kennerly, 1823–26," Missouri Historical Collections, 6:41–97.

II. SECONDARY MATERIALS

ABEL, ANNIE HELOISE. "The History of Events Resulting in Indian Consolidation West of the Mississippi," Annual Report of the American Historical Association, 1906, 1:233–450.
ABERNETHY, THOMAS PERKINS. *The Formative Period in Alabama, 1815–1828.* Montgomery, 1922.
ADAMS, JOHN QUINCY. *Lives of James Madison and James Monroe.* Buffalo, 1850.
ARTHUR, ROBERT. *The Court Artillery School, 1824–1927.* Fort Monroe, 1928.
BANCROFT, HUBERT HOWE. *History of the North Mexican States (History of the Pacific States of North America,* vol. 10). San Francisco, 1884.
————. *History of Texas (History of the Pacific States of North America,* vol. 11). San Francisco, 1889.
BASSETT, JOHN SPENCER. *The Life of Andrew Jackson.* 2 vols. New York, 1911.
BENTON, THOMAS HART. *Thirty Years' View.* 2 vols. New York, 1854.
BLANCHARD, RUFUS. *Discovery and Conquests of the Northwest with the History of Chicago.* 2 vols. Chicago, 1898.
BRYCE, GEORGE. *The Remarkable History of the Hudson's Bay Company, Including That of the French Traders of North-Western Canada and of the North-West, XY, and Astor Fur Company,* London, 1900.
BUCK, SOLON JUSTUS. *Illinois in 1818* (Illinois Centennial Commission Publications, introductory volume). Springfield, 1917.
BULGER, ALFRED EDWARD. "Last Days of the British at Prairie du Chien," Wisconsin Historical Collections, 13:154–62.
CALLAHAN, JAMES MORTON. "The Neutrality of the American Lakes and Anglo-American Relations," Johns Hopkins Studies in Historical and Political Science, 16:1–199. Baltimore, 1898.
CARTER, WILLIAM H. *The American Army.* Indianapolis, 1915.
CHITTENDEN, HIRAM MARTIN. *The American Fur Trade of the Far West: A History of the Pioneer Trading Posts and Early Fur Companies of the Missouri Valley and the Rocky Mountains and of the Overland Commerce with Santa Fé.* 3 vols. New York, 1902.
COMAN, KATHERINE. "Government Factories: An Attempt to Control Competition in the Fur Trade," Papers and Discussions of the American Economic Association, 1911, pp. 368–88.
COMFORT, BENJAMIN FREEMAN. *Lewis Cass and the Indian Treaties, 1813–1831.* Detroit, 1923.
COUES, ELLIOTT, editor. *History of the Lewis and Clark Expedition.* 4 vols. New York, 1893.
COX, ISAAC JOSLIN. *The West Florida Controversy, 1798–1813: A Study in American Diplomacy.* Baltimore, 1918.
CRANE, CHARLES J. "Our Military Policy from the End of the War of 1812–1815 to the Beginning of the Civil War," *Journal of the United States Infantry Association,* 4:677–709.
CROWE, FLETCHER STANDEFER. "The National Policy of Frontier Defense, 1815–1825." Master's thesis, Washington University, 1922.
DALLAM, PHILIP. "Dedication of Fort Edwards Monument, Warsaw, Illinois," *Journal of the Illinois State Historical Society,* 8:139–42.

DARBY, WILLIAM. *The Emigrant's Guide to the Western and Southwestern States and Territories.* New York, 1818.

DAVIDSON, GORDON CHARLES. *The North West Company* (University of California Publications in History, vol. 7). Berkeley, 1918.

DAVIS, T. FREDERICK. "MacGregor's Invasion of Florida, 1817," *Florida Historical Society Quarterly,* 7:3–71.

DUSTIN, FRED. *The Saginaw Treaty of 1819 between General Lewis Cass and the Chippewa Indians.* [Saginaw], 1919.

ELLER, W. H. "Old Fort Atkinson," Transactions and Reports of the Nebraska State Historical Society, 4:18–28.

FISHER, ROBERT L. "The Treaties of Portage des Sioux," *Mississippi Valley Historical Review,* 19:495–508.

FLAGLER, D[ANIEL] W[EBSTER]. *A History of the Rock Island Arsenal from Its Establishment in December, 1876, and of the Island of Rock Island, the Site of the Arsenal from 1804 to 1863.* Washington, 1877.

FOLWELL, WILLIAM WATTS. *A History of Minnesota,* vols. 1–3. Saint Paul, 1921–26.

FOREMAN, GRANT. *Pioneer Days in the Early Southwest.* Cleveland, 1926.

FRY, JAMES B. *The History and Legal Effects of Brevets in the Armies of Great Britain and the United States from Their Origin in 1692 to the Present Time.* New York, 1879.

FULLER, HUBERT BRUCE. *The Purchase of Florida: Its History and Diplomacy.* Cleveland, 1906.

GALLAHER, RUTH A. "The Indian Agent in the United States before 1850," *Iowa Journal of History and Politics,* 14:3–32.

GANOE, WILLIAM ANDERSON. *The History of the United States Army.* New York, 1924.

GOODWIN, CARDINAL. "A Larger View of the Yellowstone Expedition," *Mississippi Valley Historical Review,* 4:299–313.

————. *The Trans-Mississippi West, 1803–1853: A History of Its Acquisition and Settlement.* New York, 1922.

GREENHOW, ROBERT. *The History of Oregon and California.* Boston, 1844.

GREGG, THOMAS. *History of Hancock County, Illinois.* Chicago, 1880.

GRISWOLD, BERT J. *The Pictorial History of Fort Wayne, Indiana,* Chicago, 1917.

HAMERSLY, THOMAS H. S. *Complete Regular Army Register of the United States for One Hundred Years, 1779–1879.* Washington, 1880.

HANSEN, MARCUS L. *Old Fort Snelling, 1819–1858.* Iowa City, 1918.

History of Peoria County, Illinois. Chicago, 1888.

HODGE, FREDERICK W. *Handbook of American Indians North of Mexico* (Smithsonian Institution, Bureau of American Ethnology, Bulletin No. 30). 2 vols. Washington, 1907–10.

HUIDEKOPER, FREDERIC LOUIS. *The Military Unpreparedness of the United States: A History of American Land Forces from Colonial Times until June 1, 1915.* New York, 1915.

INGERSOLL, LURTON DUNHAM. *A History of the War Department of the United States with Biographical Sketches of the Secretaries.* Washington, 1879.

JOHNSON, IDA AMANDA. *The Michigan Fur Trade* (University Series, published by the Michigan Historical Commission, vol. 5, pt. 1). Lansing, 1919.

LIPPINCOTT, ISAAC. "A Century and a Half of Fur Trade at St. Louis," *Washington University Studies,* 3:205–42.

LOVE, WILLIAM A. "General Jackson's Military Road," Publications of the Mississippi Historical Society, 11:403–17.

MacGILL, CAROLINE E. *History of Transportation in the United States before 1860* (Carnegie Institution Contributions to American Economic History). Washington, 1917.

MAHAN, BRUCE E. *Old Fort Crawford and the Frontier.* Iowa City, 1926.

MARSHALL, THOMAS MAITLAND. *A History of the Western Boundary of the Louisiana Purchase, 1819–41* (University of California Publications in History, No. 2). Berkeley, 1914.

MEEKER, MOSES. "Early History of the Lead Regions of Wisconsin," *Wisconsin Historical Collections*, 6:271–96.

MEIGS, WILLIAM M. *The Life of John Caldwell Calhoun.* 2 vols. New York, 1917.

MORGAN, GEORGE. *Life of James Monroe.* Boston, 1921.

NEAL, ANNIE. "Policing the Frontier, 1816–1827." Master's thesis, University of Wisconsin, 1923.

NEVILLE, ELLA HOEA, MARTIN, SARAH GREENE, and MARTIN, DEBORAH BEAUMONT, *Historic Green Bay.* Green Bay, 1893.

OTIS, ELWELL S. *The Indian Question.* New York, 1878.

PAXSON, FREDERIC LOGAN. *History of the American Frontier, 1763–1893.* Boston, 1924.

————. *The Last American Frontier.* New York, 1910.

PECK, MARIA. "Fort Armstrong," *Annals of Iowa* (third series), 1:602–13.

PHILLIPS, ULRICH BONNELL. *A History of Transportation in the Eastern Cotton Belt to 1860.* New York, 1908.

PICKETT, ALBERT JAMES. *History of Alabama.* 2 vols. Charleston, 1851.

PORTER, KENNETH WIGGINS. *John Jacob Astor, Business Man.* 2 vols. Cambridge, 1931.

QUAIFE, MILO MILTON. *Chicago and the Old Northwest, 1673–1835: A Study of the Evolution of the Northwestern Frontier, Together with a History of Fort Dearborn.* Chicago, 1913.

————. *Wisconsin: Its History and Its People, 1634–1924.* 4 vols. Chicago, 1924.

REEVES, JESSE S. "The Napoleonic Exiles in America," Johns Hopkins Studies in Historical and Political Science, 23:531–656.

RICHARDS, GEORGE H. *Memoir of Alexander Macomb, the Major General Commanding the Army of the United States.* New York, 1833.

ROBBINS, ROY MARVIN. "The Defense of the Western Frontier, 1825–1840." Master's thesis, University of Wisconsin, 1926.

RODENBOUGH, THEODORE F., and HASKIN, WILLIAM L. *The Army of the United States: Historical Sketches of Staff and Line with Portraits of Generals-in-Chief.* New York, 1896.

ROYCE, CHARLES C. *Indian Land Cessions of the United States* (Eighteenth Annual Report of the Smithsonian Institution, Bureau of American Ethnology). 2 vols. Washington, 1899–1900.

SHERIDAN, P[HILIP] H[ENRY]. *Outline Descriptions of the Posts in the Military Division of the Missouri.* Chicago, 1876.

SMITH, EUDORA. "Stephen Watts Kearny as a Factor in the Westward Movement, 1812–1834." Master's thesis, Washington University, 1925.

SMITH, WILLIAM L. G. *The Life and Times of Lewis Cass.* New York, 1856.

STEVENS, WAYNE EDSON. "The Northwest Fur Trade, 1763–1800." University of Illinois Studies in Social Sciences, 14:407–610.

SWANTON, JOHN R. *Indian Tribes of the Lower Mississippi Valley and Adjacent Coast of the Gulf of Mexico* (Smithsonian Institution, Bureau of American Ethnology, Bulletin No. 43). Washington, 1911.

TURNER, FREDERICK JACKSON. "The Character and Influence of the Indian Trade in Wisconsin: A Study of the Trading Posts as an Institution," Johns Hopkins Studies in Historical and Political Science, 9:547–615.

VAN TYNE, CLAUDE HALSTEAD, and LELAND, WALDO GIFFORD. *Guide to the Archives of the Government of the United States at Washington* (Carnegie Institution Publication No. 92). Washington, 1907.

WALDO, S. PUTNAM. *The Tour of James Monroe through the Northern and Eastern States in 1817.* Hartford, 1819.

WAY, ROYAL B. "The United States Factory System for Trading with the Indians, 1796–1822," *Mississippi Valley Historical Review*, 6:220–35.

WESLEY, EDGAR BRUCE. "The Military Policy of the Critical Period," *Coast Artillery Journal*, 68:281–90.

————. "The Fur Trade of the Southwest, 1763–1831." Master's thesis, Washington University, 1925.

WHITE, HOWARD. *Executive Influence in Determining Military Policy in the United States* (University of Illinois Studies in Social Sciences, vol. 12). 292 pages.

WILLSON, BECKLES. *The Great Company: Being a History of the Honourable Company of the Merchant-Adventurers Trading into Hudson's Bay.* 2 vols. London, 1900.

YOAKUM, HENDERSON. *History of Texas from Its Settlement in 1685 to Its Annexation to the United States in 1846.* 2 vols. New York, 1856.

III. NEWSPAPERS AND PERIODICALS

The dates following the names of the newspapers indicate the approximate period consulted. They do not indicate the duration of the paper. Unless otherwise indicated the papers were consulted in the Library of Congress.

Alabama Republican (Huntsville), 1819–25. Several numbers are missing.

Argus of Western America (Frankfort, Kentucky), 1819–25.

Cahawba Press and Alabama State Intelligencer. December 30, 1820, to 1825.

Detroit Gazette, 1817–25. Photostatic copies are in the library of the Missouri Historical Society.

Edwardsville Spectator, 1819–26.

Halcyon and Tombeckbe Public Advertiser, 1819–22. Many issues are missing.

Louisiana Courier (New Orleans), 1819–25. Some issues are missing.

Louisiana Herald (Alexandria), 1820–25. Several numbers are missing.

Missouri Gazette and Illinois Advertiser, February 26, 1814–July 9, 1815; continued as *Missouri Gazette,* July 15, 1815–July 3, 1818; continued as *Missouri Gazette and Public Advretiser,* July 10, 1818–March 20, 1822; continued after March 27, 1822, as *Missouri Republican.* Missouri Historical Society library.

Missouri Intelligencer and Boon's Lick Advertiser, 1819–20. Continued after 1820 as *Missouri Intelligencer.*

Natchitoches Courier, scattered issues of 1825.

National Intelligencer, 1815–25. Files in the Missouri Historical Society and the Library of Congress.

Niles' Weekly Register, 1815–25.

Saginaw Courier-Herald, March 13, 1910. Courtesy of Mr. Fred Dustin.

St. Louis Enquirer, 1819–25. Many issues of 1819 missing. Missouri Historical Society library.

INDEX

Academies, military, 91, 92, 115, 131
Adams, John Quincy, on internal improvements, 96
Administration, army, *see* Army
Albany, treaty of, 16
Amelia, sloop, 121
Amelia Island, 171; troops on, 172
Amelung, Captain Ferdinand, 168, 169
American Fur Company, 51, 55n, 57, 58; opposes factory system, 48, 59; criticism of, 50; rise of, 51; St. Louis office, 59
Amusements, at garrisons, 142
Annapolis, protests removal of troops, 105
Annuities, to Indians, 23, 28
Apalachicola River, fort on, 167–70
Appropriation, for building roads, 99; refused for Missouri Expedition, 155
Arbuckle, Colonel Matthew, 180
Archer, Inspector Samuel B., on military training, 92n; on artillery school, 115; inspection by, 130
Arikara Indians, 11. *See also* Arikara War
Arikara War, 63, 160–62, 165
Arkansas River, factory on, 38, 39, 40; post on, 39, 47, 113, 178
Arkansas Territory, 178, 179
Army, protects Indians, 20; assists factors, 46; reduction and reorganization of, *1815–16*, 66–76, 100–02; Madison's recommendations concerning, 72; Calhoun's reports on, 77, 82, 83; supplies for, 78–81; contractors, 78, 79; farming activities, 81, 115, 158, 160, 184; Clay's resolution for reduction, 83; reorganization of *1821*, 84–90, 111, 113; discipline and regulation, 90, 114; constructs roads, 96–99; administration, 100–17; departments, 101; register, 101; districts and units, 101, 104; attitude of Maine congressmen toward, 106; orders, 106–09; inspec-

tors, 114–16; life, 114, 125, 129, 130, 142, 184; strength of, 194. *See also* Army staff; Frontier defense; Garrison life; Military policy; Militia; Troops
Army staff, law concerning, 72; regulation, 80; efforts to reduce, 83, 90; provision for, in act of *1821*, 89
Arrow Rock, factory at, 40
Articles of Confederation, Indian problem under, 17, 18
Artillery school, 92, 115, 131
Ashley, William H., forms fur company, 58; ascends Missouri River, 160, 162; and Arikara War, 161
Astor, John Jacob, promotes fur trade, 57; buys Canadian interests, 58; post of, on Sandy Lake, 127
Astoria, 164
Atkinson, General Henry, 141, 158, 160, 162; commander in West, 113; and Missouri Expedition, 146, 149; on steamboat transportation, 150, 154; address to army, 150
Atkinson Expedition, 165
Augusta, military headquarters at, 104; location, 112

Bainbridge, Lieutenant Henry, 129
Baker, Major Daniel, 128, 129
Bands, musical, at military posts, 142
Bank of Missouri v. Johnson, 151, 153
Bankhead, Major James, 172
Barbour, Senator James, 74, 80
Barbour, Congressman Philip P., 68, 98
Bassett, James, 169
Baton Rouge, fort at, 112, 116; distributing point, 176
Bell, John R., 50
Belle Fontaine, 88, 133, 136, 137, 145, 148, 149, 151; factory at, 40; military headquarters at, 101, 137; location, 112; troops at, 135, 137, 157
Belle Point, *see* Fort Smith

205